BRITISH AVIATION SQUADRON MARKINGS OF WORLD WAR I

BRITISH AVIATION SQUADRON MARKINGS OF WORLD WAR I

RFC • RAF • RNAS

Les Rogers

Schiffer Military History
Atglen, PA

Book design by Robert Biondi.

Library of Congress Catalog Number: 00-107619.

Printed in China.
ISBN: 0-7643-1284-7

Published by Schiffer Publishing Ltd.
4880 Lower Valley Road
Atglen, PA 19310
Phone: (610) 593-1777
FAX: (610) 593-2002
E-mail: Schifferbk@aol.com.
Visit our web site at: www.schifferbooks.com
Please write for a free catalog.
This book may be purchased from the publisher.
Please include $3.95 postage.
Try your bookstore first.

In Europe, Schiffer books are distributed by:
Bushwood Books
6 Marksbury Ave.
Kew Gardens
Surrey TW9 4JF
England
Phone: 44 (0)208 392-8585
FAX: 44 (0)208 392-9876
E-mail: Bushwd@aol.com.
Free postage in the UK. Europe: air mail at cost.
Try your bookstore first.

CONTENTS

INTRODUCTION

The origins of this book go back many years to the early 1930s, in fact, to the Hendon Air Displays and a trip along the sea shore in an Avro 504 or similar for five shillings!

To be honest, at that time the availability of information on the early flying days was almost nil – this may seem very strange to latter day enthusiasts but they must remember that the Public Records for the years 1914–1918 were not made public until 1969. Museums were not what they are now – there was no R.A.F. Museum at Hendon in those days. Perhaps also many people had unhappy memories of the terrible casualty lists in the newspapers and were trying to forget the war years. "A war to end all wars" was the slogan.

The only way to get information for the majority of would-be historians was by knowing and talking to ex-members of the services and hoping they had some photographs. This is not the best method of obtaining information although it is first hand. Memory fades and facts become distorted or embroidered (e.g., always shot down by Richthofen!). Nevertheless a few enthusiasts plodded along on their own until along came another war in 1939 which meant that research was put aside because we all had more pressing engagements. When that was over, those who survived took up their old hobby and began to build up a picture of the "old days."

Progress was still slow but, as the years rolled on, it became a bit easier. One factor supporting this was the growth of the scale model industry which introduced young people to modelling and the desire to find out more about the actual aircraft themselves. More museums opened and then three things happened quickly. First, *Cross and Cockade* starting publishing in the U.S.A.; second, the Public Records Office opened the files for 1914–1918 in 1969; and third, *Cross and Cockade G.B.* starting publishing in 1970. This meant that accurate information was finally available and could be moved around the world, and interested people could, via the columns of journals, get in touch and correspond with other people with the same interests.

And what of those early historians? Most are still about and still active. Many have specialized subjects – the contents of this book are mine.

A multitude of people have helped in the gathering of facts both large and small and I offer sincere thanks. Many were pilots, observers, or ground crew who answered my questions and loaned photographs. Alas, some are no longer with us, and to their memory I say, "Many Thanks and Rest in Peace."

To many of my later correspondants who are still around I once again express many thanks and hope they will go on discovering facts and, as important, go on passing them around.

I now come to photographs – I have tried to use as many "new" or unpublished photographs as possible and give those which, over the years have been used many times, a rest. Some, for want of alternatives, I have had to use. Some squadrons I could not find in photographs and of others I found a surplus.

I make no apologies if some are sub-standard – they will be either all that have come to light or very interesting. Taken in the field, by early cameras and wartime film, they have not the sharpness of official photographs. Remember also that cameras in active service were forbidden.

Many of my photographs have come from many friends and correspondants all over the world and sincere thanks to all of them. I have not credited photographs individually for obvious reasons but all the following are included. I must say thanks to all ex-members and their families of R.F.C., R.N.A.S., and R.A.F., from air mechanics to air marshals.

No book or magazine on British World War One aircraft can be published today without photographs from the Jack Bruce/Stuart Leslie collection – we have been in touch now for many years and this book would have been poorer without their help.

Finally I would thank again Frank Cheesmans for producing many photographs, especially those of the R.N.A.S. Thanks are due to the following – Barry Gray, Alex Imrie, Colin Owers, Ray Vann, Eric Harlin, Mike Goodall, Stew Taylor, Kevin Kelly, K.M. Molson, Bill Evans, Colin Huston, Paul Leaman, Ed Ferko, Alex Revell, Bruce Robertson, G. Quick, J. Visser, V. Koos, Peter Wright, Norman Franks, Chas Bowyer, Bernd Tötschinger, Group Captain Dye, Squadron Leader Warne, Flight Lieutenant Long, and anyone else forgotten.

Thanks of a different kind to Jacqueline Upton who plays a beautiful computer keyboard and Stephen Upton for photographic work.

INTRODUCTION TO SQUADRON, FLIGHT, AND INDIVIDUAL MARKINGS

Traditional identification within military units has had many forms over the years, from the Red Cross on the surcoat of the Crusaders, to the Napoleonic Wars with coloured facings on tunics and badges and collar flashes, to the present day.

The usual trooper, artillery man or soldier of the line was, until recently, poorly educated or uneducated and it was necessary to have some coloured visual sign so he could identify his own formation or comrades during the heat of combat or afterwards when he was likely to be shocked or confused. Coloured flags and badges were found to be most satisfactory and served up to, and including, World War One, although in keeping with the more or less camouflage colour of uniforms, the colours were muted to blend in.

In the British Army of 1914, easily recognized divisional shoulder flashes were used and on the regimental level the cap badge of long standing was used which carried on regimental tradition of many years standing.

As the Royal Flying Corps and Royal Naval Air Service were only three years old, they had no history or tradition to call on. In fact, no idea of any pattern of squadron markings had been thought of, probably because there were so many other problems to solve.

The German and French flying services were the first to realise the usefulness of some kind of unit marking. At the end of 1915 and early 1916, German Scouts started to appear with coloured tails to identify the Staffel, with coloured bands, letters or numbers as individual markings. The French usually used a coloured badge in place of the fuselage cockade and a number as individual marking.

As far as the British were concerned, no efforts were made until the early spring of 1916 when, with the increase in B.E.2 squadrons in France, it was decided to introduce some form of markings to identify the different squadrons.

Records which cover all the early correspondence about this seem to be missing, but letters that have survived show that the markings were to be used from the 23rd April, 1916 and were to be applied to aircraft of Nos.2, 4, 5, 6, 7, 8, 9, 10, 12, 13, 15, and 16 Squadrons, all of which had B.E.2s of various forms. Of the squadrons omitted, No.1 and No.3 had Moranes, No.11 had Vickers F.B.5 Gun Buses, and No.14 was in Egypt.

How this order was passed to the squadrons concerned is unclear, but on file are 13 pieces of very poor quality paper about four or five inches square. On each piece of paper was a rough drawing of a B.E.2 fuselage and tail, each one with a marking drawn on and carrying the number of the squadron to use it. Twelve of these drawings correspond to the squadrons, the thirteenth had a marking and was marked "spare."

No mention was made of any other units which prompted the C.O.s of No.18 and No.25 Squadrons who had F.E.2bs to write to H.Q.R.F.C. suggesting they paint a coloured triangle on the nacelle of their aircraft. This was refused with the comment "you are distinct enough!"

Naturally enough this prompted a rash of "unofficial" markings (including Nos.18 and 25) and in time these were accepted, or probably the principle of "Nelson's Eye" was applied, but nevertheless they remained unofficial.

During the rest of 1916 several other B.E.2 units arrived in France and in turn were issued with markings. Towards the end of 1916 and in the spring of 1917 all the B.E.2 squadrons were re-equipped with R.E.8s or A.W.F.K.8s and carried on using the markings then in use on the B.E.2s. New squadrons arrived and were issued new markings as long as they were two-seater Corps squadrons.

By mid-1917 more and more units were joining the R.F.C. and R.N.A.S in France. Incidentally, the R.N.A.S., having no B.E.2 units, had had no squadron markings. It was obvious that the present system had become dated and a review of the subject was held which led to a letter from Adv.H.Q.R.F.C. being sent to the five Brigades and the 9th Wing, dated 15th August, 1917 with outline proposals for the whole of the R.F.C. and R.N.A.S.

The Brigade and Wing Commanders were asked for their comments – all were in agreement plus a few comments. This list of markings known as the "proposed list" was amended and added to and ordered to be in use by a letter dated 26th August, 1917. Each brigade was issued with a list for its own aircraft. Rapidly "passing the buck," the instructions went down to Wing Commanders, then to Squadron Commanders, who then passed it down to the Flight Sergeant, who then passed it to a rigger who happened to be looking idle and told him to apply some white paint! Small wonder some were wrong and there was no standard pattern. Later, units made stencils and things improved, although there was still no set standard.

These markings were used successfully up to the end of 1917, but the flying services were expanding quickly, with many more squadrons planned for the coming year. To cope with this a new set of markings was issued dated 23rd December, 1917. This showed:

1. Squadrons already in France, their aircraft and markings.
2. Squadrons in France who were re-equipping with different aircraft and their markings.
3. Squadrons who were arriving in France on formation, their aircraft and markings.

This last section included several D.H.9 bomber squadrons due early in 1918 but for various reasons they did not arrive until markings for two-seat aircraft were discontinued.

All the markings on this list only lasted until 22nd March, 1918 as the day previously the German Army made its last big attack (*Kaiserschlacht*) in an effort to win the war before American forces were able to build up. As the British 5th Army retreated, so the R.F.C. units were forced to give up their aerodromes and move back to fresh quarters. It was realised that the squadron markings would indicate where units had moved to so all squadrons who were involved in reconnaissance, artillery spotting, and short range bombing were ordered on the 22nd March, 1918 to paint their markings out. This included all the two-seater squadrons. To further increase the hoped for enemy confusion, the scouts were also issued with new markings. The new instructions also stated that operations were not to be interfered with but at least one Flight was to be changed in any one day. This seems to indicate that these changes were already planned and that the German advance speeded it up.

These last squadron markings remained until the armistice and beyond except in the case of the 17th and 148th Squadron U.S.A.S., who had been attached to the R.A.F. from the end of June, 1918 and were detached in the October. To conceal their going, the squadron markings they were using were transferred to two R.A.F. units. No.210 Squadron used the dumbell and No.204 used the triangle. This was ordered in a letter dated 28th October, 1918.

Several D.H.9 squadrons in August asked permission from H.Q.R.A.F. to paint on some form of squadron marking. They were told they could "as long as it was small" and several did so.

Flight Markings

There was no official ruling on these, and often none were used. Usually, if any were used they were confined to the canvas cover of the wheel spokes. They were of help to mechanics if an aircraft landed away from the hangars and needed a "push in," ensuring the correct flight's mechanics went out to push. Once in the air their use was very limited.

Individual Markings

Again, no official ruling was issued and they were applied at squadron level. They had great value in formations and a check on pilots after combat. There was no ruling about what was used; some Wing Commanders liked all their squadrons marked in the same way, others were not concerned. Changing wing's could produce changes, but generally they remained constant throughout the unit's existence.

Markings on Other Fronts

The main front supported by British aircraft, other than the Western Front, was the Italian. When three Camel and two R.E.8 squadrons left France for Northern Italy, they went by train, arriving December, 1917. They took their existing aircraft, dismantled, with them still retaining their existing squadron markings, which they all continued to use. The only change was to change any individual figures to letters.

The other fronts all had R.F.C. or R.N.A.S. units of varying strength. No squadron markings were officially used. Most markings seen appear to have been personal ones and usually were girls' names or names of towns.

Notes to Remember When Using the Following Sections

1. For continuity, Naval squadrons are under their R.A.F. number.
2. Australian Flying Corps are under their R.F.C. numbers: 67, 68, 69, and 71.
3. Squadrons are listed numerically even if they were non-operational or never formed, i.e. "paper squadrons."
4. Home Defence squadrons often had various odd aircraft attached but only main equipment is listed.
5. Dates quoted are the official dates, but by the time the orders arrived at units a few days could have elapsed.
6. Dates of loss – i.e. "missing" or "shot down" – are taken from Casualty Returns and should be correct.
7. Aircraft recorded as "missing" – this was the term used when it had not returned. Whether its crew would be determined as POW or Killed would not have been known for several months, so I have used the term for simplicity.
8. Photographs showing serial numbers and squadron markings indicate that the aircraft was with that unit when the photograph was taken. Aircraft were often returned to depots for repairs or re-building, which meant that it could be re-issued to another squadron and seen in that squadron's markings.
9. The change from R.F.C. and R.N.A.S. to R.A.F. had no bearing on any markings or colours. The change really only affected administration, ranks, and uniforms.

Painted Flying Boats

Due to the serial numbers being painted over or too small to see, the location of squadrons in many cases is in doubt. Great Yarmouth and Felixstowe were the main bases because they gave direct access to the North Sea, but other bases around the British Isles also had a few boats. However, it has proved impossible to discover what boats were at which bases with any degree of accuracy. Because these boats are very interesting and coloured as no operational R.A.F. had been coloured before, I have included many of them even if their base is uncertain.

The R.N.A.S., operating around the Coasts of Great Britain, called all units "flights" whatever their size. After the formation of the R.A.F. on 1st April, 1918 a number of flights were called squadrons. This was mainly for administrative purposes and the process was spread over several months. For continuity I have used the R.A.F. numbers and noted the flight numbers in the text. These numbers go from No.220 to No.274.

The squadron number, followed by an asterix indicates that the aircraft illustrated may have been with other units, as their unit has not been definitely identified.

TRAINING AIRCRAFT

No official markings were allocated to these aircraft. Most training bases had some markings, although with crashes they never lasted long and were often never used.

The photographs on the following pages were selected to show training aircraft with some type of markings. Where possible I have given locations or units.

Training Squadrons in the United Kingdom

In the early days of pre-war flying, learning to fly was not organized and could be accomplished in two or three ways. Probably the easiest was to sit with one of the early flyers who, of course, were self-taught themselves, and handle the rudimentary controls first on the ground and then in the air – provided there was no wind! After this, the would-be pilot hoped to progress onwards and eventually, with luck, upwards!

As sport flying, as it was known then, became popular a number of early pioneers opened up flying schools, often to finance their own flying at meetings in England and on the Continent. Amongst others were Beatty, Hall, Flanders, and Ruffy Bauman who all started designing their own machines.

The risk to pupils and instructors was high as were the expenses, which limited the applicants to those who had the money. Quite a number of Navy and Army officers learnt in this way.

A number of commercial companies had sprung up to manufacture machines either copied from existing designs or their own ideas. Naturally, these manufactuers needed to make a profit, and to increase the chance of this opened up flying schools hoping to sell an aeroplane to successful or lucky trainees.

A number of Navy and Army officers learnt to fly in this way, paid for, reluctantly by the government of the day. Their training was elementary as perforce it had to be due to lack of knowledge of a completely new environment.

As the clock went slowly around to 1914 and the Army High Command stopped saying "they frighten the horses," the R.F.C. and the Naval Wing commenced to organize and on the outbreak of war, several squadrons had been formed and were, by standards of those days, reasonably efficient. Not much thought had been given to training other than in the squadrons themselves. Once the squadrons got to France and used make-shift aerodromes, which often had only just been harvested, plus casualities from enemy action, plus casualties from accidents, it became rapidly obvious that replacements were needed, and taking them from the two squadrons in England was not going to be enough. Training units were going to be as important as units in the field, and big efforts were made to improve the situation.

The early way was to post experienced pilots and observers back to the "Home Establishment" for a rest, form a squadron by number, add a batch of trainees, then attach the experienced crews who would bring up the learners to a higher standard. After a period of working up, the best members went to France as a new squadron, the left-overs either went to another forming squadron or to the "Pilots Pool" in France to be posted as replacements to make up losses in the units already in action.

Generally, this was the system throughout the war, although it was refined and polished as time went by and facilities improved.

As the demand for more pilots, observers, plus ground crews increased, it became necessary to form training squadrons for all categories and these sprang up in many quiet, rural areas of England. These included preliminary and advanced flying, schools for observers, schools of artillery spotting and co-operation, schools for bombing and later, schools for wireless, and later fighting schools also.

These coped well enough, but after heavy losses in France, many re-inforcements were sent poorly trained. To illustrate – No.41 Squadron R.F.C. had heavy losses in November, 1917 shortly after re-equipping with S.E.5as. The replacements arrived with only three hours solo in their log books and had no idea of keeping formation or looking out for themselves. Fortunately, the next two months were quiet and they had the chance to gain some experience.

To assist in the training programme, schools were opened in Canada and Egypt and, while not very numerous, helped with training crews. Canada made a big contribution with the large numbers of Canadian volunteers as well as those Americans who could not wait and came over the border! The schools in Egypt coped with the Middle East and Mediterranean areas.

Vickers F.B.9, 110 hp Le Rhône fitted

Squadron Markings in Training Squadrons

No official scheme was ever issued and only a few units bothered to use one, even unofficial.

The usual method was to just use individual letters or numbers, but with the rapid turn round of machines, this often was not done. In most cases the aircraft were new from the manufacturers, but many had served with the squadrons in France and been returned as war weary but suitable for training. These should have had any previous markings removed but some missed the paint brush and soldiered on in training units under false colours.

As it is impossible to establish any form of markings on trainers, I have shown a selection of types and markings with location and unit where known. Most of them are crashes of various kinds as they provided unofficial camera men with continual subjects. Nevertheless, there are hundreds more who unfortunately remain unknown and unrecorded.

Maurice Farman "Shorthorn" A'2225, Australian Training Squadron at Castle Bromwich.

Maurice Farman "Shorthorn," possibly A.F.C. Squadron.

D.H.2 A'4798 was at No.10 Reserve Squadron, Joyce Green, early 1917. Position of serial number was common to many training D.H.2s.

D.H.2 A'2582 was the personal aircraft of Capt. Bowman when instructing in U.K.

F.E.2b A'5504, Turnberry, September 1917.

F.E.2b "B."

A.W. F.K.3 A'1494.

BELOW: A.W. F.K.3 B'9554. School of Aerial Photography.

Avro 504. The swastika was painted as a good luck emblem.

Avro 504K. Standard Avro-built D'7623.

Avro 504K. Built by Brush Electrical Engineering Co. F'2283.

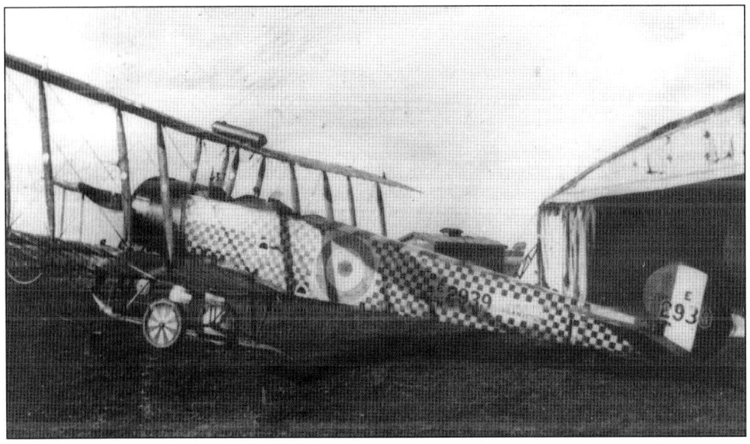

Avro 504K E'2939, built by Morgan & Co. Probably an instructor's aircraft used at Catterick.

D.H.6 C'5147, built by Kingsbury Aviation, at No.16 Training Squadron.

D.H.6 7792. The serial number does not correspond to known blocks.

D.H.6 A'9576 "1," probably from No.66 Training Squadron, Yatesbury 1918.

B.E.2c B'3995 built from spares "out on the tiles."

Curtiss JN4/4a B'1921, from Admiralty contract B'1901–1950 placed in U.S.A.

D.H.6 A'9630 "8," probably from No.66 Training Squadron, Yatesbury 1918.

D.H.6 "3012," probably B'3012, with serial below nose.

B.E.2e C'6902 presentation *Manya Krobo Gold Coast,* "V" and B.E.2 A'3129 "X" No.46 Reserve Squadron, crashed end of May or beginning of June 1918 and struck off 4.6.18. *Shall we Dance.*

B.A.T. F.K.24 *Baboon* built by British Aerial Transport Co. Only three were built.

Sopwith Scout C'514, Capt. S. Anderson, D.F.C., at Manston.

Sopwith Scout B'7525, probably at a fighting school as it is "armed" with a camera gun.

R.E.8 A'3185 from a squadron at Yatesbury.

D.H.5 A'9197 Australia No.16, N.S.W. No.15 *The Upper Hunter*, No.68 Training Squadron, Harlaxton. Presented 14.4.17.

Sopwith Scout D'4031 at No.3 Training Squadron.

Bristol M.1C C'4901, probably an instructor's machine.

R.E.8, serial unknown, with star insignia.

R.E.8 8871 fatal crash at Yatesbury.

R.E.8 "H" "The Hangar Door is Round the Front."

R.E.8, serial unknown IV. Unknown unit.

Camel D'1933 "59," No.2 Fighting School, Marske 1918.

R.E.8 "E" with a happy looking crew.

R.E.8 A'4467 "D" odd but known markings.

R.E.8 D'2626 outlined in white. "The Inspector's Aircraft." Yatesbury.

Camel, serial unknown. One of several checkerboard instructor's aircraft.

S.E.5a F'5593, pupils study cockpit layout.

Bristol F.2b C'4692 "43" Fighting School. Camera gun on top wing.

Bristol F.2b E'2224 No.66 Training Squadron, Yatesbury. Engine should have been a Falcon III.

RIGHT: Bristol F.2b C'9889 No.66 Training Squadron, Yatesbury.

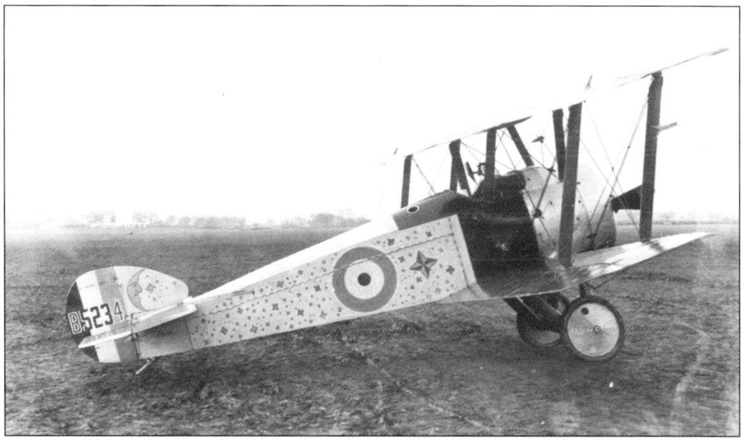

Camel B'5234 "A" Flight. Wireless experimental establishment, Biggin Hill. Moon and stars probably painted post-war.

Bristol F.2b C'1009 "85" Fighting School, Marske 1918.

Bristol F.2b probably at Yatesbury.

Bristol F.2b C'9885 outlined white "Inspector's Aircraft." Yatesbury, 1918.

Sopwith Snipe E'8123 unknown unit, *Hows That For Balance.*

D.H.9a unknown unit with a white diamond.

D.H.9a E'8557 "D" unknown unit. *Never Heard You Knock.*

Norman Thompson N.T.2b. Sunbeam Arab version, training flying boat.

Norman Thompson N.T.2b training flying boat taking off.

HOW IT ALL BEGAN

The period between the formation of the Royal Flying Corps and the Royal Naval Air Service and the outbreak of war was a time of development and experiment. In about three years the change from flying for fun to military purposes had encouraged the design and development of aircraft, engines, armament, and all the things which go with them.

One thing that had been more or less overlooked was any form of national identity markings, although France had set an example by adopting the traditional cockade. This was a blue centre spot surrounded by a white ring with a red outer one. It went back to the days of the French Revolution and was also used by the Armies of Napoleon as a cap ornament and plume holder.

Whatever the shortcomings of designers and their designs, the bureaucrats were in fully cry and required that, to keep the books right, there must be documentation of each machine. The newly formed Air Committee under the Committee for Imperial Defence of the United Kingdom ordered a common policy of numbering aircraft from both services to be effective from November, 1912.

Naval aircraft, being Senior Service, were to be numbered 1 to 200. The R.F.C. aircraft, being more numerous, were to be numbered 201 to 800. The only common component to all the varied types then in service was a rudder, and it was decreed that the number would be painted on it in 18-inch black figures; this became known as the serial number. As the standard colouring of machines then was varnished wood and doped fabric, which gave a colour of off-white to pale buff, the black figures were easily seen. Generally speaking, the size was adhered to but there were minor differences from machine to machine.

With the increase in aircraft production and the demands of the services, the first blocks of numbers were soon taken up, and by mid-1914 fresh groups were issued, Naval 801 to 1600 and R.F.C. 1601 to 3000. By mid-1915, due to big war orders, the blocks were increased again, Naval 3001 to 4000 and R.F.C. 4001 to 8000. By mid-1916 the Naval increased to 10,000. The bureaucrats realized this was getting too big and cumbersome and changes were made which would remain until the end of the war and beyond.

Before proceeding we must return to mid-1915 when the large figures on the rudder were discontinued to make way for rudder stripes. The serial numbers still from the allocated blocks were now applied to the fin, across the stripes, or on the side of the fuselage. These were much reduced in size, varying around 4–6 inches.

The new system of serial numbers again differed between the R.F.C. and R.N.A.S. R.F.C. serials would be prefixed by a letter and then a number which would cease at 9999, when a new letter would precede 9999; i.e., A1 to A9999 followed by B1 to B9999 and so on. The R.N.A.S. would use the same system but all would be prefixed by "N" only.

This system remained unchanged until the amalgamation on 1st April, 1918 when all manufacturers would deliver to one source from one order. The "N" prefix was, therefore, discontinued but machines in service retained their prefix until their loss or replacement due to war fatigue. While "N" prefixes were gradually dropped on amalgamation, they were still used on seaplanes and the various flying boats in service and, in fact, the Felixstowe and Curtiss Boats were in the range N4000–N4999, but many of the blocks of numbers were not used due to canceled or reduced orders at the armistice.

The wartime prefixes were A, B, C, D, E, F, H, and J, and G was used to identify captured German aircraft. I was not used because of confusion with 1 and J was only on very late 1918 orders, most of which were canceled or reduced. Serial numbers were either white, black, white with a black trim, or vice versa.

When the war started in early August, 1914, the pre-war squadrons moved to France within a week or two as support for the B.E.F., and the German Air Service moved in to support its armies.

With similar looking aircraft and no national markings, the aircraft provided the infantrymen with tempting targets in what was called "firing for fun." The pre-war British soldier was trained to fire ten aimed rounds per minute, so the "fun" was rather one-sided. The pilots and observers were not very happy about this situation and complaints were passed to H.Q. who passed them on to Q Branch at Farnborough, who considered the problem quite quickly.

On 2nd October, 1914 a letter from the O.C. R.F.C. arrived at the Royal Aircraft Factory asking them "to obtain a quantity of red and blue paint to paint Union Jacks on aeroplanes." This was obtained from the old paint company Robbilac in shades of Bright Red and Gentian Blue. Tests were carried out on the 19th October with Mr. Frank Goodden piloting the test aircraft which he flew over a group of ground observers at heights from 1000 feet to 6000 feet at intervals of 1000 feet. The Union Jacks showed up well and were considered very satisfactory.

Other test aircraft were also flown with the Union Jack in a shield and also the government sign of a broad arrow, but these two were not suitable.

The size of the Union Jack was stated as length seven feet, depth five feet. The cross of St. George was five inches wide. The diagonal cross of St. Patrick was 1.5 inches wide. The white outlines to these two crosses were six inches wide and the corners were filled in with blue. Orders were sent to units in the field and manufacturers to paint these below the lower wings only.

This in no way stopped the "firing for fun" as the main cross showed up very well and gave an excellent excuse for the infantry who said they were firing at aircraft with crosses on! This was, fortunately, taken seriously and it was decided on the 29th October to paint cockades as the French used but in reverse colours. A letter signed by Lt. Col. W.S. Brancker dated 2nd November, 1914 laid down the following: the then standard orders must be canceled for the painting of Union Jacks, but those now on could be left. But, this must not hinder deliveries. The circular marks should be on both lower planes as large as possible. Small Union Jacks could be made and doped on to the rudder below the serial number.

While all this was going on with the R.F.C., the R.N.A.S. was also having problems with identification, not only with the infantry but with naval gunners. Although AA guns were non existent at that time, most British ships had Vickers or Lewis Guns for local defence and with the naval tradition of shooting first, flying near ships was dangerous. Although an idea of using an anchor was considered, the R.N.A.S. adopted the Union Jack about the same time as did the R.F.C. and had the same problems. The R.N.A.S. then adopted a plan red ring with a white centre. Dating is uncertain but A.I.D. Sketch No.78 is dated October, 1914.

This, unfortunately, was the same marking used by Danish Naval Units and could cause accidents to them. The answer was to use the cockade then being used by the R.F.C. This was done by the Navy, reluctantly, and from then on national marking of both services ran, more or less, in parallel, but the red ring could still be seen well into 1915.

By mid-1915 more squadrons were arriving in France and more enemy aircraft were being encountered, several squadrons were painting Union Jacks on the fuselage sides with the risk again of the main cross being mistaken for enemy. To regulate the situation, the O.C. Admin. Wing, R.F.C. Farnborough, was ordered on 30th June, 1915 as follows:

1. To have circular red, white, and blue designs, on the top of the upper wings and below the lower wings near to the tips.
2. All covered fuselages to have the rings on both sides about midway along.
3. Rudders to have equal width striping, red, white, and blue, red to the rear.
4. No Union Jacks to be carried.

This should have cleared everything up, but whoever drafted that order forgot that a large number of British aircraft were of pusher type and no mention was made of them. It seems that some units painted on cockades and other did not. These markings proved to be satisfactory until the end of the war and beyond with minor additions or alterations.

By the spring of 1916 it was becoming necessary to introduce some form of squadron markings to all units and this is described fully in the main section.

By the beginning of 1916 the enemy was using various forms of camouflage that was proving fairly effective and this encouraged H.Q.R.F.C. to consider the same idea. Experiments were carried out in England and two covering colours were decided on. These were known as Protective Colouring No.10 and No.12 and were known as P.C.10 and P.C.12. The P.C.10 was made by mixing one part of lamp black powder to 250 parts natural iron oxide paste by weight with oil or cellulose and dryers. This produced a medium to dark brown. P.C.12 was in the same proportions of lamp black and red iron oxide which produced a red/brown colour. It is impossible to determine how the two colours were used but probably they were used as they became available to manufacturers. Due to differences in quality of pigments, careless weighing, etc., the final shades would have varied and probably account for the varied descriptions of these colours.

The use of P.C.10 was only for surfaces that could be seen from directly overhead; undersides were to remain clear doped.

The exact date of P.C.10's introduction is uncertain, but a letter dated 26 June, 1916 originating from the Quarter Master General, R.F.C., asked that P.C.10 should be used on all aeroplanes going to France. Some manufacturers were slow in complying and as late as 27th January, 1917 complaints were being made of unpainted Sopwith two-seaters arriving in France. Once the early problems were overcome, P.C.10 became the standard colouring for all the war fronts to which the R.F.C. and R.N.A.S. were sent.

Problems had arisen elsewhere; in 1915–16 there was a shortage of fighting machines and the two services were forced to purchase a fair number from France. The shortages were caused by lack of suitable designs, failure with the engine program, and, disgracefully, labour strikes in the industry for increased wages. The purchasing mission in Paris obtained Nieuport Scouts and two-seaters, Moranes of various types, and SPAD Scouts taken from the production lines.

The first problem was that the Morane Monoplane was similar to the Fokker E.I, E.II, and E.III. The then O.C. of No.60 Squadron was asked by General Trenchard to paint the cowling, spinner, under-carriage, and centre-section struts red. Capt. Smith Barry did this and it worked well, but never became a standing order, probably because the Moranes were becoming due for replacement.

The Nieuports and SPADs arrived carrying French pattern cockades on their wings and needed repainting. There were no cockades on the fuselage and the blue in the rudder stripes was too light, and were covered in codes showing doping patterns, etc. Small wonder that photographs show R.F.C./R.N.A.S. aircraft in French colours. Later Nieuports and SPADs arrived in standard French five-colour camouflage but this was not altered unless re-covering became necessary.

The only alteration to national markings was ordered on 5th May, 1917 when a one-inch wide white outline was used to make the blue stand out against the P.C.10. This was the standard, but there were several temporary markings and colour schemes:

1. Early in 1916 a B.E.2c was missing over the lines from No.7 Squadron, R.F.C. This, of course, caused little or no comment until a B.E.2c was reported over our side and then seen to land on a German aerodrome. Concern was raised that this was up to no good and could shoot down or lead our aircraft over AA batteries to be shot down. H.Q.R.F.C. ordered all brigades to obtain black paint and on a given day paint wing tips black. brigades acknowledged this on 16th April, 1916. The picture now becomes confused but on good authority, I understand that the order to paint was given and that any British aircraft would be shot down with unpainted wing tips. Whether this is the complete story or not, without doubt photographs do show black painted tips.
2.Night bombing began to build up during 1917 and was mainly by F.E.2bs that had been returned to depots by squadrons equipping with other machines. These F.E.s were in the usual colours, but when arriving at the night bombing squadrons they were given an all over coat of either P.C.10 or black, often painting out cockades, stripes, and serial numbers on the old principle of "if it doesn't move, paint it"!

Handley Page 0/100 and 0/400 aircraft started arriving mid-1918 and were treated in the same fashion. Efforts were being made to find a suitable night colour, and there is a long-held belief that a colour called "nivo," a dark slate green, was used. The following letter dated 5th November, 1918 from "Q" Branch to G.O.C. R.A.F. B.E.F.: "The problems in obtaining pigments for nivo leave no alternative than to finish 0/400s in P.C.10." Efforts were made to decrease the white in cockades and stripes but most 0/400s seem to have been untouched.

Experimental Camouflage Schemes

1. At least two 0/100s carried a mottled finish on fuselage and undersurfaces, the colours are uncertain and could be P.C.10 on the clear dope or vice versa.
2. A report dated July 1917 – Report B.62 – reports a series of practical tests carried out to determine the effectiveness of various camouflage methods. One aircraft flew between 1000 and 2000 feet, the observing aircraft flew between 5000 and 6000 feet.

Pattern No.1:
Top surface painted in 12-inch distorted squares in black and white, result – plainly visible over all types of background – camouflage – nil.

Pattern No.2:

As in No.1 but squares increased to 36 inches – same results.

Pattern No.3:
Top surfaces painted in irregular patches of light and dark khaki, result – good. Considered better than P.C.10.

Pattern No.4:
As in No.3 but using dark khaki and red brown, result – not as good as No.3 but effective over shingle.

Pattern No.5:
As in No.3 but patches of dark brown, green and light blue-green, result – not as good as No.3 but good over woodlands.

Colour mixes for No.5:
Dark brown green – 6 parts P.C.10/3 parts green/1 part blue.
Light blue green – 6 parts blue/2parts green/1 part white.
There is no evidence that this was ever used.

3. The Admiralty decided in 1917 to make a photographic reconnaissance of the Kiel Canal. Two D.H.4's modified with long range tanks to give 14 hours flying were to take off from Bacton, fly across the North Sea to Kiel, then land at Dunkerque. This scheme was abandoned in the last few days of August. These two D.H.4's were specially camouflaged all over in patches of fawn and blue.
4. A camouflage scheme for ground attack aircraft and tried on a Sopwith Salamander consisted of five different colours – dark purple, green, light earth, light green/grey, outlined in 2 inch black lines. The wing cockades were dark red centre then light earth with a dark blue outer ring and were also different in size and position. The scheme was considered quite good for Autumn and Winter but other colours would be needed for Spring and Summer.

The armistice arrived before any active trials but "seasonal" re-painting would have made the scheme difficult in any case. Whatever camouflage was used it would have been only partly effective due to changing backgrounds and the need for national identity to show.

Colours Used for Markings in the Field
Each squadron carried a set of colours in its workshop; red, white, blue, black, some dark grey, and P.C.10. These would be used for the normal purposes and any flight markings, e.g., coloured wheel covers.

Conversations over the years with numerous mechanics confirm that no one went out to buy any other colours. There have been no reports of exotic colours used.

Painted Fuselages on Flying Boats
The maximum amount of painting is on the F.2a flying boats which has been shown so well on many photographs and paintings and for long held to be official. I am indebted to Frank Cheesman for the true facts. I quote – "F/Lt. Gerry Livock and F/Lt. Bob Leckie were pilot and co-pilot at Great Yarmouth and one day when there was no flying they were talking about 'their boat' while looking at it on the hard standing. One said it could do with brightening up like the German fighters they had heard about so they got to work painting up the hull for a bit of a lark. Soon other crews followed suit.

It immediately became apparent that this painting up had great operational merits – recognition in the air between boats and making them more visible if forced down on the water.

So, the so called "official scheme" was started by two bored pilots on a dud day at Great Yarmouth!

R.E.5 – "651" in small figures. Preparing to go overseas by boat.

Sopwith Tabloid "394" large figures on white background.

Avro 504 "874" large figures on plain rudder.

B.E.2 "650" plain serial, no national markings on top surfaces.

B.E.2 "650" again, shows large union jacks below wings.

B.E.2c no serial visible. Union jack doped across rudder stripes.

RIGHT: Breguet de Chasse. R.N.A.S., Dunkerque. Cockades above and below wings double union jacks on rudder, below tailplane also.

Avro 504 "398" in small figures. No marking on top wing but on fuselage side and on rudder.

Morane Monoplane, R.N.A.S. Red rings and union jacks below wings, small jack on fuselage. "In The Arms of the Law"!

Short Type 166 "162." Red rings on wings, large union jack on fuselage, rudder stripes, large fancy serial, R.N.A.S. Salonika.

Deperdussin Monoplane "885," a civil aircraft impressed by R.N.A.S. in early marking of a red ring.

Bristol Scout "C" 1258 large serial and large union jack R.N.A.S. Eastchurch, July 1915.

F.E.8 "7616" shows poor definition between P.C.10 and cockade.

Port Victoria P.V.7 "Grain Kitten" shows the standard colours and markings 1917–18.

Sopwith Salamander test aircraft painted for camouflage trials.

B.E.2e used with the Salamander for similar trials.

D.H.4, probably A'7457 originally camouflaged fawn and blue. Planned reconnaissance of the Kiel Canal from Bacton end of August, 1917. This was abandoned and aircraft returned to Great Yarmouth for anti-zepplin patrols. Note five gun armament.

Felixstowe F.2a, probably N'4304, red and white stripes on forward hull, remainder of aircraft in P.C.10.

• • •

No.1 Squadron R.F.C.

Went to France in March 1915 with a variety of aircraft as a reconnaissance unit. Shortly after they received a number of Morane Monoplanes and Parasols. In March, 1916 a number of Nieuport Scouts were received as escorts and by January, 1917 the squadron was fully equipped with them. Early markings were numbers on the fuselage sides and on the top decking. These numbers were probably painted in red, white or blue with the white outlined in a dark colour against the silver dope.

Squadron Markings

Allotted on 26th August, 1917, a vertical bar behind the fuselage cockade. This was black on the silver dope and remained so on the later camouflaged aircraft.

Individual Markings

Numbers were still used in a similar fashion as before until late in 1917 when they changed to letters on the fuselage side just forward of the tailplane and repeated on the top decking roughly above the cockade.

In January,1918 the squadron re-equipped with the S.E.5a.

Squadron Markings

Indicated in the list of 23 December, 1917 a sloping white bar either side of the cockade.

Individual Markings

By white letters behind the squadron marking and on the top decking above the cockade:
"A" Flight used A, B, C, D, E, F
"B" Flight used G, H, J, K, L, M
"C" Flight used N, P, Q, R, S, T

Squadron Markings

Allocated 22nd March, 1918 – a white ring painted behind the cockade.

Nieuport 17 A'6605 of Lt. R.J. Bevington. P.O.W. 7.4.17.

Individual Markings

By white letters painted behind the squadron marking but now discontinued on the top decking. The letters were the same as in the earlier period, but when the squadron obtained some extra S.E5 as letters were used from the end of the alphabet.

Nieuport 17 A'313 of Lt. A.W. Wood. P.O.W. 22.4.17.

Nieuport 17 A'6644 of 2/Lt. T.H. Lines. P.O.W. 18.5.17.

Nieuport 27 B'6824–B'6768.

S.E.5a P, Q, R, S, T. "C" Flight, January/February, 1918.

S.E.5a "F" of Capt. P.J. Clayson, MC, DFC.

S.E.5a, changing from T to P.

RIGHT: S.E.5a, changing from T to P.

S.E.5a "16" in a line up, autumn 1918.

No.2 Squadron R.F.C.

Went to France in August, 1914 with a variety of early aircraft in a reconnaissance role. Eventually received B.E.2s and later variants.

Squadron Markings

Allotted on 23rd April, 1916, a triangle painted behind the cockade on the fuselage. In many cases it was repeated on the top decking. On clear doped aircraft it was in black, on P.C.10 aircraft it was painted white.

In April 1917 the first A.W. F.K.8s were received and by early June they were at full strength. These probably carried the same squadron marking.

Flight Markings

"A" Flight used red wheel covers.
"B" Flight used white wheel covers.
"C" Flight used blue wheel covers.

Individual Markings

Numbers painted on the fuselage side behind the squadron marking – originally 1–12.

Squadron Markings

Allotted on 26th August, 1917 – a white horizontal band along top edge of fuselage side. On the 27th August this was amended to a white zig-zag behind the cockade. This remained until 22nd March, 1918. The reason for this quick change was because at this time, in the 1st Brigade were three F.K.8 squadrons – 2, 10, and 35– all allotted horizontal bars (see 10 and 35 Squadrons). To avoid confusion No.2 was changed. The size and pattern of the zig-zag varied due to each flight painting their own aircraft.

B.E.2 "233," July, 1914 on Scarborough Racecourse.

B.E.2 "372," July, 1914 on Scarborough Racecourse.

Flight Markings

Remained the same as before.

Individual Markings

Still by white numbers now from 1 to 24 behind the squadron marking. Due to the large size of this marking, the number was almost underneath the tailplane and not easily seen, so it was repeated on the top decking. This was still not satisfactory and therefore it was moved in front of the cockade.

After 22 March, 1918 when the squadron marking was discontinued, the flight and individual markings remained, although some numbers were moved behind the cockade to get the white paint away from the observer's cockpit as they were not happy about being surrounded by white paint!

B.E.2c possibly in a training unit but in No.2 Squadron marking.

A.W. F.K.8 B'5782 without a number.

A.W. F.K.8 F'7421 Capt. Forsgate's aircraft 26.12.18. "B" Flight Commander.

B.E.2a "347" first British aircraft in France 13.8.14.

A.W. F.K.8 "246" "13" on the tiles.

RIGHT: A.W. F.K.8 C'8550 without squadron markings.

No.3 Squadron R.F.C.

Went to France 12th August, 1914 with an assortment of aircraft, standard for that period as a reconnaissance unit. By the end of 1915 they were equipped with Morane Parasols and a few Morane Biplanes. The Parasols were retained until September, 1917, when the squadron became a fighter unit with Sopwith Camels until the armistice.

Squadron Markings

No squadron markings issued when using Parasols.

Flight Markings

None used originally but later on, probably mid-1917, each flight carried a small marking below the cockpit. One flight used a small rectangle, one used a disc, and one used a hexagon, all painted in white and quite small.

Individual Markings

No standard markings were used but several Parasols had nicknames or mottoes around the front edge of the cowling – "Too Proud to Fight," "Archibald Certainly Not," "Pretty Damn Quick." Probably others were also used.

Squadron Markings When Using Sopwith Camels

Allocated 10th October, 1917, these were two white vertical bars behind the cockade on the fuselage sides. In December this was ordered changed to one white bar either side of the cockade on the fuselage side – there is some doubt about this second marking being used.

On 22 March, 1918 the markings were changed to two white bars just in front of the tailplane – again it is doubtful if this was used; all photographs until the armistice show two white bars behind the cockade.

Morane Parasol. Early type used by Lt. Frank Courtney.

Morane Biplane 5137 lost in action 2.3.16.

Morane Parasol *Too Proud to Fight,* January 1916.

RIGHT: Morane Parasol 5103 Lt. F.E. Goodrich. February 1916.

Individual Markings

Painted in a large block style on the fuselage side in front of the cockade and often repeated above and below wings:
"A" Flight used A, B, C, D, E, F.
"B" Flight used 1, 2, 3, 4, 5, 6.
"C" Flight used S, T, U, V, W, X.

When the establishment was raised to 24 aircraft, "A" Flight added G and H, "B" Flight 7 and 8, and "C" Flight Y and Z.

Late in 1918 orders were issued to all squadrons to delete "T" and "X." It was considered that at a distance they could be confused with the narrow, straight-sided cross then in use by the German Air Service. Therefore "C" Flight used P, R, S, U, V, W, Y, Z.

Flight Markings

From at least May, 1918 coloured wheel covers were used:
"A" Flight used red.
"B" Flight used white.
"C" Flight used blue.

Flight commanders used streamer on rudder, deputy flight commanders used streamer on strut – colour of choice.

Camel D'9443 "F."

Camel C'8333 "8" Lt. W.H. Maxted.

Morane Parasol *Certainly Not*, January 1916.

RIGHT: Camel "5."

Camel "W."

No.4 Squadron R.F.C.

Formed in August, 1912; in mid-August 1914 they moved to France with a varied collection of aircraft to provide reconnaissance for the army. In 1915 the unit gradually re-equipped with B.E.2c aircraft, later with 2d and 2e aircraft and in June, 1917 re-equipped with R.E.8s until the armistice.

Squadron Markings

None were used before 23rd April, 1916 then they were allocated a black vertical bar in front of the cockade, changed to white on later P.C.10-covered aircraft.

B.E.2 318 Seems to be down "Somewhere in France."

On converting to R.E.8s:

Squadron Markings

Remained the same as before until 22nd March, 1918, then discontinued.

Individual Markings

These are uncertain and photographic evidence is lacking; however, in mid-1918 after the squadron marking was discontinued, numbers were used on some aircraft but their extent is unknown.

B.E.2a Avro, Martinsyde, St. Omer 1914/15.

No.4a Squadron R.F.C.

Formed by withdrawing machines and crews from No.4 Squadron R.F.C. in January, 1918. Equipped with R.E.8s and attached until March to the Portuguese Army, then in France. Only about one flight in strength.

Squadron Markings

Allotted on 16th January, 1918, three white vertical bars on the fuselage side behind the cockade.

Flight and Individual Markings

No details known.

RIGHT: B.E.2b 487 Capt. G.W. Mapplebeck, left at 4.45 a.m. to bomb Lille rail junction, forced down with engine trouble and was P.O.W. but escaped back to U.K. In April, 1915, first night bombing operation by the R.F.C. Two other B.E.2bs from No.4 Squadron took part – 703, Lt. A. St.J.M. Warrand was forced down. He was P.O.W. but DOW 19.3.15. Capt. Barton crashed on take-off.

B.E.2b 705, Bailleul April/July 1915, wrecked 7.7.15.

B.E.2c 1686 at Bailleul 1915.

R.E.8 Being repaired on Naval 8's aerodrome.

R.E.8 "E" 20 "1" Capt. Stevenson, Lt. Baker, 19.5.18, with an extra Lewis on top wing.

No.5 Squadron R.F.C.

Went to France with the B.E.F. in September 1914 with a varied collection of aircraft that included both scouts and two-seat aircraft. Early in 1916 the squadron had become equipped with B.E.2cs.

Squadron Markings

Allotted on 23rd April, 1916, two bands around the fuselage, one in front of the cockade and one in front of the tailplane. The bands were painted black on clear doped aircraft and white on P.C.10.

In May, 1917 the squadron re-equipped with R.E.8s but retained the same squadron marking until 22nd March, 1918.

Individual Markings

By white numbers on the fuselage side behind the cockade. Originally 1 to 18, later increased to 24. Numbers were still retained after squadron marking was discontinued.

B.E.2c 2742 of Lt. Easom, shot down 28.9.16 by *Fl.Abt.33.*

B.E.2d 5755. Shot down 13.1.17. "Journey's End" 2/Lt. G.W. Bentley – 2/Lt. Hinckley.

B.E.2d showing controls and armament.

R.E.8 A'3685 of Lt. C.D. Smart and Lt. Hendry. Written Off 7.9.17.

RIGHT: R.E.8 "8" being rescued.

R.E.8 A'4712 "Bombay No.2" being painted on squadron. Force landed Maroeuil 29.1.18 and written off.

R.E.8 C'2536 "19" *Black Watch No.1*. Lt. Fraser, Lt. Bishop.

R.E.8 of Lt. C.F. Galbraith and Lt. V.T. Sprangle.

LEFT: R.E.8 C'2731 "1" *East Grinstead.*

OPPOSITE TOP: R.E.8 C'4590 "17."

OPPOSITE BOTTOM: R.E.8 "2" *Peach Melba.*

"EAST
GRINSTEAD."
1

17

No.6 Squadron R.F.C.

Formed 31st January, 1914 and went to France in October with the usual varied collection of aircraft in a reconnaissance role, but also had a fighter flight for escort duties. The fighter flight had Bristol Scouts, F.E.2bs and Martinsyde Scouts, etc., while the other two flights equipped with B.E.2, 2c, 2d, 2e in 1916 until re-equipping with R.E.8s in April 1917 until the armistice.

Squadron Markings

None used before 23rd April, 1916, then allocated three black vertical bars, one either side of the cockade and one in front of the tailplane, changed to white on P.C.10 covered aircraft.

On converting to R.E.8:

Squadron Markings

Remained as before until discontinued on 22nd March, 1918.

Individual Markings

No details are known; photographic evidence is lacking.

ABOVE RIGHT: B.E.2c 1756 used between 3.3.15–5.5.15.

RIGHT: B.E.2c 1748 on strength 29.1.15.

BELOW: B.E.2c 1671 to squadron 8.4.15 Wrecked 18.4.15, flying time 10.5 hours.

No.7 Squadron R.F.C.

Formed 1st May, 1914 but did not go to France until April 1915. Eventually standardized on B.E.2, 2c, 2d, and 2e aircraft until July 1917, when they were replaced by R.E.8s. Duties were reconnaissance and artillery spotting.

Squadron Markings

None used until 23rd April, 1916 then allocated two black vertical bars immediately in front of the tailplane, changed to white on P.C.10-covered aircraft.

On converting to R.E.8s:

Squadron Markings

Remained the same as before until discontinued on 22nd March, 1918.

Individual Markings

Were probably letters on fuselage sides behind the cockade; the extent of these is unknown.

B.E.2c 2750 shot down 3.6.16 by Hollebeke; note position of squadron marking bar by rudder post.

R.E.8 B'5066 "C" of Lt. Dick Combe.

Another view.

R.E.8 D'4739 "G."

No.8 Squadron R.F.C.

Formed 1st January, 1915, it moved to France in April as a reconnaissance unit equipped with B.E.2, 2c, 2d and 2e, exchanging these for Armstrong Whitworth F.K.8s in August 1917 until the armistice.

Squadron Markings

None used until 23rd April, 1916, then allocated a long black bar horizontally along the top edge of the fuselage side, later changed to white on P.C.10 covered aircraft.

On converting to F.K.8s:

Squadron Markings

Remained as before until discontinued 22nd March, 1918.

Individual Markings

It would seem from photographs that the majority of squadron aircraft did not use any.

B.E.12 Lost during Somme Battle 1916, downed by *Fl.Abt.22.*

A.W. F.K.8 C'8445 "C."

B.E.2c 1725 Flown by Lt. Harvey, P.O.W. 11.11.15 by *Fl.Abt.23.*

B.E.2c 2008. Went to France August, 1915. Shot down by *Ltn.* H.J. Buddecke.

A.W. F.K.8 C'8602 Capt. F.M. West, who won his V.C. on this aircraft.

A.W. F.K.8 D'5196.

No.9 Squadron R.F.C.

Formed on 8th December, 1914, at St. Omer from the Wireless Flight of H.Q.R.F.C. Detachments were sent to various points to spot for artillery on the British sector. These were absorbed into existing squadrons and the squadron was disbanded on 22nd March, 1915, but was reformed at Brooklands on 1st April and in July moved to the Dover area as a coastal reconnaissance unit as well as training. A variety of aircraft were used, but before returning to France in December 1915 they were equipped with B.E.2cs, later 2d and 2e in a Corps reconnaissance role until the armistice. It is doubtful that any markings were used in the early periods.

Squadron Markings
On 23rd April, 1916 they were ordered to use a white vertical band behind the fuselage cockade, usually about 12–15 inches wide, black on clear-doped aircraft. No flight or individual markings are known.

On re-equipping with R.E.8s in June, 1917:

Squadron Markings
Were as before and remained until 22nd March, 1918.

Flight Markings
Generally none were used but wheel covers may have been "marked up" on occasions.

Individual Markings
"A" Flight used number 1–8, "B" Flight 9–16, "C" Flight 16–24 in white behind the squadron marking and on the top decking, in use from June to early December, 1917. After December up to the armistice letters were used instead but between the cockade and squadron marking. "A" Flight used A–H, "B" Flight used J–Q, "C" Flight used R–Y.

R.E.8 "A" 3920 "B" at Proven, Belgium.

B.E.2d 7195 of Lt. G.E. Hicks lost 29.4.17. Note black bar on lower wing.

B.E.2c 2508. Crashed.

B.E.2c 4119. Crashed, London Colney.

R.E.8 "A" 4366, "21" crashed through engine failure near Boesinghe.

R.E.8 E'1207 "L" at Bickendorf, early 1919.

No.10 Squadron R.F.C.

Formed 1st January, 1915, as a reconnaissance unit equipped with B.E.2cs, later 2d and 2e. Went to France in July. In July/August 1917 re-equipped with Armstrong Whitworth F.K.8s until the armistice.

Squadron Markings

None were officially used until 23rd April, 1916, when they were allocated a black disc behind the cockade, changed to white on P.C.10-covered aircraft. However, ten days before, a B.E.2c was lost night bombing, so the disc was in use then. On converting to F.K.8s the same marking was used as before until new ones were issued:

Squadron Markings

Allocated 26th August, 1917, a long white bar along the bottom edge of the fuselage side. In practice the length varied from full to half length of the fuselage. This was discontinued 22nd March, 1918.

Flight Markings

By coloured wheel covers: "A" Flight used red, "B" Flight used white, "C" Flight used blue.

Individual Markings

By numbers 1–18 on fuselage side behind the cockade and above the squadron marking, repeated on the top decking. Later in 1918 numbers were replaced by letters in the same place; "A" to "U" at least were used.

B.E.2c 2567 lost on a night raid 14.4.17, flown by 2/Lt. Holmes.

A.W. F.K.8 B'233. On strength 7/17–11/17.

LEFT: A.W. F.K.8 F'7425 "S."

A.W. F.K.8 "L."

A.W. F.K.8 F'7489 "O" of "B" Flight flown by 2/Lt. Morford.

A.W. F.K.8 B'263 "11" Punjab No.22 *Simla Hills,* of 2/Lt. A. Muir, Gnr. R. Dunsmuir, lost 24.11.17. Fuselage in a wrecks graveyard.

BELOW: A.W. F.K.8 D'5197 "U" of Lt. E.W. Swann and 2/Lt. S.G. Watson.

No.11 Squadron R.F.C.

Formed 14th February, 1915 and went to France in July with Vickers F.B.5. "Gunbuses" as a two-seater fighter unit. Early in 1916 a few Nieuport "Bebe" were on strength. In June 1916 they re-equipped with F.E.2bs and replaced these with Bristol Fighters in June, 1917, which were used until the armistice in a fighter/reconnaissance role.

Squadron Markings

None used before the Bristols, but several photographs show F.E.2bs with a hollow white triangle on the nose. If this was a form of squadron marking it was unofficial.

Flight Markings

"B" Flight marked their aircraft with "B" on the port side of the top wing and number on the starboard as well as the hollow triangle, possibly below the lower wings also. Although unconfirmed it is likely that the other flights did the same.

On converting to Bristol Fighters:

Squadron Marking

Some form of unofficial markings were used to begin with – one aircraft had two vertical red bars with blue outlines. Another had a broad red bar with blue outlines. No other details are known.

The official marking allocated 26th August, 1917 was two white bars, one either side of the cockade, sloping inwards at the top. This remained in use until 22nd March, 1918.

Flight Markings

By coloured wheel covers:
"A" Flight used white.
"B" Flight used red.
"C" Flight used blue.

Individual Markings

"A" Flight used 1, 2, 3, 4, 5, 6.
"B" Flight used A, B, C, D, E, F.
"C" Flight used U, V, W, X, Y, Z.

All individual markings were painted behind the second bar of the squadron marking. Some Bristols were also marked on the centre section.

F.E.2b 4290. Note the triangle on nose. M.I.A. 2.9.16

Nieuport 11 A'126.

Bristol F2b A'7131 "5" September, 1917.

ABOVE: Bristol F2b A'7130 "3"; 2/Lt. N.J. Taylor and Lt. G.W. Mumford M.I.A. 19.9.17 during an Offensive Patrol over Bullecourt.

LEFT: Bristol F2b C'4846 "6."

Bristol F2b A'7127 "U" *Trainbourne*. Shot down by *Flak Batterie 102*.

Bristol F2b E'2428 "Y" In the Cabbage Patch.

Bristol F2b E'2586 "6."

Bristol F2b "W" and "X."

Bristol F2b "4" of Lt. Ashlin, *Me and My Bus*.

BELOW: Bristol F2b C'4814 "D."

Bristol F2b A'7231 "1" of "A" Flight. Shot Down 17.10.17 S.W. Cambrai by Vzfw. Bey of *Jasta* 5.

In R.F.C. colours on being shot down.

B. F. (Bristol-Fighter) D.D. — Zweisitzer

wird von Engländern geflogen.

1. Ansichten des Flugzeuges.

2. Besondere Merkmale:

Seitensteuer abgerundet mit anschließender leicht gewölbter Kielflosse; leicht abgerundetes, geteiltes Höhensteuer mit anschließender Dämpfungsfläche; untere Tragdecks zurückgestaffelt, je zwei Strebenpaare, vierflügelige Zugschraube, Verwindungsflächen an oberen und unteren Tragdecks.

3. Besatzung:

Zweisitzer, Führer vorne (meist Offizier), Beobachter (M.G.-Schütze) hinten

4. Leistungen:

Standmotor 250 (275) PS Rolls-Royce, 12 Zylinder mit Stirnkühler. An Steigfähigkeit dem Albatros D III und V besonders in größeren Höhen etwas überlegen, dem Pfalz D III gleich, an Schnelligkeit Albatros und Pfalz D III ungefähr gleich, an Wendigkeit dem deutschen Einsitzer unterlegen, dem deutschen Aufklärungs-C-Flugzeug mindestens gleich.

LEFT: In German colours on identification leaflet.

BELOW: Well written message "Don't Shoot, Good People."

No.12 Squadron R.F.C.

Went to France in September 1915 with a varied collection of aircraft types as a bombing and reconnaissance unit. In February 1916 B.E.2cs fully equipped the squadron, followed by the B.E.2d and 2e. It thereafter served as a Corps reconnaissance unit until the armistice, receiving R.E.8s in June 1917 and at least one Bristol Fighter late in 1918.

Squadron Marking

Allocated 23rd April, 1916, a long black band along the top side of the fuselage immediately below the top longeron. Shortly after this the marking was changed, possibly to avoid confusion with the marking of No.8 Squadron. The original long band was retained and a similar band added just above the bottom longeron. When the P.C.10 covering was used the black bands became white.

Flight Markings

Were used from the time of squadron markings or possibly earlier. Each flight's aircraft were marked with the flight letter on the side panels behind the cylinder blocks.

Individual Markings

None are believed to have been used.

On converting to R.E.8s:

Squadron Markings

Allocated 26th August, 1917, a white horizontal band along bottom sides of the fuselage.

Flight Markings

Were combined with the individual markings:
"A" Flight used "A1" to "A6" on fuselage sides in white behind the cockade.
"B" Flight used "1B" to "6B" in same position.
"C" Flight used "C1" to "C6" in same position.

On 22nd March, 1918, the squadron markings were discontinued but the flight/individual markings remained. When the establishment was increased "A7" and "A8," "7B" and "8B," "C7" and "C8" were added.

Just before the armistice the squadron received a Bristol Fighter (Arab) for "special jobs." It is not believed to have had any markings.

A Personal Marking

One of the pilots in mid-1918 was Lt. Ralph Metcalfe, later Sir Ralph. He had been in the wine trade pre-war and as a fluent French speaker often visited French Escadrilles in the area. On a visit to S.P.A.3 (*le Cigognes*) they painted a red stork on his R.E.8 fuselage saying they would know him and could protect him.

B.E.2c 4128 shows one bar along fuselage bottom.

B.E.2c 2502 "C" of Lt. Hayes, M.I.A. 9.11.16 near Vrancourt.

Bristol Fighter C9982 "A1."

R.E.8 "4B."

LEFT: B.E.2c Shot down.

R.E.8 "C."

Bristol F2b E'2233 "B4" "Alresford Rural District." Crashed 21.4.19.

Bristol F2b (Arab engine); some crews pose at 11 a.m., 11th November, 1918 – the moment the armistice started. Crews did not like the Bristol issued for special duties, preferring the R.E.8. (Comment from Capt. B.J. Purefoy, Flt. Cmdr. 1918.)

No.13 Squadron R.F.C.

Was formed on 10th January, 1915, and moved to France in the following October as a Corps reconnaissance unit equipped with B.E.2cs, later using 2d and 2e, retaining this role until the armistice. On moving to France they took twelve new aircraft in clear dope finish with white wheel covers. Re-equipped with R.E.8s in April, 1917.

Squadron Markings

Allocated 23rd April, 1916, a narrow black horizontal bar along the centre of the fuselage running from the pilot's cockpit to the tail. On P.C.10-covered aircraft this would have been white.

This marking was used on the R.E.8s until discontinued on 22nd March, 1918.

Individual Markings

No definite details are known. One R.E.8 was marked "A" behind the cockade with the white bar broken on either side of it. Photographs of the squadron are very scarce but those known show no individual markings.

B.E.2c lined up before leaving for France, 12.10.15.

B.E.2c 4076. Lt. Powell's crash, July 1916.

B.E.2c 2625. Lt. Atkinson's crash, June 1916.

B.E.2c 2535. Note wheel cockade.

R.E.8 "A," no details.

RIGHT: R.E.8 "B" Flight, Etrun Aerodrome, July, 1917.

No.14 Squadron R.F.C.

Formed in February 1915 and after training went to Egypt to provide reconnaissance units for the Army operating against Turkey. Small units were provided to work with the Army against the Senussi in the Western Desert, the campaign across the Sinai Desert, and in Arabia.

A variety of aircraft were used – D.H.1a., D.H.2, Vickers F.B.19, Martinsyde Elephant, and Bristol Scouts.

Early in 1916 the squadron began to equip with B.E.s of assorted types and in 1917 received a flight of Nieuport 17s.

November 1917 saw the B.E.s replaced with R.E.8s, but some Nieuports were retained until the armistice.

There is no record of any type of marking used.

D.H.1a with skull and bones on nose.

D.H.2.

Martinsyde G.100.

D.H.2 and Vickers F.B.19.

RIGHT: Bristol Scout 4689 with Lewis gun on top wing.

BELOW: R.E.8 B'5054 white rectangle, a possible squadron marking.

B.E.2c 4356 at Dabaa.

No.15 Squadron R.F.C.

Went to France in December 1915 equipped with B.E.2cs.

Squadron Markings

Allotted on 23rd April, 1916 a white vertical band in front of the tailplane.

In June, 1917 the squadron re-equipped with R.E.8's, the same squadron marking was retained until 22nd March, 1918. In several cases the white band was carried over the lower front edge of the fin.

Individual Markings

White numbers were painted on the sides of the fuselage behind the cockade and repeated on the top decking. Originally these were 1 to 18 but were later increased to 24.

After squadron markings were discontinued the numbers were still used.

Bristol Scout "C" 5314, May 1916, 2/Lt. Elliott.

R.E.8 B'2260 "12" 1.5.18 Capt. Hill, Capt. Pett, and dog.

B.E.2e 2810, March 1917.

BELOW: R.E.8s on the roadside 25.3.18 during March retreat.

ABOVE: R.E.8 D'4847 "15" of Capt. R.A. Cross and Lt. Alder, shot down 8.10.18.

RIGHT: R.E.8 "8."

No.16 Squadron R.F.C.

Formed at St. Omer 10th February, 1915, from flights of No.2, 5, and 6 Squadrons. Various aircraft were used until February 1916 when the squadron was issued with B.E.2cs.

Squadron Markings

Allotted 23rd April, 1916, two bands around the fuselage, one either side of the cockade. These were black on clear-doped aircraft and white on the later PC.10-covered ones.

In May 1917 the squadron re-equipped with R.E.8s and retained the same squadron marking until 22nd March, 1918.

Individual Markings

By white numbers painted on the fuselage side behind the squadron marking and repeated on the top decking. Numbers originally were 1–18, later increased to 24. Extra or spare machines were marked 25 onwards.

After squadron markings were discontinued the numbers were still used.

B.E.2c 4494; force landed 9.10.16 behind German lines.

RIGHT: B.E.2d 5746; shot down.

B.E.2c 2633; presentation "Punjab No.11 Kalabagh," S/Off April, 1917.

R.E.8 A'3839 "16" in the snow.

R.E.8 E'1104 "11" *Dorothy* of Lt. S.H. Hughes, 2/Lt. J.P. Taylor-Jones at Camblain-L'Abbe.

BELOW: R.E.8 C'2248 "2," "A" Flight at Auchy, November 1918. The pilot was Lt. B. Boyter.

No.17 Squadron R.F.C.

Formed February 1915. After training went to Egypt in November. After a short stay at Suez went to Salonika in July 1916 to support the Army in Macedonia, mainly in the reconnaissance role although a number of fighters were on strength. These were handed to No.150 Squadron in April 1918 and until the armistice the unit served as a reconnaissance unit. Aircraft were varied B.E.2c, Bristol Scout, B.E.12, A.W. F.K.8, and S.E.5a.

No markings are on record but some S.E.5a' had names on the cowling, usually a girl's name or a town.

When the fighter flight was withdrawn it was replaced by a flight of six D.H.9s and these made up "B" Flight. At the armistice the squadron had nine A.W. F.K.8s, six D.H.9, and one B.E.12.

A.W. F.K.8 (B'3359?) crashed by Lt. Ackery at Lahana, Macedonia.

No.18 Squadron R.F.C.

Went to France on 19th November, 1915, equipped with Vickers Gun Buses but in April 1916 they were replaced with F.E.2bs.

Squadron Markings

None allotted, but when the B.E.2c squadrons were given squadron markings on 23rd April, 1916, the O.C. of 18 Squadron asked permission to paint a red triangle on the nacelle side behind the lacing. The reply on 28th April was "this is unnecessary as the F.E.s are distinct enough!" However, on 22nd September, 1916, F.E.2b 6937 was lost over the lines and under the paint on the nose of the nacelle could be seen a light coloured diamond, which could have been a version of the proposed unofficial marking.

In May/June, 1917 the F.E.s were withdrawn and the squadron re-equipped with D.H.4s. No record of markings for this period.

A.W. F.K.8 C'3560 at Lahana, Macedonia.

Squadron Markings

Allotted 26th August, 1917, a white square on the fuselage side behind the cockade. This was painted fairly large.

Flight Markings

"A" Flight used red wheel covers.
"B" Flight used white wheel covers.
"C" Flight used blue wheel covers.

B.E.2e *Baroda No.9* – A'3084 and A'1334 #5 at Lahana.

F.E.2b 6937 'Punjab No.29 Rawlpindi' of Sgt. T. Jones, 2/Lt. F.A.A. Hewson, captured 22.9.16.

RIGHT: D.H.4 A'8043 "F" of 2/Lt. R.A. Mayne and Lt. V. Scott, M.I.A. 16.3.18. Crashed Fromelles, downed by *Flak Batterie 107*.

Individual Markings
"A" Flight used A, B, C, D, E, F; spare aircraft used G.
"B" Flight used 1, 2, 3, 4, 5, 6; spare aircraft used 7.
"C" Flight used S, T, U, V, W, X; spare aircraft used Y.

Painted in white behind the squadron marking, on the centre section, and sometimes on the top decking. After the deletion of squadron markings the same individual markings were used.

D.H.4. Another view of A'8043. Rudder has been "souvenired."

No.19 Squadron R.F.C.

Went to France on 30th July, 1916, equipped with B.E.12s.

Squadron Markings
None allotted

Flight Markings
"A" Flight used white wheel covers.
"B" Flight used red wheel covers.
"C" Flight used blue wheel covers.

Some time, probably in October, the squadron used as an unofficial squadron marking a white dumbbell on the fuselage sides behind the cockade. The flight markings were still used but began to disappear due to high loss rate.

D.H.4 A'7818 "C" Major Bowman (in centre) O.C. 41 Squadron "Pinching Wood." Caption on original!

Individual Markings
By large numbers on the fuselage sides painted roughly above the lower wing. The numbers went from 1–6 and were in flight colours.

The B.E.12s proved completely useless and the squadron re-equipped with SPAD Scouts. The first one arrived in October 1916 but they were not completely equipped until late February 1917.

Squadron Markings
None allocated, but the squadron still used unofficially the Dumbbell usually painted in black on the clear doped fuselage sides.

In May of 1917, the squadron moved to Liettres where SPADs were unknown. After several attacks by Naval squadrons the squadron adopted various devices to shown that they were R.F.C.:

SPAD A'6633, 2/Lt. S.S. Purves P.O.W. 19.3.17, Offensive Patrol over Cambrai.

BELOW: SPAD A'6706, Lt. H.P. Baker P.O.W. 24.3.17, Offensive Patrol near Lens.

1. A canvas sleeve, doped dark brown, was laced around the rear fuselage.
2. A flight letter in white on the sleeve.
3. A flight letter in white on the fuselage without the sleeve.
The identity problem did not improve so more drastic measures were taken:
4. Red, white, and blue bands were painted around the fuselage behind the cockade.
5. Red, white, blue, white, and red bands were painted on.
6. Wheel covers were painted as a cockade.

These bands were painted in varying widths and patterns and were used at least until August, 1917.

Squadron Markings
Allotted on 26th August, 1917 – a white square on the fuselage side behind the cockade.

However, there seems no evidence that this was ever used, although it was still recorded by G.H.Q. in December 1917 and was ordered to be used also on the forthcoming Dolphins. In fact, the Senior Flight Sergeant who was with the squadron all the time states that no square was ever used. In November 1917 SPADs were seen with letters and dark bands around the rear fuselage.

Sopwith Dolphins began to arrive in January 1918 and in a few weeks the squadron was fully equipped. Again, there is no evidence that the white square was ever used and it is doubtful if it ever was. On 22nd March, 1918, the squadron was allocated a white dumbbell painted behind the cockade.

Flight Markings
"A" Flight used white wheel covers.
"B" Flight used red wheel covers.
"C" Flight used blue wheel covers.

Individual Markings
White letters behind the dumbbell and on the upper wing:
"A" Flight used A, B, C, D, E, F.

SPAD B'1627, Lt. S.F. Allabarton P.O.W. 19.5.17 By A.A. fire.

SPAD B'6776, 2/Lt. L. Whitehouse P.O.W. 17.10.17.

Sopwith Dolphin E'4514 "E."

SPAD A'6634, Lt. A.T. Shipwright P.O.W. 16.8.17.

Sopwith Dolphin "G."

"B" Flight used G, H, J, K, L, M.
"C" Flight used N, O, P, Q, R, S.

Flight commanders flew a red, white, and blue streamer from the rudder. Deputies flew one from each interplane strut.

On 27th May, 1918, Lt. J.T. Parkinson, No.201 Squadron reported that when at 14,000 feet East of Arras he fired at long range at a group of enemy aircraft with coloured tails; on closing he saw they were Dolphins. A message from 3rd Brigade to Dolphin squadrons asked for information. No.19 replied that "A" Flight had white tails, "B" had red, and "C" had blue. They were ordered to paint these back in P.C.10 immediately. However, red-tailed Dolphins were seen again on 22nd July and were once more ordered to remove the colour.

No.20 Squadron R.F.C.

Arrived in France on 23rd January, 1916 equipped with F.E.2bs. It would appear that none of the squadron's aircraft carried any markings.

During the second half of August, 1917 the squadron was re-equipped with Bristol Fighters.

F.E.2d A'27 of Lt. W. Anderson and Lt. D.B. Woolley, M.I.A. 17.3.17 by *Fl.Abt. 227.*

Sopwith Dolphin C'3828 "P" of Lt. Aldridge March 1918 at St. Marie Cappel. C'3828 was lost 3.5.18 when flown by Lt. Chadwick.

Squadron Markings

Allotted on 26th August, 1917 – two vertical white bars, one in front of the fuselage cockade and one behind. On 5th October this was canceled and they were ordered to use one vertical bar in front of the cockade, retaining this until 22nd March, 1918.

Individual Markings

These were not painted on until some time in 1918. Then letters were painted roughly below the pilot's cockpit. The letters ran from "A" to "S."

F.E.2d 6356 of 2/Lt. L.R. Heywood and 2/Lt. D.B. Gayford P.O.W.

RIGHT: F.E.2d A'5 (not of 20 Squadron) delivered in error direct to the Germans 1.6.16! Included to shown the interior of the nacelle.

F.E.2b 6359, presentation "Baroda No.17" Shot down 16.5.16 and wrecked. Lt. E. Trafford-Jones, K.I.A., Capt. E. Forbes, W.I.A.

Bristol F.2b B'1125 of Lt. W.D. Chambers and 2/Lt. F.H. Berry, P.O.W. 9.10.17. Special reconnaissance Roulers-Menin shows second bar of squadron marking painted out.

Bristol F.2b B'1307 "K."

Bristol F.2b D'7939 "P" *Toronto*, Lt. Finch and Lt. Russell shot down 15.9.18.

Bristol F.2b "M."

No.21 Squadron R.F.C.

Formed 23rd July, 1915, moved to France in January 1916 with R.E.7s as a bomber-reconnaissance unit. In August re-equipped with B.E.12s in the fighter-bomber role. In February/March 1917 re-equipped with R.E.8s and flew them in a reconnaissance role until the armistice.

Using B.E.12s no official squadron marking was used, but some time in the autumn a white dumbbell was painted behind the fuselage cockade as an unofficial marking. No details are known about this period.

On re-equipping with R.E.8s the dumbbell was still used and it was used until 22nd March, 1918.

Squadron Markings

Allocated 26th August, 1917 – a white dumbbell on fuselage sides behind the cockade.

Flight Markings

Probably by coloured wheel covers.

Individual Markings

In the first period numbers were used painted between the cockade and the squadron marking. Late in 1917 or early in 1918 letters replaced the numbers and were used until the armistice.

R.E.7 force landed at Chateau Forestal, Pas de Calais, 17.6.16, Lt. Coombe and Mlle de Roquigny in aircraft.

R.E.8 "11."

R.E.8 "M" and Capt. B.E. Catchpole.

R.E.8 A'3224 "15" at Droglandt.

R.E.8 C'2601 "K" with Capt. J.R. Hopkins, Lt. Watney, and F/Sgt. Monery.

R.E.8 B'8889 "M" with Capt. B.E. Catchpole, May 1918.

No.22 Squadron R.F.C.

Formed September 1915 and moved to France 1st April, 1916, equipped with F.E.2bs as a reconnaissance unit. Re-equipped in August 1917 with Bristol Fighters. Their role changed to fighter-reconnaissance until the armistice.

There is no known date when the squadron first marked its F.E.2bs; it was probably not until the autumn of 1916.

Squadron Markings
None used on F.E.2bs.

Flight Markings
The flight letter was marked in white either side of the fuselage in front of the cockade.

Individual Markings
By numbers 1–6 behind the flight letter. Repeated below the lower wings, often on white on a dark disc.

On converting to Bristol Fighters:

Squadron Markings
Allocated 26th August, 1918, three white vertical bars on fuselage sides; one in front of the cockade, one behind, and one immediately in front of the tailplane.

Flight Markings
"A" Flight used red wheel covers.
"B" Flight used white wheel covers.
"C" Flight used blue wheel covers.

Individual Markings
By letters in white on the fuselage side, roughly midway between the second and third bars of the squadron marking:
"A" Flight used A, B, C, D, E, F.
"B" Flight used G, H, J, K, L, M.
"C" Flight used N, O, P, Q, R, S.

The squadron marking was deleted officially on 22nd March, 1918. The letters remained the same but were moved closer to the cockade and repeated on the centre section and again beneath the lower wing.

Flight commanders usually flew A, G, N and also carried rudder streamers.

F.E.2b 4883 "B1" *Kookaburra*, Major Learmont, D.S.O., MC., C.O. at Chippilly, early 1917.

F.E.2b A'857 "B" of Capt. F.P. Don and 2/Lt. Harris, shot down 5.6.17 over Lesdain.

A'85.7 Just captured "a family photo."

Bristol F2b A'7163.

Bristol F2b "H."

Bristol F2b "L" shot down, date unknown, being repainted by Germans.

Bristol F2b B'1112 "F." Later to 16 Squadron.

Bristol F2b "F" with extra Lewis guns.

Bristol F2b "I." Another version of extra guns.

No.23 Squadron R.F.C.

Formed 1st September, 1915, and after training moved to France in March 1916 equipped with F.E.2bs as a fighter-reconnaissance unit. In January 1917 re-equipped with SPAD Scouts and became a fighter squadron. In March 1918 was re-equipped with Sopwith Dolphins, retaining them until the armistice.

On using F.E.2bs:

Squadron Markings
None allocated.

Flight and Individual Markings
Each flight marked its flight letter on the nose of the nacelle with the individual number either side of it.

On using SPAD Scouts:

Squadron Markings
None used on re-equipment.

Flight and Individual Markings
It appears from photographs that each flight painted the nose cowling in a different fashion. One used black and white narrow stripes, one blue and white, and one plain red. Other markings seem to be a mixture of stripes and numbers on fuselage.

Squadron Markings
Allocated 26th August, 1917 a white triangle behind the fuselage cockade.

Individual Markings
By letters painted behind the squadron marking:
"A" Flight used A, B, C, D, E, F.
"B" Flight used L, M, N, O, P, Q.
"C" Flight used T, U, V, W, Y, Z.

In addition, "C" also painted the letter on the nose. The wheel covers of all aircraft were painted white.

On changing to Sopwith Dolphins, March/April, 1918:

Squadron Markings
Allocated March/April a white disc behind the fuselage cockade.

Individual Markings
By letters as before on the SPADs behind the squadron marking and repeated on the top decking.

F.E.2b 4852 "C6." Lt. F.G. Thierry, Lt. Buck, P.O.W. 17.9.16 by *Hptm.* Zander, *K.G.1.*

F.E.2b 4852 "C6" as above.

F.E.2b A'5449 "A1" presentation N.S.W.No.7, exchanged for SPAD 7, 12.2.17. Later to 100 Squadron.

RIGHT: SPAD B'1524 "1" 2/Lt. F.W. Illingworth P.O.W. (wounded) 7.6.17 by *Off.Stellv.* Aue of *Jasta* 10.

SPAD B'3460 2/Lt. Count L.T.B. di Balme P.O.W. 7.6.17 near Rumbeke by *Gefr.* Brettel, *Jasta* 10.

SPAD "Z" "C" Flight Capt. W.M. Fry in centre.

SPAD A'6682 "4" Lt. Craig, P.O.W. 22.7.17.

SPAD. Squadron Line up at La Lovie. Mostly SPAD 13s.

SPAD 13 B'6732 "A." Lt. Doyle, P.O.W. 26.2.18, shot down north of Laon by *Oblt.* von Tutschek.

Sopwith Dolphin "B."

SPAD 13 B'6732 "A" as at left.

Sopwith Dolphin E'4717 "M."

Sopwith Dolphin E'4147 "S" Crashed 3.5.18 St. Omer.

Sopwith Dolphin C'4150 "Y."

LEFT: Sopwith Dolphin "E."

No.24 Squadron R.F.C.

Went to France 7th February, 1916 with 12 D.H.2's. By the start of the Somme Battle (1st July, 1916) strength had increased to 18 D.H.2's with two or three Morane Monoplanes as reserves.

Squadron Markings
None allocated.

Flight and Individual Markings
Originally the wheel covers and outer interplane struts were painted in a flight colour:
"A" Flight was red.
"B" Flight was white.
"C" Flight was blue.

In June 1916 it was decided to adopt some kind of individual markings but this was difficult due to lack of space on the nacelle. To overcome this problem a unique system was adopted. The coloured struts were painted with a contrasting colour band or bands, never more than two – white on the red and blue struts, black on the white. If the sequence of bands was ever recorded no details have survived.

Again unique to the squadron was the saw-tooth pattern painted around the underside edges of the nacelle in grey or P.C.10. Early in 1917, large numbers were used as identity, painted on the nacelle and on the wings, possibly in flight colours.

Using D.H.5s:
The first D.H.5 arrived on 1st May, 1917, although it was not until the third week in June that the change-over was complete. No details of markings have been recorded but possibly the numerals of the earlier period were used.

Squadron Markings
Allocated on 26th August, 1917 – one white vertical band on the fuselage side in line with the trailing edge of the lower wing.

Individual Markings
"A" Flight used letters A, B, C, D, E, F.
"B" Flight used numbers 1, 2, 3, 4, 5, 6.
"C" Flight used letters U, V, W, X, Y, Z.

The letters and numbers were behind the cockade on fuselage. On Christmas Day, 1917, the first S.E.5a arrived and before long the squadron was fully equipped. Markings were as before.

Squadron Markings
Allocated on 22nd March, 1918, two white bands, one on either side of the cockade on the fuselage.

Individual Markings
Again by letters and figures behind the cockade and also painted on the upper centre section below the Foster mounting:
"A" Flight used A, B, C, D, E, F.
"B" Flight used 1, 2, 3, 4, 5, 6.
"C" Flight used U, V, W, X, Y, Z.

D.H.2 5930, 2/Lt. O. Lerwill, P.O.W. 25.3.16.

D.H.2 5983, Capt. J.O. Andrews. Red struts, white band.

D.H.2 6000, red struts, white bands, red wheel.

RIGHT: D.H.5 A'9463 "6."

D.H.2. Lt. P.A. Langan Byrne KIA 16.10.16 by *Hptm.* Oswald Boelcke of *Jasta* 2 for his 34th victory. Note sawtooth edging.

S.E.5a B'548 "Z" crashed.

D.H.5 A'9435 "E" Lt. G.P. Robertson P.O.W. 10.9.17.

D.H.5 A'9272 "3" Lt. Cowper.

S.E.5a C'1057 "C," Lt. Wigan P.O.W. 6.3.18 by *Oblt.* A. von Tutschek, C.O. *J.G.2.*

RIGHT: S.E.5a F'5689 "F," Lt. Seymour.

S.E.5a E'1293 "4," Capt. C.N. Lowe, "B" Flight Commander.

S.E.5a F'5459 "Y," wings with reduced dihedral.

No.25 Squadron R.F.C.

Went to France in February, 1916 equipped with F.E.2bs, later receiving the more powerful 2ds.

Unofficial markings were used which identified the squadron and flights. Across the noses of the Fees were painted either one, two, or three horizontal black bands usually outlined in white:
"A" Flight used one band.
"B" Flight used two bands.
"C" Flight used three bands.

During June/July 1917 the squadron was re-equipped with D.H.4s and these also carried on the unofficial black band tradition.

A black horizontal band was painted along the centre line of the fuselage behind the cockade; this band was repeated on the fin. The fuselage band was broken to enable the individual letter to be painted on. The letter was repeated on the side of the engine panel. The original 16 aircraft were lettered:

A, B, C, D, E, F, G, H, J, K, L, M, N, O, P, R, Z.

Squadron Markings

Allotted on 26th August, 1917, a white crescent painted on the fuselage side behind the cockade.

Individual Markings

By letters in white behind the squadron marking:
"A" Flight used A, B, C, D, E, F.
"B" Flight used G, H, J, K, L, M.
"C" Flight used N, O, P, Q, R, S; Spare – Z

After the squadron marking was discontinued on 22nd March, 1918, the individual markings were retained but moved closer to the cockade.

F.E.2b 6341, Presentation "Zanzibar No.1," Capt. D. Grinnel-Milne and Cpl. D. MacMaster.

F.E.2b 6341, *Scotch Express* on other side. P.O.W. 16.5.16.

In October 1918 some D.H.9as were received but the squadron was not fully equipped with the type before the armistice. If any individual markings were painted on they were probably the same as on the D.H.4.

LEFT: F.E.2b 6940, Lt. C.S. Rogers K.I.A., Sgt. H. Taylor P.O.W., shot down at Noyelles 8.6.16.

D.H.4 A'2170 "L" of 2/Lt. R. Main and Lt. J.M. Leach shot down and turned over.

D.H.4 A'2170 After being pulled upright.

D.H.4 A'7563 "O" of 2/Lt. C.J. Fitzgibbon and 2/Lt. W. Rudman, M.C., lost 21.4.18 Valenciennes/Cambrai.

No.26 Squadron R.F.C.

Formed on 8th October, 1915, at Netheravon from personnel from the South African Flying Unit which had operated against the Germans in South West Africa. It returned in the December and operated in the campaigns in German East Africa. When this campaign was finished the squadron returned to England and was disbanded in July, 1918. It used various Farman pushers and later the B.E.2c. No markings are known.

No.26 Sqdn 'A' Flight 2.17, Njombe, German East Africa.

LEFT: No.26 Sqdn BE2c 8424 up country, German East Africa.

No.27 Squadron R.F.C.

Went to France on 1st March, 1916, with 10 Martinsyde G100s, later known as "Elephant." By the beginning of July the strength had been increased to 18 aircraft.

Originally no markings were used but around the middle of 1916 small wooden shields were fixed on the fuselage sides between the centre section struts. On this was painted an Elephant in flight colours:
"A" Flight – Red.
"B" Flight – White.
"C" Flight – Yellow.

These colours were repeated on the wheel covers. All aircraft were marked with a flight letter and were numbered 1 to 6. The flight letter was painted in white on the upper port wing and below the starboard in black. The individual number was in white on either side of the nose, repeated on the upper side starboard wing and in black below the port wing.

The first replacement D.H.4 arrived on 29th September, 1917, but it was not until the end of December that the squadron was completely equipped with them.

Squadron Marking

Allocated one white vertical bar painted on the fuselage side behind the cockade. This was notified in a letter from H.Q.R.F.C. dated 5th November, 1917, but may have been in use before that date. Probably used also on "Elephants" in November/December 1917.

Martinsyde 7266, 2/Lt. S. Dalrymple, going to France, February, 1916.

Martinsyde A'6263 "A5," June 1917.

Martinsyde Mixed flights "bombed up."

Martinsyde "2," "3," and "5" of "A" Flight at Fienvilliers, 1916.

Flight Markings
By coloured wheel covers as on the "Elephants" but at a later date "C" Flight may have changed to blue.

Individual Markings
By white letters painted on the sides of the nose, repeated twice on the upper wing either side of the centre section, repeated in black below the lower wings:
"A" Flight used A, B, C, D, E, F.
"B" Flight used G, H, J, K, L, M.
"C" Flight used N, O, P, Q, R, S.

Various aircraft had letters behind the cockade; these may have been used by "C" Flight. After the deletion of squadron markings on 22nd March, 1918, the letters were still used.

In May 1918 the squadron received its first D.H.9, but was still only partly equipped by the armistice. The flight and individual markings were the same on the D.H.9s as on the D.H.4s.

Martinsyde "A" 3978 "B4." 2/Lt. W.R. Skinner, P.O.W. 9.8.17.

RIGHT: D.H.4 "E" "bombed up."

BELOW: D.H.4 "A" Flight at Serny, Pas de Calais 17.2.18.

D.H.4 "G" with Fiat engine.

D.H.4 B'2071 "R."

D.H.9 C'6109 "P," 2/Lt. H. Wild and Sgt. E. Scott K.I.A. 16.6.18.

No.28 Squadron R.F.C.

Went to France at the beginning of October, 1917 equipped with Sopwith Camels.

Squadron Marking

Allocated on 10th October, a white square painted on the fuselage side behind the Cockade. It was repeated on the top wing, starboard of the centre section. Flights were marked with a flight letter painted very small in white just behind the cockpit.

Individual Marking

Each flight's aircraft were marked with large white numbers painted in front of the fuselage cockade. Numbers used were 1 to 6.

At the end of October, 1917 the squadron stood down and moved to Italy, flying operationally on 14th November, 1917. The squadron marking remained the same as in France, but shortly after arrival the individual markings were changed to white letters painted on the fuselage sides forward of the cockade, repeated on the top wing, port of the centre section.

"A" Flight used A, B, C, D, E, F.
"B" Flight used G, H, J, K, L, M.
"C" Flight used N, O, P, Q, R, S.

Spare aircraft used letters not allocated, for example "X." These markings were used until the armistice. Usually the white square used in Italy was smaller than that used in France.

Camel B'6345 "F" in Italy.

Camel B'6344 "G" of Capt. J. Mitchel MC, DFC, in Italy.

Camel B'5178 "C3" of Lt. R.A. Cartledge, lost 27.10.17.

Camel B'6362 "1" being shown to French aircrews.

Camel B'6344 "1" in France.

Camel B'5401 "E" of 2/Lt. H. Butler in Italy, K.I.A 22.2.18.

Camel D'8209 "H" of Lt. A.R. Strange, P.O.W. 13.7.18 in Italy.

Camel B'5169 "B" of Capt. C.M. McEwan MC, DFC, in Italy.

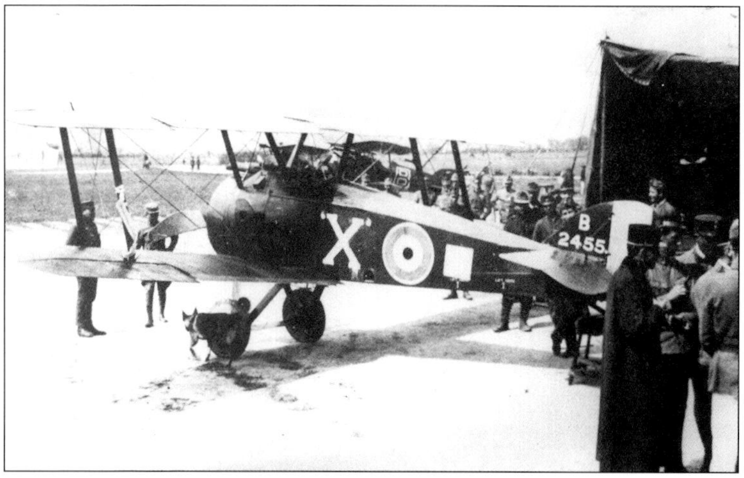

Camel B'2455 "X" of Lt. E.C. Forder, P.O.W. 11.5.18 in Italy.

Camel B'9310 "D" of Lt. S.M. Robins, P.O.W. 19.6.18 in Italy.

BELOW: Camel? "C" Italy, of Capt. Wilson, post armistice.

No.29 Squadron R.F.C.

Went to France in March, 1916, the second unit to have D.H.2s.

Squadron Markings

None allocated.

Flight Markings

Originally the wheel covers were painted red, white, or blue. During the summer, numbers were painted on the nose of the nacelle on the port side of the upper wing and below the port lower wing:
"A" Flight used red, outlined in shadow-shaded white.
"B" Flight used white, outlined in shadow-shaded blue.
"C" Flight used blue, outlined in shadow-shaded white.

The same colours were used below the wings, but white was used on upper wing.

Nieuport Scouts were received in March, 1917.

Squadron Markings

No official marking was used, but an unofficial marking of a broad red band was painted around the fuselage roughly midway between the cockade and tail.

Flight Markings

Cowlings were painted either blue, red, or blue and red quartered, although this was not used on aircraft all the time.

Individual Markings

Numbers were used in front of the cockade, probably the same colours as on the D.H.2s.

Squadron Markings

Allocated 26th August, 1917 – two vertical bands, one either side of the cockade, black on the silver aircraft and white on any in P.C.10 finish.

Flight Markings

Believed to have been by coloured wheel covers.

Individual Markings

By letters on fuselage side in front of the front band of the squadron marking, in white on P.C.10 covered aircraft and black on silver air craft. This was often repeated on the wings.

Squadron Markings

Allocated 27th December, 1917 when they expected to re-equip with S.E.5as – two white vertical bars behind the fuselage cockade. In fact, the S.E.5as did not arrive until March, 1918 and the squadron was not fully equipped with them until 19th April.

It is not known if any of the Nieuports used the new marking or if any of the early S.E.5as did so. In any case it was changed again.

Squadron Markings

Allocated 22nd March, 1918 – one vertical white band in front of the tailplane.

Flight Markings

None appear to have been used.

Individual Markings

"A" Flight used letters A, B, C, D, E, F in white on fuselage sides above the lower wing and repeated on the upper centre section on the starboard side and below the lower port in black.

"B" Flight used G, H, J, K, L, M on nose panels below exhaust and on wings as before.

"C" Flight appear to have painted the letters either on the nose panels or on the rear fuselage. Letters known to have been used are S, Q, U, Y, Z.

D.H.2 7849 "4" September, 1916

Nieuport 17 B1546 of Lt. B. Hill, P.O.W. 24.7.17.

RIGHT: Nieuport 17 B3598 of Lt. F.J. Ortweiler, P.O.W. 16.10.17 by *Oblt.* Erwin Bohme, *Jasta* B.

F. E. 8 (Fighting-Experimental) — Kampfeinsitzer (Scout)
wird von Engländern geflogen.

1. Ansichten des Flugzeuges:

2. Besondere Merkmale:
Gitterrumpf. Ovales Seitensteuer ohne die kurze Ausgleichsfläche von F.E.-Doppelsitzer 1a, keine dreieckige Kielflosse, kein Stoßrad, vierflügelige Druckschraube, Verwindungsklappen an oberen und unteren Tragdecks.

3. Besatzung:
Einsitzer.

4. Leistungen:
110 PS 9 Zylinder Gnome. An Geschwindigkeit und Steigfähigkeit dem Pfalz D III, sowie dem Albatros D III und V unterlegen, an Wendigkeit überlegen, fällt jedoch stark in der Kurve.

5. Bewaffnung:
1 Lewis-M.G., das festgestellt werden kann, mit mehreren Trommeln zu 100–200 Schuß, kein Zielfernrohr.

D.H.2 7925 "4" of 2/Lt. H.A. Hallam, P.O.W. 9.11.16. German identification leaflet but titled as F.E.8.

S.E.5a "L" Presentation No.5 Reserve Brigade R.F.A.(T).

S.E.5a F927 "A" at Bickendorf, 1919.

BELOW: S.E.5a "D," "E," and "F" from "A" Flight.

ABOVE: S.E.5a C8904 "H" at Bickendorf, 1919, with "L" in background.

RIGHT: S.E.5a "S" of 2/lt. D. O'Leary, P.O.W. (W.D.) 28.9.18.

BELOW: S.E.5a F934 "F" of Capt. Harrison (from South Africa).

No.30 Squadron R.F.C.

Formed at Ismailia in March, 1915 and served in Mesopotamia as a general purpose squadron flying a mixture of B.E.2c,s Martinsydes, R.E.8s, SPAD Scouts, and anything else available.

No squadron marking was issued but the squadron used a broad white band around the fuselage roughly midway between the cockade and the tailplane.

Martinsyde S.1.

R.E.8 B'6612.

SPAD A'8812 at Faluja, Mesopotamia.

R.E.8 A'4352.

BELOW: R.E.8 crashed, no details.

No.31 Squadron R.F.C.

Formed 11th October, 1915 for service in India. At the end of November one flight sailed, followed by one in January, 1916, and one in April, 1916. Equipped with B.E.2c and B.E.2e, used to stand guard on the N.W. Frontier. No markings are recorded.

No.32 Squadron R.F.C.

Went to France on 28th May, 1916 as a fighter unit equipped with D.H.2s, retaining them until June, 1917 when they became fully equipped with D.H.5s. These were replaced by S.E.5as in December, 1917 which were used until the armistice.

Using D.H.2s

No squadron markings were used.

Flight Markings

In July/August, 1916 the flights were marked with coloured wheel covers. They were painted in black and white rings.
"A" Flight one white narrow ring on a black background.
"B" Flight one black narrow ring on a white background.
"C" Flight a white central spot on a black background.

This method was of limited use and later in the year additional markings were applied. The flight letter was painted in white on the top port wing and an individual number on the top starboard wing. The letters and numbers were repeated on the underside of the nacelle in black.

Using D.H.5s

Any markings for the earliest period are unknown but were probably the same as using the D.H.2s.

Squadron Markings

Allocated on 26th August, 1917 – one white vertical band immediately behind the fuselage cockade.

Flight Markings

The flight letter was painted in white in various positions:

"A" and "C" Flights painted the letter on the fuselage sides in line with the trailing edge of the lower wing.

"B" Flight painted the letter on the top of the fuselage about half way along and in black below the fuselage.

Individual Markings

"A" and "C" Flights had a number on the upper wing port side and often the flight letter on the starboard. "B" Flight had the number immediately behind the flight letter on the fuselage top and bottom.

Using S.E.5As

The order from H.Q. R.F.C. dated 3rd December, 1917 shows that the squadron was allocated the same marking as on the D.H.5s.

Squadron Markings

Allocated 22nd March, 1918, two white bars sloping in at the top behind the fuselage cockade.

B.E.2c probably at Risalpur, N.W. India. *Do You Want a Tow.*

B.E.2c 4340 "2" and Skull and Crossbones, "Many Helping Hands."

D.H.2 "B" Flight used 24.8.16 to 9.9.16

RIGHT: D.H.2 7851 "C" Flight of 2/Lt. F.G. Wagner, M.I.A. 7.1.17.

Flight Markings

Flight letter in white in the area of the leading edge of the lower wing, the position varied slightly.

Individual Markings

By numbers on the top of the upper wing in white and in black below the lower wing. Each flight used 1 to 6.

D.H.2 7862 used 19.7.16 to 28.3.17 when damaged in action. The pilot was 2/Lt. A.V. Gompertz. Note rockets on struts.

D.H.5 A'9340 "C" Flight. These markings are incorrect but are believed to be a "mock up" for War Savings Exhibition in London.

S.E.5a of Lt. W. Tyrell, "3" on wing, showing camouflage.

RIGHT: S.E.5a E'5937 "B" Flight, of 2/Lt. J.O. Donaldson (USAS and RAF) P.O.W., shot down 1.9.18 on an Offensive Patrol near Cambrai.

D.H.2 7851 "C" Flight of 2/Lt. F.G. Wagner, M.I.A. 7.1.17.

D.H.5 "B1" crashed on aerodrome.

S.E.5a B'166 "A" Flight "2" on wing.

No.33 Squadron R.F.C.

Formed at Filton 12th January, 1916 as a training squadron but in March became part of the Home Defence Force. Moved to Yorkshire as defence for the industrial areas around Leeds and Sheffield against Zeppelin attacks. After these ceased the squadron remained in the area and took up a subsidiary role as a Training Unit.

Equipment

B.E.2c and e, B.E.12, F.E.2b and d, Avro 504K.

Squadron Markings

None allocated.

Individual Markings

None known to have been used officially. Personal names were probably used in some cases.

F.E.2d A'6356 Presentation "Ceylon No.4," *Flying Fox,* used 24/25.9.17 by Lt. Carruthers.

No.34 Squadron R.F.C.

Went to France in July, 1916 equipped with B.E.2es.

Squadron Markings

Date of allotment is unknown, probably shortly after arriving in France – a sloping white bar either side of the cockade on the fuselage. Re-equipped with R.E.8s in January, 1917 and retained the same squadron marking.

Individual Markings

By numbers painted on the fuselage side behind the squadron marking. Numbers 1 to 18 were used. In November, 1917 the squadron moved to Northern Italy, taking their R.E.8s with them. For a while the squadron marking and individual markings were retained, but early in 1918 the numbers were changed to letters to conform with the other squadrons then in Italy.

Squadron Markings

The sloping bars are believed to have been retained until the armistice.

Individual Markings

By letters painted in white on the fuselage side mid-way between the tailplane and the cockade. Letters "A" to "S" were used.

R.E.8 "8."

R.E.8 "14."

BELOW: R.E.8s, possibly on arrival in Italy.

R.E.8 "M" in Italy.

R.E.8 B'793 "P."

R.E.8 D'4780 "N."

No.35 Squadron R.F.C.

Formed 1st February, 1916 as a Corps reconnaissance unit and moved to France end of January, 1917 equipped with Armstrong Whitworth F.K.8s. Before going overseas, the squadron had been especially trained for co-operation with the Cavalry. It was immediately attached to the Cavalry Corps, remaining until March, 1918, then undertaking general reconnaissance duties.

Squadron Markings

Allocated 26th August, 1917 – a white band along the centre of the sides of the fuselage broken by the cockade.

Individual Markings

By numbers on the fuselage side, usually behind the cockade in white. Numbers 1 to 18 were used.

The squadron had a few Bristol Fighters during 1918 for "special jobs." These were marked as the F.K.8s with numbers greater than 18, e.g. 19.

When the squadron markings were discontinued from 22nd March, 1918 the individual markings remained. A number of squadron aircraft flew without any individual markings. Some observers were not happy with large amounts of white around their cockpits.

A.W. F.K.8 A'2707 flown by Lt. Jenkins. Crashed 16.2.17, repaired, flown on Offensive Patrols by Jenkins. On 4.9.17 crashed on aerodrome by Blackie and Shaw.

A.W. F.K.8 C'3549 "8."

ABOVE: B.F.2b B'1134 "19." Previously with No.48 Squadron.

RIGHT: November, 1918. Observer A.H. Coles.

No.36 Squadron R.F.C.

Formed at Cramlington 1st February, 1916 as a Home Defence Unit for the North of England. Operated in the Tyne and Tees area until the armistice.

Equipment

B.E.2c and e, B.E.12 and 12a, F.E.2b and d, Bristol Fighter, Sopwith Scout. The squadron was scheduled to re-equip with Avro 504Ks at the armistice.

Squadron Markings

None Allocated.

Individual Markings

Probably none other than personal names, etc.

Sopwith Scout B'1807 "A7" which later went to No.198 N.T.S.

B.E.2d with three Le Prieur rockets on the port side.

No.37 Squadron R.F.C.

Formed at Orfordness as an experimental unit but became part of the establishment. Re-formed 15th September, 1916 as a Home Defence Unit to cover the north-eastern approaches to London from Zeppelin attacks.

Equipment

B.E.2d and e, B.E.12, 12a, 12b, Sopwith two-seater, Sopwith Scout, S.E.5a. Shortly before the armistice the squadron was equipped with Sopwith Camels.

Squadron Markings

None allocated.

Individual Markings

None known to have been used. Personal names were probably used in some cases.

Sopwith Scout A'653 used 7.7.17 by Capt. G.A. Ridley, later it was transferred to No.61 Squadron and written off in a ground collision 6.10.17.

No.38 Squadron R.F.C.

Formed as a Training Unit 1st April, 1916, re-formed 14th July 1916 as a Home Defence Unit at Castle Bromwich. Operated from fields in Lincolnshire as protection for industrial targets in the Midlands against Zeppelin attacks. When these stopped, acted as a Night Training Unit. On 31st May, 1918 moved to France as a night bombing unit, taking their F.E.s with them.

Equipment

B.E.2c, 2d, 2e, B.E.12, B.E.12a, F.E.2b, F.E.2d.

Squadron Markings

None allocated.

Individual Markings

Probably personal markings only.

Camel "H" of Hollington at Stow Maries, 1918.

Camel F'1333 "M" of Lt. Murray at Stow Maries, 1918.

No.39 Squadron R.F.C.

Formed at Hounslow, 15th April, 1916 as a Home Defence Unit, operated from fields in Essex and Kent to cover the north-eastern approaches to London. Remained in this role until a few days before the armistice and then moved to France with their Bristol Fighters.

Equipment

B.E.2c and d, B.E.12, 12a, A.W. F.K.8, S.E.5a, Sopwith Camel. On the night of 5th December, 1917 they introduced the Bristol Fighter to Home Defence duties and by mid-January, 1918 were fully equipped with them.

Squadron Markings

None allocated.

Flight and Individual Markings

Up until the Bristol Fighters there is no evidence of any markings. Photographic evidence shows the following on Bristol Fighters:

RIGHT: F.E.2b C'9795 night bomber. There is a narrow white stripe on rudder.

1. A horizontal line along the centre of the fuselage side with a number painted behind the cockade. Line and numbers were probably blue outlined in white. Numbers 1, 2, 8 seen in use February/March 1918.

2. A large black diamond outlined white on fuselage side behind the cockade in use February/March 1918.

3. "A" "6" painted on each side of the fuselage cockade in black, shadow-shaded white, in use May,1918.

B.F.2b B'1262 "8" presentation "Maharajah of Bahadur, Sir Rameswar Singh of Darbhanga No.2."

B.F.2b "2" Presentation as above No.5.

RIGHT: B.F.2b C'4645 "4" black diamond.

BELOW: B.F.2b "1" and "2."

No.40 Squadron R.F.C.

"A" Flight went to France 2nd August, 1916 followed by "B" and "C" on the 19th. It was initially equipped with F.E.8s.

Squadron Markings

None at this time.

Flight Markings

By coloured wheel covers:
"A" Flight used red covers.
"B" Flight used white covers.
"C" Flight used blue covers.

Individual Markings

By large numbers on the nacelle forward of the cockade:
"A" Flight used 1 to 6 in red outlined in white.
"B" Flight used 1 to 6 in white.
"C" Flight used 1 to 6 in blue outlined in white.

During March, 1917 the squadron re-equipped with Nieuport Scouts, eventually having Types 17, 23, and 27 and had a change of markings.

F.E.8 7624 "6" of Capt. Mapplebeke, P.O.W. 9.11.16.

Flight Markings

By coloured wheel covers as before.

Individual Markings

"A" Flight used numbers, 1, 2, 3, 4, 5, 6 in black behind cockade.

"B" Flight used Roman Numerals I, II, III, IV, V, VI behind the cockade in white with black trim. These were repeated on the top wing in various ways.

"C" Flight used numbers, 1, 2, 3, 4, 5, 6 behind the cockade in blue with white trim.

Squadron Marking

Allotted 26th August, 1917, these were three white vertical bands around the fuselage, one in front and one behind the cockade and one just in front of the tailplane.

In the beginning the other markings remained the same as before but very soon changes took place. There is no official reason but the squadron marking changed to one band in front of the cockade and two in front of the tailplane. The flight markings remained but the individual markings changed to letters behind the cockade. These were often based on names, nicknames, or fancies.

During October, 1917 the squadron converted to S.E.5as.

Squadron Markings

Officially these were the same as on the Nieuports but again were painted with two bands in front of the tailplane.

Flight Markings

As before.

Individual Markings

By white letters behind the fuselage cockade, repeated on the top port wing:

"A" Flight used A, B, C, D, E, F.

"B" Flight used G, H, J, K, L, M.

"C" Flight used N, O, P, Q, R, S.

Squadron Marking

Allotted 22nd March, 1918 this was a "white sloping 'N'" on the rear fuselage.

F.E.8 6388 "4" of 2/Lt. J. Hay, K.I.A. 23.1.17 near Lens.

F.E.8 6456 "4" of Lt. T. Shepard, Missing 9.3.17.

F.E.8 A'4874 "4" of 2/Lt. G.F. Haselar, P.O.W. 9.3.17.

F.E.8 "3" with Capt. F.J. Powell, MC, in Centre.

Flight Markings
As before.

Individual Markings
By letters as before but again in some cases, initials and names, etc., were used to indicate the pilot.

Some time in mid-1918, "B" Flight painted their letters in black with a white trim – possibly this was also done by the other flights in their flight colours. Struts were also banded.

The squadron marking as allotted was shown as a "sloping 'N;'" most photographs show it being painted as a "backward sloping 'N.'"

Nieuport 17 "VI" at Bruay, 1917.

Nieuport 27 "L" used by MacLanachan and Mannock.

S.E.5a with tail trolley in foreground.

Nieuport 17 A'6680 "III."

Nieuport 17 "IV" A'6667 of 2/Lt. H.S. Pell, K.I.A. 6.4.17 during a special mission attacking a balloon at Sallaumines.

S.E.5a "O" leaving for France.

RIGHT: S.E.5a D'3511 of Major R.S. Dallas DSO, DSC, in camouflaged S.E.5a May, 1918.

S.E.5a D'3540 "K" Capt. Gwilym Lewis, DFC.

"S" Bi89 on strength 20.3.18, struck off 21.5.18, crashed.

"U" unknown serial. Both 'C' Flight. Chevron is unknown, may be flight marking.

No.41 Squadron R.F.C.

Went to France 15th October, 1916 equipped with F.E.8s. During the settling in period the aircraft were marked as follows:

"A" Flight – Red wheel covers, Nos.1 to 6 in red outlined in white.
"B" Flight – Blue wheel covers, Nos.1 to 6 in blue outlined in white.
"C" Flight – White wheel covers, Nos.1 to 6 in white.

The numbers were painted on the sides and bottom of the nacelle and on the centre line of the top wing. During the period, May/June 1917 Pilots complained that the number on the wing was a natural aiming point and it was then moved outwards.

During July the F.E.8s were withdrawn to be replaced by D.H.5s. In the beginning the D.H.5s were marked in the same fashion as the earlier F.Es.

Squadron Markings

Allotted on 26th August, 1917, two white vertical bars painted one either side of the cockade.

Flight Markings

Coloured wheel covers as on F.E.8.

Individual Markings

By white letters and numbers painted on the fuselage side in front of the squadron marking below the cockpit. These were repeated on the starboard top wing and below the starboard bottom wing:

"A" Flight used A, B, C, D, E, F
"B" Flight used 1, 2, 3, 4, 5, 6
"C" Flight used U, V, W, X, Y, Z

The D.H.5s were gradually replaced by S.E.5a during October/November 1917 and by the 7th November the squadron was fully equipped.

The squadron, flight, and individual markings remained the same but to improve identification the individual letters and numbers were painted behind the squadron marking. These markings remained until March, 1918.

Squadron Markings
Allotted 22nd March, 1918, two white vertical bars painted behind the cockade on the fuselage side.

Flight Markings
Had been discontinued although a few coloured wheel covers lingered on.

Individual Markings
"A" Flight used A, B, C, D, E, F.
"B" Flight used 1, 2, 3, 4, 5, 6.
"C" Flight used U, V, W, X, Y, Z.
Spare Aircraft "O."
Squadron Commander (Major Bowman) "M."

The squadron painted its squadron markings with much wider bars than usually seen on S.E.5as of other units.

F.E.8 7626 of Capt. G. Leaske over Ypres Salient.

F.E.8 of Lt. Soundy "B" Flight.

F.E.8 6454 of 2/Lt. G.S. Deane, P.O.W. 26.11.16.

F.E.8 used by Lt. C. Porter, Capt. G. Leaske, and Lt. Soundy.

RIGHT: F.E.8 6465 of 2/Lt. N.B. Hair, P.O.W. 7.6.17.

D.H.5 A'9276 of 2/Lt. J.L. Haight, P.O.W. 28.9.17.

S.E.5a C'1752 "E" used by Lt. F.H. Taylor, MC.

BELOW: D.H.5 A'9474 of 2/Lt. F.S. Clarke, P.O.W. 29.10.17.

S.E.5a "1" used by 2/Lt. Hemmings and 2/Lt. Jones.

S.E.5a E'3977 "C" of Lt. E.H. Barksdale with Capt. F.R. McCall showing off squadron dogs.

S.E.5a F'5910 "A" of Lt. W.G. Claxton, DSO, DFC, P.O.W. 17.8.18 in this aircraft.

RIGHT: S.E.5a C'5301 "C" used by Lt. A. Goby.

BELOW: S.E.5a F'912 "3" of Capt. E.J. Stephens, "B" Flight/Commander.

No.42 Squadron R.F.C.

Formed 1st April, 1916 and moved to France in August equipped with B.E.2c, later changing to 2d and 2e as a Corps Reconnaissance Unit. In April 1917 converted to R.E.8s.

In November moved to northern Italy for the same duties on the Austrian Front, returning to France in March 1918 and remaining until the armistice.

Squadron Markings

No exact date given for adopting any markings but in the later part of 1916 they were allocated a white square painted behind the fuselage cockade. After receiving the R.E.8s this square was retained and also used in Italy. In many cases it was also painted on the top decking and below the fuselage, probably in black.

Individual Markings

By Letters on fuselage sides behind the squadron marking. On returning to France in March, 1918 the white square was discontinued and the letters retained.

ABOVE RIGHT: R.E.8 "E."

RIGHT: R.E.8 "E" showing cockpit details.

BELOW: R.E.8 A3843 with cellon centre section.

No.43 Squadron R.F.C.

Went to France in January, 1917 equipped with Sopwith two-seaters. Originally no form of markings were carried but in February all the aircraft were marked with a flight letter and an individual number. These varied considerably in style and application:

"A" Flight aircraft were marked A – 1, 2, 3, 4, 5, 6.
"B" Flight aircraft were marked B – 1, 2, 3, 4, 5, 6.
"C" Flight aircraft were marked C – 1, 2, 3, 4, 5, 6.

During the last few days of August and the first days of September, these markings were painted out and all aircraft were marked with a letter painted in front of the fuselage cockade:

"A" Flight used A, B, C, D, E, F.
"B" Flight used G, H, J, K, L, M.
"C" Flight used N, O, P, Q, R, S.

Sopwith two-seater A'8337 "A-4."

Squadron Marking

Allotted on 26th August, 1917, it was a solid white triangle painted behind the fuselage cockade. This was painted on the two-seaters and also on the Camels as they arrived. Early in October, the squadron was fully equipped with Camels.

Individual Markings

By white letters painted on the fuselage sides in front of the cockade:

"A" Flight used A, B, C, D, E, F.
"B" Flight used G, H, J, K, L, M.
"C" Flight used N, O, P, Q, R, S.

Some extra Camels arrived early in 1918 and took up some of the unused letters.

Sopwith two-seater A'8784 "B-2."

Squadron Marking

Allotted 22nd March, 1918, this was two white sloping bars, one either side of the cockade. In many cases this was repeated on the upper wing, one bar either side of the centre section.

Individual Markings

By white letters painted behind the squadron marking:

"A" Flight used A, B, C, D, E, F, G, H.
"B" Flight used I, J, K, L, M, N, O, P.
"C" Flight used R, S, T, U, V, W, Y, Z.

These were repeated on the port side of the upper wing.

Sopwith two-seater A'1100 "C-5."

Personal Markings

During this period some Camels had names painted on the front edge of the cowling, such as *Sunbeam* and *Fortuna*. Others had a heraldic badge below the cockpit.

In September, 1918 the Camels were replaced with Sopwith Snipes. Squadron and flight markings remained the same.

When Capt. Woollett started to specialize in balloon strafing, he painted patches of white on his Camel and added two white bands around the fuselage. The Wing Commander thought this could lead to an accident and advised their removal. It is not known if this Camel flew so marked.

RIGHT: Sopwith two-seater A'993 "A-6" of 2/Lt. C.M. Reece and 2 a.m. A. Moult. Shot down 28.4.17 while on line patrol over Lens-Neuvireuil.

Sopwith two-seater B'2552 "X" marking change.

Camel "A" Flown by Capt. H. Balfour.

Camel B'3839 "W."

RIGHT: Camel "Z," etc., a line up of "C" Flight.

BELOW: Camel "S" painted up for a balloon attack by Capt. H. Woollett. He was ordered to paint it out.

Camel "T," etc., a line up of "C" Flight.

Camel showing the badge on Capt. H. Woollett's aircraft.

Camel showing the badge on Lt. Lingham's aircraft.

Snipe E'8015 "E" at Bickendorf early 1919.

Camel C'8215 "I" of Capt. L.G. Loudoun, P.O.W. 29.8.18. Note markings on top wing.

Snipes "J, K, L, Q" at Fienvillers September, 1918.

Snipe E'8006 of E.G. Weaver.

Snipes lined up at Bickendorf, 1918/19.

No.44 Squadron R.F.C.

Formed 24th July, 1917 at Hainault Farm as a Home Defence Unit for the London area until the armistice.

Equipment

Initially Sopwith two-seaters but the squadron was re-equipped with Sopwith Camels in August, 1917 and flew their first operation on the 12th.

Squadron Markings

None allocated.

Flight Markings

Originally no markings were used. Later in the autumn, flights were marked:
"A" Flight a white cartoon terrier dog on fuselage side.
"B" Flight a white crescent moon on fuselage side.
"C" Flight a white helmet and plume on fuselage side.

These signs were also on the front of the hangars. These did not last long and more conventional markings were used:
"A" Flight used numbers on fuselage sides behind cockade.
"B" Flight used a broad white band flanked in blue behind the cockade.
"C" Flight same as "B" but flanked in red.

At the same time wheel discs and fins were white.

The squadron appeared to change or vary their markings at will.

Camel B'2402 in original form.

Camel and "Comic" line up.

Camel. Flight/Commander's aircraft with running dog insignia.

Camel with Viking helmet insignia.

Camel B'2402 after modification to "comic" version.

Camel squadron line up at Hainault Farm.

No.45 Squadron R.F.C.

Was formed 1st March, 1916 and went to France in October equipped with Sopwith two-seaters as a fighter-reconnaissance unit. In July, 1917 was re-equipped with Sopwith Camels with a fighter role. In November, 1917 it went to northern Italy for operations on the Austrian Front, returning to France in September, 1918.

It was re-equipped with long-range Sopwith Snipes and attached to the Independent Force to escort to their day bombing squadrons. The armistice came before this occurred so that normal offensive patrols took place.

Squadron Markings

Using Sopwith two-seaters no official marking was allocated but some confusion occurred when the squadron operated in the same areas in which Naval Sopwiths were also flying. To alleviate this, the squadron painted a vertical band behind the cockade on the fuselage. This was painted black on the clear-doped fabric of the older aircraft and white on the more recent aircraft in P.C.10.

Individual Markings

About early May, 1917 individual markings were painted on. They are believed to be:

"A" Flight – A to F.
"B" Flight – 1 to 6.
"C" Flight – N to T.

All were in white below the cockpit.

During August the two-seaters were replaced and by 1st September the squadron was fully equipped with Sopwith Camels.

Squadron Marking

Allocated 26th August, 1917 a white dumbbell on the sides of the fuselage behind the cockade, repeated on the top decking.

Individual Markings

"A" Flight used A, B, C, D, E, F.
"B" Flight used G, H, J, K, L, M.
"C" Flight used N, O, P, R, S, T.

The squadron "acquired" a few spare Camels; these were marked as the flights "U" and "V" at least.

On 16th November, 1917 the squadron was withdrawn and moved to Italy by train, leaving on 12th December, and was operational by the end of the year. Markings remained the same but in some cases the individual letters were of a more fancy pattern.

To try and deceive the Austrians that another Camel squadron had arrived, "A" Flight moved from Grossa to Easoni Airfield. The dumbbell was painted out and a broad white vertical band was painted around the fuselage behind the cockade. Individual letters remained the same, "A" to "F." This was known as "D" Flight from about August, 1918.

On the 20th September, 1918 the squadron was withdrawn and returned to France to join the Independent Force, where it should have received long-range Snipes to become an escort squadron to day bombers of the Force. The Snipes never arrived and the squadron flew normal patrols with Camels.

Nieuport 12 A'6740; the band could be red.

Sopwith two-seater A'1083 with black band.

Sopwith two-seater with white band.

Camel"5" whose engine failed; Lt. Bush crashed on British side of the lines.

RIGHT: Camel "4."

Camel "L."

Camel "J" in the Marshes.

Camels "A" Flight at Istrana, Italy 1918.

Camels "B" Flight at Istrana, Italy 1918.

Camel "G."

Camel "K" of 2/Lt. J.E. Child.

Camel "R."

No.46 Squadron R.F.C.

Went to France in October, 1916 and were equipped with Nieuport two-seaters. These carried no markings but may have had coloured wheel covers. In April, 1917 the squadron re-equipped with Sopwith Scouts – 12 to begin with and later increased to 18.

Squadron Marking

None used at this period.

Flight Markings

"A" Flight used blue wheel covers.
"B" Flight used white wheel covers.
"C" Flight used red wheel covers.

Individual Markings

Each flight was marked 1, 2, 3, and 4 behind the fuselage cockade, repeated twice on the upper wing just inboard of the cockades, all in white, and probably marked below the lower wing in black.

In May, there was a change of markings which coincided with the increase in strength.

Flight Markings

Again by coloured wheel covers, but at this time some pilots had additional markings on the covers but there was no set system. Some were painted as a cockade, others as blue and white halves, red, white and blue segments, skull and crossbones, etc. In some cases these markings were painted on the centre section.

Individual Markings

"A" Flight used A, B, C, D, E, F.
"B" Flight used 1, 2, 3, 4, 5, 6.
"C" Flight used U, V, W, X, Y, Z.

During the period 10th July–30th August, the squadron was in England on Home Defence duties and some "painting up" took place, mainly names on the fuselage sides. On returning to France these were painted out.

Squadron Markings

Allocated 19th September, 1917, two white vertical bands in front of the tailplane. Individual markings remained the same.

Allotted 22nd March, 1918 – a long white bar along the top, bottom, and centre of the sides of the fuselage. In practice the top and bottom bars were usually not used.

Flight Markings

By blue, white, and red wheel covers as before.

Individual Markings

Establishment increased to 24 aircraft – painted on fuselage sides.
"A" Flight used A, B, C, D, E, F, G, H.
"B" Flight used 1, 2, 3, 4, 5, 6, 7, 8.
"C" Flight used S, T, U, V, W, X, Y, Z.

In many cases these were not painted on the wings.

Sopwith Scout A'7327 "1" of Capt. Pratt with cross bones on wheels.

Sopwith Scout A'7327 "1" of Capt. Pratt showing cross bones on centre section.

Sopwith Scout B'1727 "2" of Lt. N. Dimmock with half-and-half wheels.

Sopwith Scout "3" of Capt. Heath.

Sopwith Scout B'1719 "4" of Lt. Ferrie with three-colour wheels.

Sopwith Scout A'7325 "1" of Lt. Marchant with Three-colour wheels.

Sopwith Scout B'1777 "4" of Lt. A. Gould Lee. *Chin Chow* painted out 12.9.17.

Sopwith Scout A;6157 "6" of Lt. A.P. Mitchell, P.O.W. 7.6.17 over Polygon Wood. Cockades on wheels and centre section.

Sopwith Scout A'673 "5" of 2/Lt. L.M. Shadwell, P.O.W. 16.9.17, claimed by *Ltn.* Joerfe, *Jasta* 12.

Sopwith Scout B'1777 "4" of Lt. A. Gould Lee, *Chin Chow.*

Sopwith Scout B'1862 "W" at gun butts, Izel-le-Hameau.

Sopwith Scout, captured, no details. Note wing markings.

Camels "1 and 5" in the snow. "5" is B'5419 used by Lt. H.N.C. Robinson, MC. Struck off charge 29.1.18.

Camel "W" December, 1917.

Sopwith Camel B'5209 "X" of Lt. A.L. Clark, P.O.W.

Camel C'1659 "W" of Capt. Debenham.

Camel F'6253 "B" of Lt. Lazenby at Baizeux.

Camel D'6681 "A" of Lt. H.L. Cross, shot down 19.7.18, while ground strafing, made P.O.W.

No.47 Squadron R.F.C.

Formed on 1st March, 1916 and in September left for Greece to support Allied Forces in Salonika as a Reconnaissance Unit. Until April, 1918 it had a fighter flight attached, but this was withdrawn to help form No.150 Squadron.

The squadron flew reconnaissance missions over the Macedonian front until the Bulgarians surrendered on 30th September, 1918. Various aircraft were used; B.E.2e, B.E.12, Bristol Scouts, A.W. F.K.8s, Bristol Monoplanes, and S.E.5as. At the end of hostilities it was almost fully equipped with A.W. F.K.8s.

Markings

No markings seem to have been used although some names may have been used on the S.E.5as. When the Fighter Flight was withdrawn the squadron operated two flights, "A" and "C" each of five A.W. F.K.8s. On 21st August, 1918, six D.H.9' were added and made up "B" Flight.

D.H.9. Field Marshall Milne, G.O.C. Salonika Forces, about to fly in a D.H.9 of No.47 Squadron R.F.C. There appears to be a two-colour stripe on fuselage, perhaps blue and white.

A.W. F.K.8 B'3347 at Salonika.

A.W. F.K.8 B'5399 crashed by Christie 22.11.18.

RIGHT: Vickers F.B.19. at Salonika, one of the Fighter Flight.

BELOW: A.W. F.K.8 with Bulgarian aircraft on Sveta-Urae Aerodrome after armistice.

No.48 Squadron R.F.C.

Went to France March, 1917 equipped with Bristol F.2a, the first squadron to have them. These were replaced by the improved F.2b.

Squadron Markings

None allotted initially.

Individual Markings

By white numbers painted behind the cockade on the fuselage and repeated on the top decking:
"A" Flight used 1, 2, 3, 4, 5, 6.
"B" Flight used 7, 8, 9, 10, 11, 12.
"C" Flight used 13, 14, 15, 16, 17, 18.

Squadron Marking

Allotted 26th August – two white vertical bars behind the fuselage cockade. There is evidence that the "proposed" squadron marking of a sloping "N" behind the cockade was painted on for a short time.

Flight Markings

"A" Flight used red wheel covers.
"B" Flight used white wheel covers.
"C" Flight used blue wheel covers.

Individual Markings

As before.

Squadron Markings

By 23rd December, 1917 the squadron was using one white vertical bar in front of tailplane.

Flight Markings & Individual Markings

After 22nd March, 1918 the flight markings as before.

Individual Markings

"A" Flight used 1, 2, 3, 4, 5, 6, 7, 8.
"B" Flight used 9, 10, 11, 12, 13, 14, 15, 16.
"C" Flight used 17, 18, 19, 20, 21, 22, 23, 24.

B.F.2b "21."

B.F.2a A'3322 "5" of Lt. H.D. Davies and 2/Lt. R.S. Worsley, shot down east of Arras 13.4.17.

B.F.2a A'3322 shows fuselage markings in detail.

B.F.2b "9."

RIGHT: B.F.2b C'841 "11" of Lt. R.H. Little 26.4.18 to 26.6.18.

B.F.2b C'814 "12" of Major Keith Park.

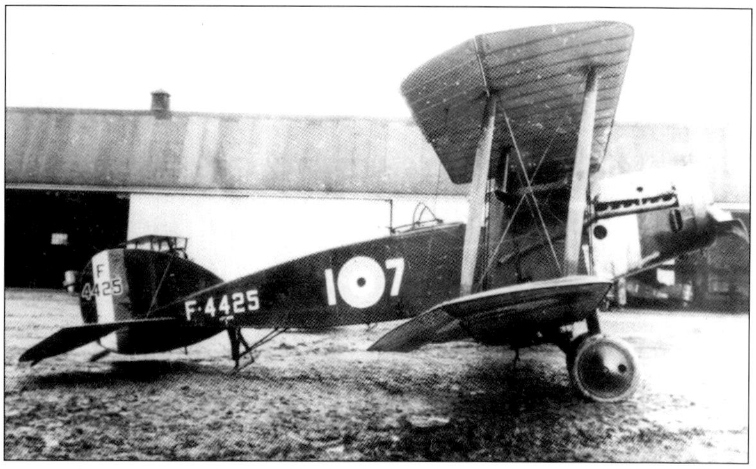

B.F.2b F'4425 "17" at Bickendorf 1918/19.

B.F.2b B'1124 of 2/Lt. J. Frost and 2/Lt. F.L. Smith landed in Holland 29.9.17 after an air combat.

B.F.2b B'1124 in Dutch colours with squadron marking visible.

B.F.2b B'1124 was used by the Dutch until 1924.

No.49 Squadron R.F.C.

The unit went to France on 12th November, 1917 fully equipped with D.H.4s. It re-equipped with D.H.9s during late March, 1918 and used them until the armistice.

Squadron Marking

Used from November until 22nd March, 1918 – a white dumbbell on the fuselage sides behind the cockade.

Flight and Individual Markings

Numbers and letters on the centre section and probably below lower wing:
"A" Flight used letters painted on sides of the cowling; A, B, C, D, E, F.
"B" Flight used numbers painted on sides of the cowling; 1, 2, 3, 4, 5, 6.
"C" Flight used letters painted on sides of the cowling; U, V, W, X, Y, Z.

Flight commanders were usually identified by a two-colour streamer fixed to the rear port outboard interplane strut.

D.H.4 B'7747 flown regularly by Lt. A.H. Curtis carried a personal marking originally inspired by a squadron artist who drew a number of very "eyeable" girls who wore a green cap. Lt. Curtis had a metal cone made and fixed to the propeller boss and painted green. From then on his aircraft was always known as "Miss Green Cap."

It was common practice in 49 Squadron to cross-post crews and machines from one flight to another to make up losses or crashes. This meant that the sequence of flight markings was often disrupted. If there was time, the original letter or number was painted out and a new one painted on. Lt. Morris was flying A'7694 "Z" when he was given one of the Fiat-engine aircraft; "Z" was transferred to another flight and his "Z" was over-painted "6."

They changed their D.H.4s to D.H.9s commencing in March 1918, becoming fully operational in April. Squadron markings were discontinued from 22nd March and at the same time the individual markings also changed. Letters were painted on the fuselage sides behind the cockade and probably on the centre section, repeated underneath the nose behind the propeller. The letters ran from "A" to "S" with "I" not used – if any extra machines were acquired they were marked with any of the remaining letters.

D.H.9 "Z."

D.H.4 B'7747 "6" of Lt. A.H. Curtis and 2/Lt. V. Gordon, crashed 16.2.18.

D.H.4 A'7694 "6," a replacement for B'7749.

D.H.9 C'6114 "M;" note "M" below nose.

D.H.9 C'6114 "M."

D.H.9 "N" shot down at Ostende.

No.50 Squadron R.F.C.

Formed at Dover 15th May, 1916 as a Home Defence Unit to protect south east England and the approaches to London. Operated from fields in Kent and later became part of the London Air Defence. Retained this role until the armistice.

Equipment

B.E.2c and 2e, B.E.12, 12a, 12b, A.W. F.K.8, Sopwith Scout, S.E.5a, Sopwith Camel.

Squadron Markings

None allocated.

Individual Markings

There is no evidence of any markings on the various B.E.s and F.K.8s in use.

Sopwith Scouts were received in small numbers in July 1917, but were withdrawn quickly. In May 1918 some S.E.5as were received and flew with B/E.12a and bs. Two S.E.5as were marked with coloured band around the fuselage, red with narrow white outlines on one and a mixture of red and blue on the other. During May 1918 S.E.5a D'5995 was marked with a broad red band around the fuselage with a white "1" superimposed.

July/August 1918 saw the squadron equipped with Sopwith Camels. No official markings were used but some carried two leaping dogs painted below the cockpit.

As a footnote to No.50 Squadron, the then C.O., Major M.G. Christie (15th May, 1916 to 23rd February, 1917), decided that the clear-dope finish on the B.E.2cs was useless for night flying. He had all his aircraft doped over-all black. However, when they were airborne during the day they had no national markings and were at risk from friendly aircraft and unfriendly A.A. guns. Therefore, white rings were painted on wings and fuselage which destroyed any value of the black covering. The idea was accepted by H.Q. Home Forces. who promulgated it for adoption by "all night flying aircraft" on 29th August, 1916. Photographs show this scheme was not always used.

B.E.2e at Detling 1917. Note under-wing marking.

RIGHT: B.E.12 6510 used 12.8.16 by 2/Lt. McClaughry with five Le Prieur rockets either side.

S.E.5a of Capt. C.J. Chabot, Bekesbourne.

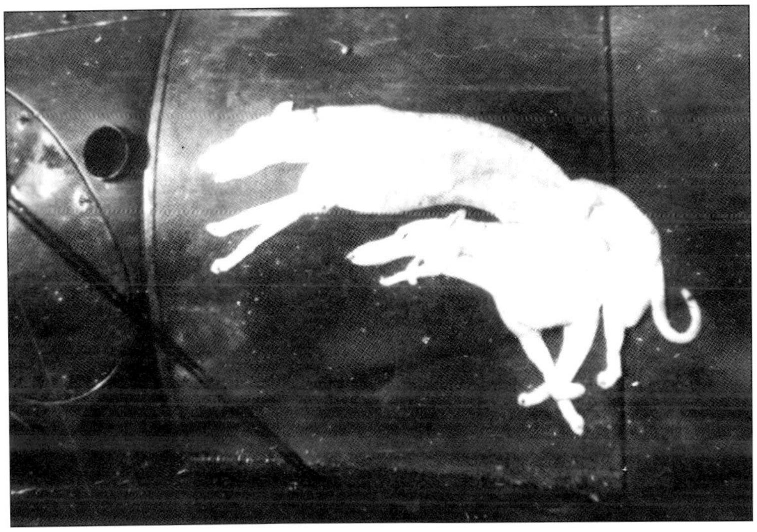

S.E.5a of Capt. Insall. Note crude flame dampers.

S.E.5a D'5995. Flight Commander's aircraft, Bekesbourne, 1918.

LEFT: S.E.5a line up at Bekesbourne, 1918.

BELOW: Camel, detail close up of "Dingo Dogs" insignia designed by G.S.M. Insall, VC, autumn 1918.

No.51 Squadron R.F.C.

Formed at Thetford 15th May, 1916 as Home Defence Unit for defence of the industrial midlands from fields in East Anglia. It retained this role until the armistice.

Equipment

F.E.2b, F.E.2d. Shortly before the armistice some Sopwith Camels arrived, but did not fly in the defence role.

Squadron Markings

None allocated.

Individual Markings

None known to have been used, probably personal names in some cases.

No.52 Squadron R.F.C.

Went to France 16th November, 1916 equipped with R.E.8s, exchanging these in February, 1917 for the B.E.2es of No.34 Squadron, re-equipped with R.E.8s again in May.

Squadron Markings

Date of allotment is unknown but probably dates from arrival in France – a white zig-zag on the fuselage sides from the fin to the cockade, repeated on the top decking. This was painted on both B.E.2es and R.E.8s and retained until 22nd March, 1918.

Individual Markings

On the B.E.s the marking for "A" and "B" Flights is unknown. "C" Flight – the letter "C" was painted on the fin above the serial number followed by a "Domino" marking, one spot to six spots. These were not used on the R.E.8s which were marked with numbers on the fuselage sides in front of the cockade. Originally numbers 1 to 18 were used; these were later increased to 24. After squadron markings were discontinued the numbers were still used. The zig-zag squadron marking was seen painted in various fashions.

RIGHT: R.E.8 A'4267.

BELOW: B.E.2e "C" Flight. Note "Domino" spots on fin.

F.E.2b A'5548 used 24/25.9.17 by Lt. H.D. Montgomery.

B.E.2e captured after forced landing 20.3.17. Presented by European & Indian Staff, Bombay Baroda & Central Indian Railway Company.

R.E.8 A'4267 "7."

R.E.8 "2" in background is "12."

R.E.8 "9" "Wind Up" below observer's cockpit.

No.53 Squadron R.F.C.

Formed 15th May, 1916 as a training unit but in the December it was moved to France and equipped with B.E.2e' as a Corps reconnaissance unit. In April, 1917 it re-equipped with R.E.8s and used these until the armistice.

Squadron Markings

Allocated a white crescent behind the cockade, date is uncertain but it was in the B.E.2e period.

On re-equipping with R.E.8:

Squadron Marking

Allocated 26th August, 1917 as before, this remained until 22nd March, 1918 when it was discontinued.

Individual Marking

By letters on fuselage sides behind the crescent squadron marking.

B.E.2e 7240; crescent is crossways on fuselage top, wheel is in colours, two Lewis guns carried.

B.E.2e 7250, overturned, fuselage broken behind cockade.

R.E.8 B'6598 at Villeselve March, 1918.

R.E.8 "M" crashed.

ABOVE: RE8 crashed in ditch.

RIGHT: RE8 'P' crashed.

No.54 Squadron R.F.C.

Went to France in December, 1916 equipped with Sopwith Scouts, the first R.F.C. squadron to do so. In the beginning no formal markings were used, instead pilots used their names, initials, or nicknames painted on the fuselage sides and also on the centre section. This expanded to include various paintings, e.g. a kangaroo and a girl's head. Due to the rapid turn round of aircraft, these markings began to disappear and ceased altogether when the pilot/artist was lost in early June, 1917. Some time in April or May a system was started which remained until the armistice.

Individual Markings

"A" Flight used 1, 2, 3, 4, 5, 6.
"B" Flight used 7, 8, 9, 10, 11, 12.
"C" Flight used 13, 14, 15, 16, 17, 18.

These were painted in white in front of the cockade on the fuselage.

Squadron Marking

Allotted 26th August, 1917, a long white bar along the top edge of sides of the fuselage, from the cockade to the tailplane.

Individual Markings

In December, the squadron was withdrawn to equip with Sopwith Camels and at the same time a change of squadron marking was notified but was not used until late January 1918. The squadron marking and individual markings which were used earlier were transferred to the Camels.

Squadron Marking

Used from late January, 1918 – a single white vertical bar painted in front of the cockade on the fuselage.

Individual Markings

Again by numbers in white but now painted behind the cockade:
"A" Flight used 1, 2, 3, 4, 5, 6.
"B" Flight used 7, 8, 9, 10, 11, 12.
"C" Flight used 13, 14, 15, 16, 17, 18.

There is a strong possibility that "13" was not used. These markings were retained until March 1918.

Squadron Marking

Allotted 22nd March, 1918 – a white sloping "N" behind the cockade on the fuselage. However, due to some misunderstanding, they still used a vertical white bar either side of the cockade. On 29th June, 1918 the squadron was ordered to use the correct marking as allotted in March.

Individual Markings

Were as before but now increased to 24.

Sopwith Scout flown by Lt. Oliver Stewart, spring 1917.

Sopwith Scout B'1721 "3" of Lt. F.W. Kantel shot down 30.5.17 while escorting F.E.2bs.

ABOVE RIGHT: Sopwith Scout A'6174 "Canada" of 2/Lt. G.C. Hadrill shot down 9.5.17 while escorting F.E.2bs.

RIGHT: Camel B'5423 "6" of 2/Lt. F.M. Ohrt, shot down 19.1.18 during an offensive patrol over Ramicourt.

Camel C'1576 "18" of 2/Lt. E.B. Lee, missing 18.3.18 after an offensive patrol to Busigny.

Camel B'5417 "11" of 2/Lt. G.A. Manley shot down 9.2.18 on wireless interruption patrol near Sissy.

Reverse photo of B5417 above right. Cowling became detached, and Lt. Manley was forced to land.

C'6720 Capt. F.L. Luxmore. O.P. Busigny 18.3.18. Shot down by Lt. H. Kirschstein of Jasta 6. Became PoW.

No.55 Squadron R.F.C.

Went to France 6th March, 1917 equipped with D.H.4s, the first squadron to use them.

Squadron Marking

None used at this period.

Flight Marking

By coloured wheel covers:
"A" Flight used red.
"B" Flight used white.
"C" Flight used blue.

Individual Markings

By names of gods and goddesses painted about three inches (75mm) high in white below the exhaust manifold. Examples include:

Juno used by Major John Baldwin, the C.O.
Psyche used by Lt. Barnett.
Mars used by Lt. G.W. Murray of "C" Flight.

Other names known to have been used include *Apollo, Jupite*r, and *Saturn*.

Once the squadron became operational it was realized that the names were not enough to identify individual aircraft. About the middle of April the following scheme was used:
"A" Flight used red wheel covers and Nos. 1, 2, 3, 4, 5, 6.
"B" Flight used white wheel covers and Nos. 1, 2, 3, 4, 5, 6.
"C" Flight used blue wheel covers and Nos. 1, 2, 3, 4, 5, 6.

The numbers were painted on the fuselage sides just behind the rear cockpit. The names were still in use but as aircraft were lost or written of they started to disappear and that fashion did not appear again.

Squadron Markings

Allotted 26th August, 1917 a solid white triangle painted behind the fuselage cockade. At the same time the numbers were moved from the sides to the nose panels.

In October 1917 the squadron flew south to Ochey to the 41st Wing. Either before or just after this move the squadron marking was removed and not re-used, and no other marking was used. At the same time the numbers were also discontinued and a new system adopted.

Individual Markings

"A" Flight used letters A, B, C, D, E, F, G, H.
"B" Flight used letters J, K, L, M, N, O, P, Q.
"C" Flight used letters R, S, T, U, V, W, Y, Z.

All were in white on the cowling sides. Wheel covers were still in flight colours but again, due to losses this often was not done. These markings were used up to the armistice.

Flights were made up to eight aircraft shortly after joining 41st Wing (this later became the Independent Force).

Formation Leader's Markings

Red, yellow, and black streamers on outer rear interplane struts and on rudder; the Deputy Leader's were on rudder only.

D.H.4 A'7140 "2" of Lt. R.A. Logan and Lt. F.R. Henry, P.O.W. 8.4.17. while bombing Chateau Hardenpont.

D.H.4s on 6.3.17. The squadron left Lilbourne, Northamptonshire for France. Bad weather intervened and they put down at Hendon until it cleared. They were photographed there by Major John Baldwin, C.O., later Sir John Baldwin.

Personal Markings

Some pilots painted various names on their aircraft (*Auld Reekie, P.D.Q.*), but usually a town or girl's name was used.

Transport

A snail was painted in flight colours on the sides of vehicles.

D.H.4 A'2140 "2" being repainted in German colours. This was the first R.F.C. D.H.4 lost.

BELOW: D.H.4 "1" and "B."

BOTTOM: D.H.4 A'7624 "M."

No.56 Squadron R.F.C.

Was formed on 8th June, 1916 and after training on various types were equipped with S.E.5s and moved to France 7th April, 1917. Shortly afterward they re-equipped with S.E.5as. Other than two weeks in June, 1917 when they returned to England as part of the defence of London, they remained on the Western Front until the armistice.

Squadron Marking
None allocated.

Flight Markings
"A" Flight wheel covers painted red.
"B" Flight wheel covers painted blue and white quarters.
"C" Flight wheel covers painted blue.

Individual Markings
None were used initially. Shortly after arriving in France, the squadron was grounded while modifications were made to improve the aircraft and the first patrol was flown on the 22nd April. Some time after this, probably in May, markings were painted on.

Squadron Markings
None allocated.

Flight and Individual Markings
"A" Flight used the letter "A" and numbers 1, 2, 3, 4, 5, 6.
"B" Flight used the letter "B" and numbers 1, 2, 3, 4, 5, 6.
"C" Flight used the letter "C" and numbers 1, 2, 3, 4, 5, 6.

These were painted in various styles and positions. Most commonly seen was the letter in front of the cockade and the number behind it. Usually these markings appeared also on the top decking. This style of marking was in use while the squadron was on Home Defence duties and was still used on return to France on 5th July, 1917.

About the mid-July period some aircraft were "painted up" in bright colours after the fashion of some German aircraft. This was strictly forbidden and was ordered to be removed.

In August, squadron markings were issued.

Squadron Markings
Allocated a dumbbell on either side of the fuselage behind the cockade. This was probably in flight colours; certainly in the case of "C" Flight the dumbbell was a dark colour.

Individual Markings
Had changed to large white letters behind the cockade repeated on the upper starboard wing in white and below the lower starboard in black often outside the cockade:
"A" Flight used A, B, C, D, E, F.
"B" Flight used G, H, I, J, K, L.
"C" Flight used M, N, O, P, Q, R.

On 25th September, 1917 the squadron marking was ordered to be changed to an 18-inch (450mm) white band completely around the fuselage from the leading edge of the tailplane towards the cockade. This remained until 22nd March, 1918. The letters remained as before.

About January 1918 there was a change in "B" Flight's identity markings. Letters were discontinued and replaced with numbers 1, 2, 3, 4, 5, 6 in the same positions. About the same time "C" Flight changed their letters to U, V, W, X, Y, Z. There is no known reason for these changes. "Possibly" the squadron was anticipating an increase in numbers and made the changes to accommodate another six aircraft. In fact, no S.E.5a squadron had an extra six aircraft on strength (as did many Camel squadrons), mainly because of problems with Hispano engines.

There was a change in squadron markings 22nd March, 1918.

Squadron Markings
Two sloping white bars, sloping inwards at the top of the fuselage side immediately in front of the tailplane remained until the armistice.

Identity Markings
Letters and Figures remained the same.
"B" Flight – the flight commenced using the blue and white quartered wheel covers on going to France and finished the war with them. From photographs it appears they were not always used between these times.

S.E.5 A'8909 "A1" of Capt. P.B. Prothero.

S.E.5 A8913 "B2." Sgt. Vousden with Lt. Muspratt's S.E.5.

RIGHT: S.E.5 A'4862 "C3" of Lt. H/D. Spearpoint, P.O.W. 17.6.17.

S.E.5 A'4853 "C2" of Lt. D.S. Wilkinson.

S.E.5a B'502 "A." Lt. G. Maxwell's S.E.5a.

S.E.5a "Q" and "R" with dark dumbbells on fuselage.

S.E.5a B'4863 "G." Capt. J.B. McCudden's S.E.5a.

S.E.5a B'505 "V." Flown by various pilots.

S.E.5a C'5303 "X" of Lt. L.N. Franklin, K.I.A. 14.7.18.

S.E.5a "1" of Lt. W.S. Maxwell, K.I.A. 27.3.18.

S.E.5a "V" of Lt. H.J. Burden.

S.E.5a B'628 "4" of Lt. W.R. Irwin at Baizieux, 1918.

S.E.5a B'1444 "D" of Lt. C. Parry, April–June 1918.

S.E.5a "W" of Capt. Grinnel-Milne October, 1918.

No.57 Squadron R.F.C.

Formed on 8th June, 1916 and went to France in the December equipped with F.E.2ds in the two-seat fighter-reconnaissance. role. In June 1917 the squadron began to re-equip with D.H.4s in the day bombing role, retaining these until the armistice.

Using F.E.2ds

No squadron markings were used.

Flight and Individual Markings

Flight letter and individual number painted on either side of the nacelle, in some cases painted on the nacelle nose also.

Using D.H.4s

Originally believed to have carried on with the earlier system.

Squadron Markings

Allotted 26th August, 1917, a white disc painted on the fuselage side behind the cockade.

Individual Markings

"A" Flight used A, B, C, D, E, F in white on the nose below the exhaust.
"B" Flight used 1, 2, 3, 4, 5, 6 in white on the nose below the exhaust.
"C" Flight used S, T, U, V, W, Y in white on the nose below the exhaust.

After squadron markings were deleted on 22nd March, 1918 the individual markings were still used until the armistice. Size and position varied slightly due to different engine installations.

D.H.4 A'7439 of Sgt. S.F. Edginton and 2/Lt. H.T. Hearn, K.I.A. 11.9.17 while bombing Courtrai sidings.

D.H.4 A'7583 "2" of Lt. C.G. Crane and 2/Lt. A.L. Inglis, P.O.W. 2.10.17.

F.E.2d A'6355 of 2/Lt. F.A. Handley and 2/Lt. E. Percival, last seen attacking enemy aircraft near Noyelles, M.I.A. 29.4.17.

D.H.4 A'7422 "A."

D.H.4 A'7645 "C" of Lt. F.L. Mond and Lt. E.M. Martin, missing 15.5.18 in this D.H.4.

No.58 Squadron R.F.C.

Formed on 8th June, 1916 and served as an Advanced Training Unit until December, 1917. It was then mobilized for overseas and equipped with F.E.2bs in a night bomber role. In September 1918 it began to re-equip with Handley Page 0/400s.

No markings have been recorded for the F.E.2bs. The H.P. 0/400s had white letters on fuselage sides roughly mid-way along. The sequence of letters is unknown, but A, B, C, F, H, M, N, P are known. These letters may have not been used before the armistice but they were on when the unit flew to Egypt in May, 1919.

F.E.2d with air and ground crew.

No.59 Squadron R.F.C.

Went to France on 23rd February, 1917 equipped with R.E.8s.

Squadron Marking

Used after arriving in France, two vertical bands around the fuselage behind the fuselage cockade. Retained until 22nd March, 1918. For some reason, these bands were painted black or red or in some form of flight colours.

Flight Markings

Aircraft of each flight were marked with the flight letter painted in white on the fuselage side behind the squadron marking and repeated on the upper centre section.

Individual Markings

By white numbers either in front or behind the flight letter and repeated on the centre section. Originally used "A1" to "A6," "B1" to "B6," "C1" to "C6," later increased to "7" and "8." When squadron markings were discontinued the flight letter and number were retained.

R.E.8 B'5106 "1A" taking off.

R.E.8 A'3213 "4A" of Sgt. Smith, and Lt. Dilnutt, captured 25.4.17.

R.E.8 E'1209 "6A."

R.E.8 A'3213 "4A" as above.

LEFT: B.F.2b E'2016 *Rita,* Lt. A.S.R. Burt, early 1919.

No.60 Squadron R.F.C.

Went to France end of May, 1916 obtaining their aircraft on arrival (four Morane Bullets, four Morane parasols, and four Morane Biplanes). During August these were gradually replaced with Nieuport Scouts but not until mid-October was the change-over complete.

During this period no type of markings were used, but as from 19th July, the spinner, cowling, and under-carriage struts on Moranes were painted bright red to distinguish them from Fokker Monoplanes.

Morane Monoplane A'128 about June 1916.

Flight Markings

By mid-October, flight letter painted in front of fuselage cockade.

Individual Markings

By numbers painted behind the fuselage cockade – letter/numbers were repeated on the top decking painted black on silver aircraft and white on dark coloured aircraft. These markings remained until 11th July, 1917 when S.E.5's were received. During the last months of the Nieuports service the wheel covers and some cowlings were painted in flight colours:

"A" Flight used red.
"B" Flight used yellow or white.
"C" Flight used blue.

Morane Biplane 5182 about June 1916.

Flight Commanders

Had one streamer on trailing edge of rudder, Deputy Leader had streamer on each interplane strut, usually a yellow or blue message bag.

The early S.E.5s were painted in flight colours on engine cowlings, lower wing root fairings, footstep, fin, and on a diagonal band around the rear fuselage, all outlined by a two-inch (50mm) white line, but this was short lived.

Morane Parasol 5134 about June 1916.

Squadron Marking

Allotted 26th August, 1917 – a solid white disc painted on the fuselage behind the cockade and repeated on the top decking. By now S.E.5as had replaced the S.E.5.

Flight Marking

By coloured wheel covers:
"A" Flight used red.
"B" Flight used white.
"C" Flight used blue.

Individual Markings

"A" Flight used letters A, B, C, D, E, F painted in white on the fuselage side in front of the cockade.
"B" Flight used numbers 1, 2, 3, 4, 5, 6 painted in white on the side of the nose below the exhaust manifold.
"C" Flight used letters U, V, W, X, Y, Z painted in white on the fuselage side in front of the cockade.

These were repeated in white on either the centre section or, at a later date, on the port upper wing and in black below port wing.

Squadron Marking

Allotted 22nd March, 1918 – two white vertical bands painted immediately in front of the tailplane.

Flight Markings

Wheel covers as before.

Individual Markings

"A" Flight used A, B, C, D, E, F in front of the cockade.
"B" Flight used G, H, J, K, L, M on engine panels.
"C" Flight used U, V, W, X, Y, Z in front of the cockade.

Some time in the summer of 1918, "A" Flight used A, B, C, D, E, F behind the cockade.

During 1918 the wing markings were often not used but no hard and fast rules applied. Many aircraft showed no signs of having wheel covers in flight markings. Spare aircraft used Letters between "M" and "U," e.g. "N."

Morane Biplane 5167 with two Lewis guns.

Nieuport 16 and 17s A'6766 "A5" of 2/Lt. C.S. Hall, A'6718 "A3" of Lt. H. Kirten, A'6645 "A2" of Lt. G.O. Smart, of "A" Flight January/March 1917.

Nieuport 17 B'1514 "A4" of 2/Lt. McKissock, P.O.W. 6.5.17.

Nieuport 17 A'200 "A6" used by Capt. Molesworth and others.

Nieuport 17 "C6" with unknown pilot P.O.W.

Nieuport 17 A'6718 "A3" of Lt. D.C. Murray, P.O.W. 27.6.17.

RIGHT: S.E.5 First issue to squadron. Could be Bishop's machine, A'8936.

S.E.5 A'8898. First issue flown by Capt. K.L. Caldwell.

S.E.5a B'507 "A." Engine failure forced to land 5.10.17, 2/Lt. J.J. FitzGerald P.O.W.

S.E.5a A'8918 "W" of Lt. H.T. Hammond shot down by ground fire near La-Bassee 14.9.17.

S.E.5a "B" Flight line up, September 1917.

S.E.5a E'3919 "G" of 2/Lt. M.D. Sinclair crashed due to engine failure.

S.E.5a E'1306 "V" of Lt. G.L. du Cros crashed 6.7.18.

S.E.5a "A" of Lt. J.W. Rayner.

S.E.5a "D" of Lt. F.W. McCarthy.

S.E.5a E'4095 "V" of Lt. M.D. Sinclair, right way up.

S.E.5a F'5687 "G" Presentation "Sallie Parker," 16.11.18.

S.E.5a "B" Flight line up, April 1918.

No.61 Squadron R.F.C.

Formed 24th July, 1917 at Rochford as a Home Defence Unit covering the London area. Retained this role until the armistice.

Equipment

Sopwith Scouts, S.E.5as in January, 1918, Sopwith Camels a few weeks before the armistice.

Squadron Markings

None allocated.

Flight and Individual Markings

Personal markings probably, but unconfirmed on Sopwith Scouts.

Several S.E.5as carried a colour scheme of coloured diamonds mid-1918, colours are believed to be black and white on one and blue and khaki on the other. These may have been unofficial camouflage schemes by the squadron, although official schemes were taking place using diamonds in a wide range of colours and patterns.

Both S.E.5as B'658 and D'3459 were with the squadron together, February to 20th May (at least) 1918, in diamond markings.

The squadron was due to receive Camels as from July 1918 but probably was not fully equipped for some weeks.

S.E.5a B'652 believed to be in experimental camouflage scheme tried in 1918, although several were so painted.

Sopwith Scout B'5904 "A1," "1" repeated on decking.

Sopwith Scout "2" of Lt. A.H. Bird, Rochford.

RIGHT: Sopwith Scout "5" at Rochford.

Sopwith Scout "7" of Capt. Collier (?) at Rochford.

Sopwith Scout "A" at Rochford.

No.62 Squadron R.F.C.

Went to France in January, 1918 equipped with Bristol Fighters.

Squadron Marking

Allocated in December, 1917, three white bands, one in front of the fuselage cockade and two behind. The bands were painted across the top of the fuselage. Discontinued from 22nd March, 1918, to the relief of the observers who were unhappy about the large amount of white paint around them.

Individual Markings

By white letters painted on the nose panels below the exhaust pipe, repeated on the top wing, to port of the centre section:
"A" Flight used A, B, C, D, E, F.
"B" Flight used J, K, L, M, N, O.
"C" Flight used P, Q, R, S, T, U.
Spare aircraft used letters not allocated, e.g. "W."

C'4630, "J" of 2/Lt. H.A. Clarke and Capt. H. Claye.

RIGHT: "L" at Planques February/March, 1918.

"R" at Planques 1st May, 1918, of Lt. W.E. Staton and Lt. J.R. Gordon.

C'4619. "P," probably at Croisette, September, 1918.

E'2595 "K" with modified Foster mounting on centre section for Lewis gun to increase firepower.

"N" Date unknown but before 19th May, 1918 as tail of C'4630 in background.

C'4630 "J" after being shot down 19th May, 1918. Victory claimed by *Ltn.* Delling of *Jasta* 34b.

No.63 Squadron R.F.C.

Formed 31st August, 1916 and was intended as a day bomber unit with D.H.4s for service in France. This did not take place and in June 1917 it left for Mesopotamia as a Corps Reconnaissance Unit having a Fighter Flight attached, arriving in August. The main equipment was R.E.8s with Bristol Scouts and some SPAD Scouts as fighters.

Shortly after arriving, the fighters were withdrawn and the squadron became a reconnaissance unit only, taking part in the allied advance up the Tigris and the final battles with the Turkish Army. No markings have been recorded.

D.H.5 A'9507 "E" presentation "Christchurch Old Boys Club" flown by Capt. E.R. Tempest.

No.64 Squadron R.F.C.

Went to France 14th October, 1917 equipped with D.H.5s.

Squadron Marking
Allotted on 10th October, 1917 a solid white triangle behind the fuselage cockade.

Individual Markings
"A" Flight used letters A, B, C, D, E, F in white below the cockpit.
"B" Flight used numbers 1, 2, 3, 4, 5, 6 in white below the cockpit.
"C" Flight used letters U, V, W, X, Y, Z in white below the cockpit.

These were usually repeated on the top wing and below the lower.

During January/February 1918 the squadron was equipped with S.E.5as, becoming operational the beginning of March. The squadron marking was still retained and probably the individual ones also.

S.E.5a C'6418 "2" over turned by Lt. M.L. Howard, 30.6.18.

Squadron Marking
Allotted 22nd March, 1918, a white vertical bar immediately behind the fuselage cockade.

Individual Markings
"A" Flight used letters A, B, C, D, E, F in white behind the squadron marking.
"B" Flight used numbers 1, 2, 3, 4, 5, 6 in white behind the squadron marking.
"C" Flight used letters U, V, W, X, Y, Z in white behind the squadron marking.

From at least August, the "X" in "C" Flight was replaced by "N." The C.O., Major Smythies, used "S" as his marking. The flight commanders usually flew "E," "6," and "U."

S.E.5a D'336 "5" flown by Lt. W.C. Daniel.

RIGHT: S.E.5a D'389 "E" has white fin and wheels.

No.65 Squadron R.F.C.

Formed at Norwich 1st August, 1916 as a fighter unit and trained with a variety of aircraft. Moved to France at the end of October,1917 equipped with Sopwith Camels. Flew over Western France until the armistice.

Squadron Markings
Allocated 10th October, 1917 a white horizontal band along the centre of the sides of the fuselage.

Flight Markings
Believed to have been by coloured wheel covers in the usual red, white, and blue.

Individual Markings
By letters on the fuselage sides in white behind the cockade:
"A" Flight used A, B, C, D, E, F.
"B" Flight used G, H, J, K, L, N.
"C" Flight used R, S, T, U, V, W.

Squadron Markings
Allocated 22nd March, 1918, two white vertical bars one either side of the fuselage cockade, remaining until the armistice.

Flight Markings
"A" Flight used red wheel covers with white edge.
"B" Flight used blue wheel covers with white edge.
"C" Flight used white wheel covers with red edge.

Individual Markings
Again by letters but now painted in front of the cockade:
"A" Flight used A, B, C, D, E, F, G, H
"B" Flight used J, K, L, M, N, O, P, Q
"C" Flight used R, S, T, U, V, W, Y, Z

Camel "G" probably end of war, *Teddy Comes Too.*

Camel B'2458 "R" of 2/Lt. J.P. Morgan, P.O.W. 15.11.17.

Camel "C" crashed, no details.

Camel B'6393 "F" of 2/Lt. Whitehead, crashed 20.10.17.

Camel F'3991 "V" Lt. A.G. Jones-Williams *Peggy.*

No.66 Squadron R.F.C.

Formed 30th June, 1916, and went to France in March 1917 as a fighter squadron equipped with Sopwith Scouts. In October was re-equipped with Sopwith Camels. In November was withdrawn and sent to Northern Italy and flew Camels in that area until the armistice.

Squadron Markings

Using Sopwith Scouts between March and August, 1917, none allocated.

Individual Markings

"A" Flight used letters in front of the cockade "A to F."
"B" Flight used numbers in front of the cockade (probably blue with white trim).
"C" Flight used letters, probably end of alphabet.

Squadron Markings Using Sopwith Scouts

Allocated 26th August, 1917, a long horizontal white bar along the centre-line of the fuselage broken for the cockade and letters.

Individual Markings Using Sopwith Scouts

By letters behind the cockade. The letters ran from "A" to "S."

Squadron Markings Using Sopwith Camels

Re-equipping of the squadron with Sopwith Camels commenced in October 1917 and was completed early in November. A change of squadron marking was ordered 5th November, 1917, as one white vertical bar in front of the cockade and one horizontal bar behind on the fuselage centre-line. Shortly after this, the squadron moved to Italy and was in action in December, 1917. The squadron marking was used continually in Italy while the squadron remained as a whole.

Individual Markings Using Sopwith Camels

By white letters on the fuselage sides behind the cockade and repeated on the top of the upper wing. The letters ran approximately from "A" to "T."

When No.45 Squadron left Italy on 20th September, 1918 the remaining Camel Squadrons each painted a flight in 45's dumbell markings to mislead the enemy into believing that there were still three Camel squadrons at the front. There is no evidence whether the deception was successful or not, but it was retained up to the armistice so H.Q. R.A.F. probably considered it helpful.

Sopwith Scout B'2142 "N," with Lewis gun on wing.

Sopwith Scout A'6194 "4" of Capt. L.H. Smith, M.I.A. 24.5.17 during an offensive patrol near Croisilles-Hermies.

Sopwith Scout A'6194 "4" *Train Bourne*.

Sopwith Scout B'2167 "L," of 2/Lt. W.C. Heathcote, damaged landing 28.9.17.

Sopwith Scout A'635 "D" of 2/Lt. M. Newcombe, P.O.W. 12.10.17 during ground attack mission.

Camel D'8101 "P," flown by Lt. G.A. Birks.

Camel B'6413 "J" of Lt. Rudge, damaged in a landing collision with hangar 3.4.18.

Camels "J," "K," and "T" in the long grass.

Camel F'1923 "A" at San Pietro Aerodrome in fake 45 Squadron markings.

Camel B'5181 "C" at San Pietro Aerodrome in fake 45 Squadron markings.

Camel B'5648 "E" of Lt. Alan Jerrard, who crashed and was P.O.W. after his combat on 30.3.18 which lead to his V.C.

No.67 Squadron R.F.C.

In March 1916 a draft of Australian personnel arrived in Egypt and were mustered to become No.67 Squadron, which served as a general duties squadron flying a variety of aircraft.

In January 1918 the squadron started to re-equip with Bristol Fighters and soon became a fighter squadron, playing an important part in General Allenby's offensive against the Turks.

No squadron or individual markings were allotted, but aircraft were in a variety of finishes.

On 6th February, 1918, No.67 Squadron became No.1 Squadron Australian Flying Corps, but this made no difference to its aircraft or duties.

Bristol M.1c A'5141 at Deir-el-Belah.

Martinsyde 7488 flown by Capt. A.W. Ellis.

Bristol FB.19 A'5236 at Deir-el-Belah.

B.F.2b B'1146 Capt. Ross Smith and Lt. E.A. Mustard discussing their mission.

LEFT: B.F.2b B'1146 presentation "N.S.W. No.1," *The White Belltrees* of Capt. D.W. Rutherford, April 1918.

ABOVE: No.67 Sqdn. Mesopotamia, two RE8s between two Martinsydes. October 1917 at the time of reequipping with RE8s.

RIGHT: B.F.2b A'7196 showing coloured fuselage flash.

No.68 Squadron R.F.C.

Formed in England from Australians and went to France on 21st September, 1917, equipped with D.H.5s.

Squadron Marking as No.68 Squadron R.F.C.

Allotted on 19th September, is was a single white vertical bar in front of the tailplane.

Individual Markings

"A" Flight used letters A, B, C, D, E, F behind the cockade.
"B" Flight used numbers 1, 2, 3, 4, 5, 6 behind the cockade.
"C" Flight used letters U, V, W, X, Y, Z behind the cockade.

In January 1918 the squadron re-equipped with S.E.5as and on the 20th became No.2 Squadron, Australian Flying Corps.

Squadron Marking as No.2 Squadron, A.F.C.

Allotted to coincide with change of title, it was a white boomerang in front of the tailplane. The squadron marking was changed on 22nd March, 1918, to a single white vertical bar in front of the cockade.

Individual Markings as No.2 Squadron, A.F.C.

"A" Flight used letters A, B, C, D, E, F in front of the cockade with the boomerang marking, and behind the cockade with the bar marking.
"B" Flight used numbers 1, 2, 3, 4, 5, 6 behind the cockade.
"C" Flight used letters U, V, W, X, Y, Z behind the cockade.

All individual markings were repeated on the upper port wing.

LEFT: D.H.5 A'9542 "Z" of Lt. McKenzie, shot down 6.12.17 near Fremicourt. Lt. McKenzie survived.

D.H.5 A'9344 "C" of Reg Holden badly shot up.

D.H.5 A'9449 1 "B" Flight Commander.

S.E.5a C'5382 "Z."

S.E.5a C'9539 "V," of the "C" Flight Commander.

S.E.5a "C" "A" Flight, end of war.

S.E.5a "B" "A" Flight.

S.E.5a B'8392 "1" of "B" Flight, Capt. Davies.

BELOW: S.E.5a D'6950 "V" of "C" Flight, Capt. Howard.

S.E.5a E'9565 "X" of "C" Flight, Capt. Manuel.

S.E.5a B'8400 "Y" of "C" Flight.

No.69 Squadron R.F.C.

Formed from a draft from Australia, went to France 9th September, 1917, equipped with R.E.8s.

Squadron Markings

Allotted on 19th September, it was a solid white disc painted behind the cockade on the fuselage side.

Individual Markings

Large white numbers behind the squadron marking; the numbers ran from 1 to 18.

On 20th January, 1918, the squadron became No.3 Squadron Australian Flying Corps. About this time the individual markings changed:

"A" Flight used A, B, C, D, E, F.

"B" Flight used G, H, J, K, L, M.

"C" Flight used N, O, P, Q, R, S.

These were painted behind the squadron marking and repeated centrally on the upper centre section.

After the deletion of squadron markings the individual markings remained the same.

R.E.8 "13" leaving on a night bombing raid.

R.E.8 A'3662 "J" presented by Mr. H. Teesdale Smith of Adelaide.

R.E.8 F'6016 "K" *Marjorie*.

R.E.8 B'4048 "S."

LEFT: R.E.8 C'2309 "O" *The Danby*.

ABOVE: R.E.8 A'4397 "D," this was usually flown by Capt. R.G.D. Francis D.F.C.; it amassed 440 hours 35 minutes flying time and made 147 flights across the lines.

RIGHT: R.E.8 "D" and *Kewpie Doll* – see A'4397.

No.70 Squadron R.F.C.

Equipped with newly issued Sopwith two-seaters, the squadron went to France by flights as the machines became available:
"A" Flight arrived 24th May, 1916.
"B" Flight arrived 29th June, 1916.
"C" Flight arrived 30th July, 1916.

The original Sopwiths were clear-doped and the first P.C.10 finish was not seen until August, 1916. Until then no markings were used, but some time in the autumn markings were applied.

Squadron Markings Using Sopwith Two-Seaters

None allotted.

Flight Markings Using Sopwith Two-Seaters

Aircraft of each flight were marked with the flight letter. The position varied but "A" Flight's letter was in front of the cockade, "B" Flight's was behind, and"C" Flight's was in front.

Individual Markings Using Sopwith Two-Seaters

By numbers 1 to 6 behind the cockade in "A" and "C" Flights, behind the "B" in "B" Flight.

In July 1917 the squadron re-equipped with Sopwith Camels. They were marked in the same fashion as the earlier two-seaters except that "B" Flight conformed with the other two flights. Markings were also applied on the centre-sections and below the lower wings.

Squadron Markings Using Sopwith Camels

Allotted 26th August, 1917, this was a white zig-zag on the fuselage side behind the cockade. New markings were allocated 22nd March, 1918; these were three vertical white bands around the fuselage behind the cockade.

Individual Markings Using Sopwith Camels

By white letters painted in front of the cockade on the fuselage, repeated on the centre section and below the lower wing:
"A" Flight used A, B, C, D, E, F.
"B" Flight used G, H, J, K, L, M.
"C" Flight used N, O, P, Q, R, S.

After 22 March 1918 these were originally as in the earlier period, but when the squadron increased to 24 Camels these were changed:
"A" Flight added G and H.
"B" Flight used J, K, L, M, N, O, P, Q.
"C" Flight used R, S, T, U, V, W, Y, Z.

Around July 1918 "B" Flight changed to numbers, using 1, 2, 3, 4, 5, 6, 7, 8. These were in use at the armistice.

Post Armistice

It was planned to convert the squadron to Sopwith Snipes, but the armistice stopped this. However, when they moved to Germany on occupation duties they were with the 4th A.F.C. and when they disbanded, their Snipes went to 70 Squadron on 22nd February, 1919. The three white bands were still used but individual markings were by numbers at least up to 20.

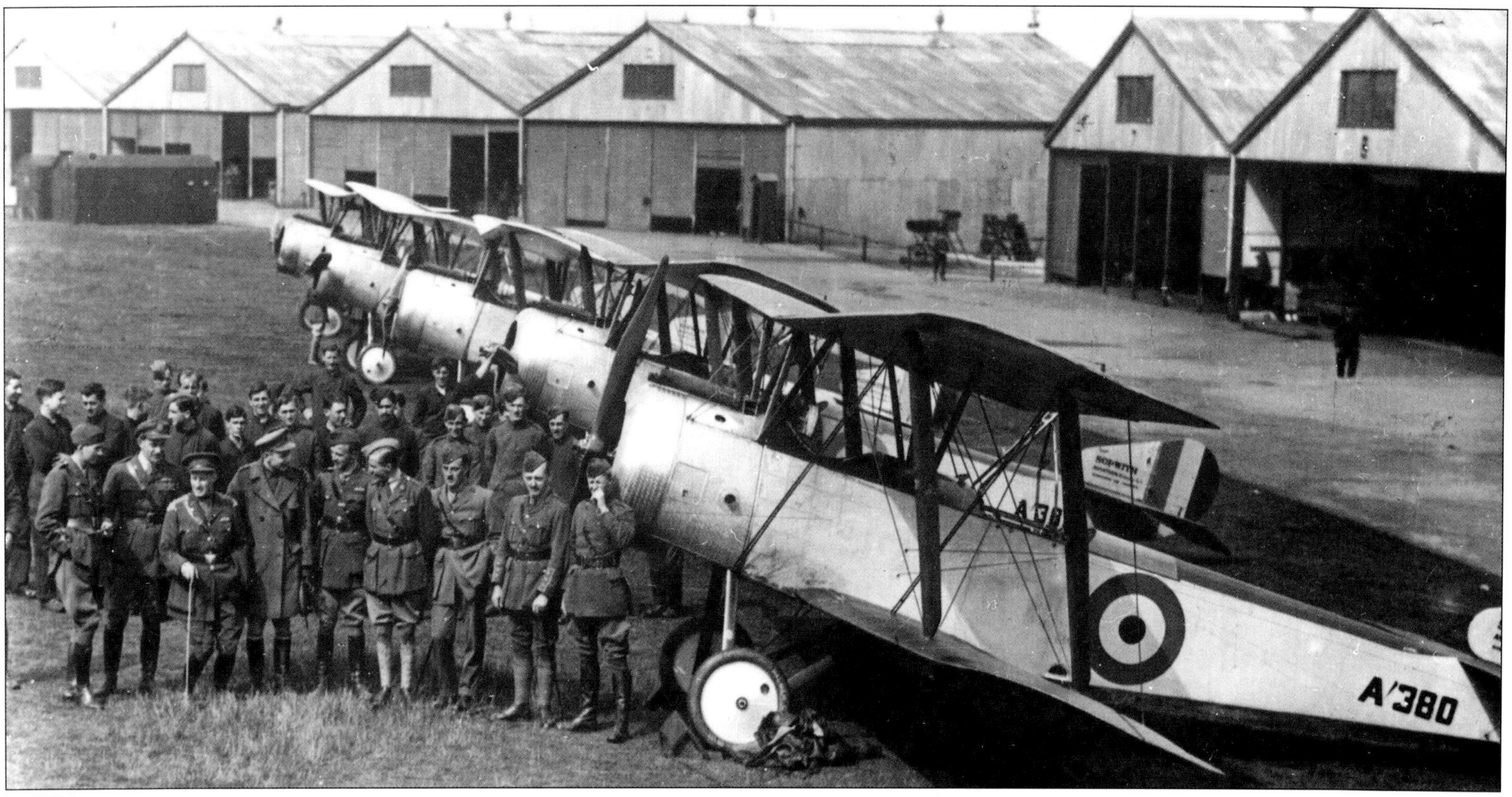

"B" Flight; brand new Sopwith two-seaters ready to leave for France, June 1917.

Early loss believed to be claimed by *Jasta* 2.

"B" Flight, July 1917 at Estree Blanche.

B'3823 "C5" of Lt. R.C. Hume shot down 28th July, 1917, and P.O.W. Victory claimed by *Ltn*. Mohnicke of *Jasta* 11.

B'7320 of Lt. Todd. It was damaged by A.A. fire 24th February, 1918; the pilot was unhurt.

B'3823 being removed for scrap.

"D" abandoned on Marieux Aerodrome March, 1918.

"U" Collided in the air. Pilot unhurt. "U" is a horseshoe.

BELOW: Squadron line up December 1918 at Bickendorf bei Cologne Aerodrome.

BOTTOM: Sopwith Snipe squadron line up, February, 1919.

"B" abandoned on Marieux Aerodrome March, 1918

"B" in the snow on Bickendorf bei Cologne Aerodrome.

E'8057 "14" with striped cowling, February, 1919.

No.71 Squadron R.F.C.

Formed in England from Australian personnel and went to France in December 1917 equipped with Sopwith Camels. On 20th January, 1918, it became No.4 Squadron A.F.C.

Squadron Marking

Allotted by 23rd December, a white boomerang behind the cockade and repeated on the top decking. A new squadron marking was allotted 22nd March, 1918; this was a single white bar in front of cockade.

Individual Markings

"A" Flight used letters A, B, C, D, E, F in front of the cockade.
"B" Flight used numbers 1, 2, 3, 4, 5, 6 in front of the cockade.
"C" Flight used letters U, V, W, X, Y, Z in front of the cockade.

In March, 1918 the establishment was raised to 24 aircraft. "A" Flight added "G" and "H," "B" Flight added "7" and "8," and "C" Flight added "S" and "T." All were repeated on the upper starboard wing.

After the new squadron marking was allotted on 22 March 1918:
"A" Flight used letters A, B, C, D, E, F, G, H behind the cockade.
"B" Flight used numbers 1, 2, 3, 4, 5, 6, 7, 8 behind the cockade.
"C" Flight used letters S, T, U, V, W, X, Y, Z behind the cockade.

All markings were repeated on the upper starboard wing.

In September, 1918 the squadron re-equipped with Sopwith Snipes. The individual markings remained the same but were deleted from the wing. The height of the squadron marking was considerably reduced but made broader.

RIGHT: Camel and Major W.A. McCloughry M.C.

Camels at Bruay, March 1918.

Camels possibly at Bruay, 1918.

Snipe E'8082 "X" of "C" Flight used by Ross.

Snipe "A" used by Capt. Roy King.

Snipe E'8205 "F."

Snipe E'8198 "U."

Snipe E'8100 "B," E'7345 "E," and "H."

No.72 Squadron R.F.C.

Formed 2nd July, 1917 after training as a fighter unit. By mid-December it commenced moving to Mesopotamia arriving at Basra in January, 1918 and was ready for operations in March. The squadron then split into detached flights:

"A" Flight moved to Samarra with Spads, S.E.5as, and D.H.4s which were withdrawn later.

"B" Flight stayed at Baghdad with Martinsydes.

"C" Flight moved to Mirjana with Bristol Monoplanes.

No squadron marking was allocated.

Individual Marking

One Bristol Monoplane had zig-zag markings early in May; possibly these were a personal marking or denoted the Flight Commander.

Bristol Monoplane in Persia.

BELOW: Bristol Monoplane and R.E.8 in Persia, end of war.

No.73 Squadron R.F.C.

Went to France on 9th January, 1918, equipped with Sopwith Camels.

Squadron Marking

Allotted in December, 1917, this was three vertical white bars painted on the fuselage side behind the cockade. There are no details of any flight or individual markings at this time. A squadron marking was allotted 22nd March, 1918; this was two vertical white bands around the fuselage behind the cockade.

Individual Markings

After 22nd March, 1918, large white letters on the fuselage size in front of the cockade were used:

"A" Flight used letters A, B, C, D, E, F, G, H.

"B" Flight used letters I, J, K, L, M, N, O, P.

"C" Flight used letters Q, R, S, T, U, V, W, Y.

These were used when the squadron strength was made up to 24 Camels. Many of the Camels had the wheel covers painted white.

At some time while Major T.O. Hubbard was in command a badge showing "Old Mother Hubbard, bare cupboard and dog" (English nursery rhyme) surmounted with a large "C" was painted on a Camel, below the cockpit. It was used by the C.O. and it is unlikely that other Camels were marked in this fashion.

RIGHT: Camel "D" Lt. E.J. Lussier.

Camel "B" of Capt. Stevenson, M.C., D.F.C. POW 28.7.18.

Camel "N" of Lt. G. Carr-Harris.

Camel "K" *Edith* of Lt. R.H. Gowan.

Camel E'1532 "1" of Lt. E. Barker.

LEFT: Camel "O" of Lt. E. Barker.

Camel D'9398 of Lt. R.F. Lewis, KIA 25.7.18 at Fresnes.

No.74 Squadron R.F.C.

Went to France 31st March, 1918, equipped with the S.E.5a.

Squadron Marking

A white horizontal band on the top, bottom, and sides of the fuselage behind the cockade. This varied considerably in size and position.

Individual Markings

"A" Flight used white letters between cockade and squadron marking, using A, B, C, D, E, F.
"B" Flight used white numbers painted either side of the nose using 1, 2, 3, 4, 5, 6.
"C" Flight used white letters between cockade and squadron marking using G, H, J, K, L, M.

Some time in the early summer various pilots decided to change their individual letters to something more personal. Letters were still used but now indicated names or nicknames. For example, Lt. L.A. Richardson used "R," Lt. "Taffy" Jones used "T," and Lt. "Mike" Hunt used "M."

S.E.5a of Capt. Mannock departing for France 31.3.18.

LEFT: S.E.5a F'8990 "R."

S.E.5a "B" and "A" Flights mixed.

"B" and "A" Flights mixed.

No.75 Squadron R.F.C.

Formed at Goldington 1st October, 1916, as a Home Defence Unit operating detached flights from fields in Bedfordshire to fly anti-Zeppelin patrols. In September, 1916 they flew to Lincolnshire as cover for the north midlands. In June 1918 they became part of the London Air Defence, retaining this role to the armistice.

Equipment
B.E.2c and e, B.E.12, 12a, 12b, and Avro 504K.

Squadron Markings
None allocated.

Flight and Individual Markings
Probably personal markings only.

No.76 Squadron R.F.C.

Formed at Ripon 15th September, 1916, as a Home Defence Unit for the industrial areas of Yorkshire. Had detached flights at Copmanthorpe, Helperby, and Catterick until the armistice.

Equipment
B.E.2c and e, B.E.12, 12a, 12b, and Avro 504K.

Squadron Markings
None allocated.

Flight and Individual Markings
Probably personal markings only.

RIGHT: S.E.5a "Z" of Lt. F.S. Gordon.

B.E.12 6478.

B.E.12b C'3094 used by Lt. R. MacDonald.

No.77 Squadron R.F.C.

Formed at Edinburgh 1st October, 1916, as a Home Defence Unit for Central Scotland, operating from fields on the east coast until the armistice.

Equipment

B.E.2c and e, B.E.12, 12b, and Avro 504K.

Squadron Markings

None allocated.

Flight and Individual Markings

Flights had coloured wheel discs, most likely red, white, and blue. Probably personal markings only.

ABOVE RIGHT: Avro 504 E'3273 and E'3278 preparing to take off.

RIGHT: BE12 C'3087 ready to take off.

BELOW: BE2bs and BE12s. Night line up at Penstone.

No.78 Squadron R.F.C.

Formed at Harrietsham 1st November, 1916, as a Home Defence Unit covering the south coast and approaches to London. Operated from fields in southern counties until moving to Suttons Farm as part of the London Air Defence.

Equipment

B.E.2e, B.E.12, B.E.12a, B.E.12b, Sopwith two-eater, F.E.2d, and Sopwith Camel.

Squadron Markings

None allocated.

Flight and Individual Markings

While using the various B.E. types, no markings were used. The F.E.2ds were only used while the squadron was awaiting Sopwith two-seaters and carried no markings.

F.E.2d 1882 and 1883 being prepared for flight. These later went to No.33 Squadron R.F.C.

The first Sopwith arrived in the first week of August 1917 but deliveries were slow and by Christmas 12 were on strength, some B.E.12as making up the numbers. One flight of Sopwith two-seaters had a white diamond just in front of the tail, repeated on the top decking and white numbers in front of the fuselage cockade and repeated on the top decking. Another flight had three bands of checks together around the fuselage, probably red, white, and blue, and white numbers below the cockpit, on the top decking, and on the top of the top wing. Other two-seaters were seen with various stripes and numbers in white.

Sopwith Camels started arriving early in 1918 and eventually the squadron was fully equipped.

It is believed that personal markings were the only kind used.

Sopwith two-seaters with the band of checks.

Sopwith two-seater, probably, B'762, converted to a single-seater with twin upward-firing Lewis guns. This also had band of checks.

LEFT: Sopwith two-seater "1" at Suttons Farm, 1917.

No.79 Squadron R.F.C.

Went to France in February 1918 equipped with Sopwith Dolphins.

Squadron Marking

Before arriving in France they were allocated a white dumbell painted on the fuselage side behind the cockade. On 22nd March this was changed to a white square behind the cockade.

Individual Markings

By white letters on the fuselage side behind the squadron marking, repeated on the upper port wing just in board of the cockade. There was a lot of variation in the style of letters:

"A" Flight used A, B, C, D, E, F.
"B" Flight used G, H, J, K, L, M.
"C" Flight used N, O, P, Q, R, S.

After the armistice, when at Bickendorf, extra Dolphins were on strength, and other letters known to have been used were U, V, and X. Also at this period some aircraft had the squadron marking and letter in reversed positions.

Sopwith Dolphin C'3898 "D."

Sopwith Dolphin D'7927 "K" of 2/Lt. Snyder.

LEFT: Sopwith Dolphin C'3944 "N" of Capt. F.I. Lord D.F.C.

Sopwith Dolphin F'7052 "R."

Sopwith Dolphin F'7065 "U."

No.80 Squadron R.F.C.

Went to France 25th January, 1918, equipped with Sopwith Camels.

Squadron Marking

Allotted in December 1917, this was one vertical white bar just in front of tailplane which was repeated on the upper starboard wing.

Flight Markings

"A" Flight used red wheel covers.
"B" Flight used white wheel covers.
"C" Flight used blue wheel covers.

Individual Markings

"A" Flight used A, B, C, D, E, F, G, H.
"B" Flight used J, K, L, M, N, O, P, Q.
"C" Flight used R, S, T, U, V, W, Y, Z.

The position of these letters varied. In the beginning they were painted in front of the cockade, but by May/June they had been moved to behind it. This may have been due to Pilots not liking a large area of white paint below the cockpit area.

Squadron Transport

Was marked by the painting of a Camel (four-legged variety) in a bell. This was due to the association of the Sopwith Camel and Major V.D. Bell, who was the O.C. during the squadron's period in France.

Sopwith Dolphin C'8043 "Y."

Camel C'3378 "B" flown by Capt. Preeston.

No.81 Squadron R.F.C.

Formed in August, 1917 as a training unit, it was expected to become a fighter squadron and go to France with Sopwith Dolphins in the spring of 1918. Due to shortages of machines and pilots it did not go and was disbanded July, 1918. It was reformed two days after the armistice and re-titled No.1 Squadron Canadian Air Force with several Dolphins on strength.

Camel C'6724 "R" flown by 2/Lt. G. Millar, shot down south of Bapaume 25.3.18.

Line up showing various maple leaves.

Squadron Marking

Allotted on 22nd March, 1918, this was a white hexagon painted on the fuselage side behind the cockade. It is unlikely to have been used.

After reforming as No.1 Squadron C.A.F., the Dolphins carried a maple leaf in various colours on the fuselage side behind the cockade.

No.82 Squadron R.F.C.

Formed 7th January, 1917, as a corps reconnaissance unit equipped with the Armstrong Whitworth F.K.8. Moved to France in November,1917, remaining there until the armistice.

Squadron Markings

Allocated 5th November, 1917, these were two white vertical bars on the fuselage sides behind the cockade.

Flight Markings

"A" Flight used red wheel covers.
"B" Flight used white wheel covers.
"C" Flight used blue wheel covers.

Individual Markings

"A" Flight used 1, 2, 3, 4, 5, 6.
"B" Flight used 7, 8, 9, 10, 11, 12.
"C" Flight used 13, 14, 15, 16, 17, 18.

After 22nd March, 1918, squadron markings were discontinued; the other markings remained.

F.K.8 B'5837 "7" crashed by R. Fagan at Bonneuil. Returned to A.D. 3.3.18.

F.K.8 "17" early 1918 with G. McM. Findley on board.

F.K.8 "12" and "11."

RIGHT AND BELOW: F.K.8 C'8636 "14" *Chips*.

No.83 Squadron R.F.C.

Formed at Montrose 7th January, 1917, and then trained at Spittlegate as a night bombing unit. In March 1918 it moved to France equipped with the F.E.2b and remained in the night bombing role until the end of the war.

Squadron Markings

None allocated.

Flight and Individual Markings

None known.

S.E.5a "H" of Lt. W.E. Watts, P.O.W. 20.10.17.

No.84 Squadron R.F.C.

Went to France in September 1917 equipped with the S.E.5a.

Squadron Marking

Allotted on 19th September, this was a white square behind the fuselage cockade. On 1st October this was replaced by a white horizontal line along the centre of the fuselage top, bottom, and sides from the cockade to the tailplane. This was painted on all squadron aircraft on 2nd October. This was changed on 22nd March, 1918 to two white sloping bars, one either side of the fuselage cockade. Flight markings were as before but no individual markings were used from this time.

Flight Markings

"A" Flight used red wheel covers.
"B" Flight used white wheel covers.
"C" Flight used blue wheel covers.

Individual Markings

White letters painted on the fuselage sides in front of the cockade roughly below the cockpit:
"A" Flight used A, B, C, D, E, F.
"B" Flight used G, H, J, K, L, M.
"C" Flight used N, O, P, Q, R, S.

S.E.5a B'574 "F" in German hands.

RIGHT: S.E.5a E'6024 crashed by Capt. C.P. Falkenburg.

BELOW: S.E.5a B'544 "E" of 2/Lt. G.R. Gray, P.O.W. 31.10.17, and B'566 "J" of 2/Lt. E.W. Powell.

S.E.5a C'5329 "G" of Lt. A.E. Davies shot down by A.A.

S.E.5a of Lt. Peter Reid.

S.E.5a of 2/Lt. W.J. Nel.

LEFT: S.E.5a of Lt. J. Boudwin (U.S.A.S.)

BELOW: S.E.5a F'5685 "Pulling and Pushing."

No.85 Squadron R.A.F.

Went to France in May 1918 equipped with the S.E.5a although they were originally expected to have Dolphins. As a Dolphin squadron they were due to go to France early in 1918.

Squadron Marking

Allotted by December, 1917, this was two sloping white bars behind the cockade. This marking was not used. A new squadron marking was allotted 22nd March, 1918; this was a white hexagon painted on the fuselage side and sometimes on the top decking behind the cockade.

Individual Markings

By white letters below the cockpit, repeated on the upper starboard wing roughly mid-span:
"A" Flight used A, B, C, D, E, F.
"B" Flight used G, H, J, K, L, M.
"C" Flight used T, U, V, W, Y, Z.
Other aircraft carried letters between "M" and "T," e.g. "N."

S.E.5a D'6933 "N" presentation "Newport Fife No.4" flown by Lt. J.C. Rorison, July, 1918.

S.E.5a squadron line up leaving for France.

S.E.5a "D."

S.E.5a "D" with pilot and ground crew.

No.86 Squadron R.F.C.

Formed in September 1917 but did not become operational before disbanding on 4th July, 1918. It began to reform at Brockworth on 30th October, 1918 but the armistice, two weeks later, caused it to be suspended. No markings were ever allocated.

No.87 Squadron R.A.F.

Originally the squadron was scheduled to have gone to France in January 1918, but due to the problems with the Hispano-Suiza engine, it did not leave until the last week in March. On arrival the Dolphins were taken as replacements for the existing squadrons, the pilots returning to England to re-equip. On completion of this the squadron returned to France on 26th April equipped with 19 Dolphins.

Squadron Marking

Allotted by 23rd December, 1917, this was two white vertical bars, one either side of the cockade on the fuselage. It is doubtful if this was ever used. New markings were allotted on 22nd March, 1918, a large white letter "S" lying on its side painted behind the individual letter. This marking is reported as not being painted on until late in May.

Individual Markings

By white letters behind the cockade on the fuselage, repeated in white on the upper starboard wing inboard of the cockade, and in black below the port wing.

"A" Flight used A, B, C, D, E, F.
"B" Flight used G, H, I, J, K, L.
"C" Flight used M, N, O, P, Q, R.

The O.C. was Major J.C. Callaghan M.C. He flew "S" all painted on before leaving England.

Some Dolphins were marked with figures, for example "2" and "6." These are believed to be spare aircraft.

Flight Markings

"A" Flight used standard P.C.10-coloured wheel covers.
"B" Flight used white-centred wheel covers.
"C" Flight used white wheel covers.

Flight Commander's Markings

"A" Flight Commander flew "A."
"B" Flight Commander flew "G."
"C" Flight Commander flew "M."
Streamers were also used.

"L" of Lt. C.E. Worthington at Petit Snythe, April 1918.

C'3912 "F" Crashed by Lt. N. Sales.

C'8163 "A" of Capt. J.H. Larkin, "A" Flight.

"I" showing two Lewis guns on lower wings fired by cords from cockpit.

LEFT: C'4225 "R" of Lt. E.B. Crickmore, 16th July, 1918. Victory claimed by *Ltn.* Steinbrecker of *Jasta* 46.

Another view of C'4225.

Dolphin C'4137 "V" shows why the Dolphin was called "Blockbuster."

B'7935 "Y" and C'8197 "M" at Cambrai, November 1918.

No.88 Squadron R.A.F.

Went to France in April, 1918 and became operational the first week in May. It was equipped with Bristol Fighters.

Squadron Markings

No marking used. Originally 88 Squadron was to have been an S.E.5a squadron and as such had been allocated a marking of three vertical white bars behind the cockade.

Flight Markings

"A" Flight had wheel covers and front cowling white.
"B" Flight had wheel covers and front cowling red.
"C" Flight had wheel covers and front cowling blue.

Individual Markings

By large white numbers painted on the fuselage side behind the cockade:
"A" Flight used originally 1, 2,3, 4, 5, 6.
"B" Flight used originally 7, 8, 9, 10, 11, 12.
"C" Flight used originally 13, 14, 15, 16, 17, 18.

Towards the end of 1918 extra aircraft were added to the squadron and these used higher numbers such as 19 and 22.

F.2.b F'5814 "1."

RIGHT: F.2.b E'2458 "9" crashed.

F.2.b E'2459 "12."

F.2.b "19."

F.2.b E'2220 "22" used by Lt. F. Jeffries.

F.2.b "8" crashed.

F.2.b F'4311 "19" at Bickendorf 1919.

No.89 Squadron R.F.C.

Formed July 1917 at Netheravon as a Home Defence and training unit with a variety of aircraft, including the B.E.12, Camel, and Avro 504s. It became non-operational and was disbanded on 4th July, 1918. It was reformed on Armistice Day and was immediately suspended. No markings were allocated.

Dolphin C'4151 "P" during original mobilisation.

No.90 Squadron R.F.C.

Should have gone to France in January 1918, but due to delays in receiving its Dolphins it was held back and its pilots used as reinforcements. It was eventually disbanded on 3rd August, 1918.

Squadron Markings

Allotted by December, 1917, this was a single white vertical bar behind the cockade on the fuselage. A new marking was allotted on 22nd March, 1918, a diagonal white band from the top of fuselage behind the cockade to the bottom of the fuselage in front of tailplane. It is unlikely that either of these were used. After being disbanded it was reformed on 22nd August, 1918, at Buckminster as a Home Defence Unit to cover the industrial Midlands, becoming part of the Northern Air Defence.

Equipment

Avro 504K. No markings are known.

Sopwith Dolphin J9 "2."

No.91 Squadron R.F.C.

Formed in September 1917 as a fighter squadron expecting to be equipped with Sopwith Dolphins. It should have gone to France in the spring of 1918 but due to a shortage of aircraft, the pilots did not go. Remaining at Chattis Hill, it became a Radio Training Unit with a variety of aircraft until disbanded in July, 1918.

Squadron Markings

Allotted on 22nd March, 1918, this was a white triangle painted on the fuselage behind the cockade. Although the squadron was disbanded quickly, it did start to mark up with the triangle.

S.E.5a "F."

No.92 Squadron R.F.C.

Formed on 1st September, 1917, to be equipped with the S.E.5a. Due to delays with engines they did not go to France until July 1918.

Squadron Marking

Allotted in December, 1917, this was a white dumbell on the fuselage side, but it was not used.

Squadron Marking

Allotted on 22nd March, 1918, this was three white bars, one in front of the cockade and two behind, but it was not used. Three white vertical bars behind the cockade were used from July, 1918.

Individual Markings

When used were by white letters painted in front of the cockade.

S.E.5a F'943 "S."

S.E.5a H'691 of Lt.Gasgoyne stunting.

S.E.5a's F'903 and H'697 with pilots.

No.93 Squadron R.F.C.

Formed in September 1917 as a fighter squadron expecting to be equipped with Sopwith Dolphins. It should have gone to France in the spring of 1918, but due to a shortage of aircraft and pilots, it did not go. It was disbanded in October, 1918.

Squadron Markings

Allotted on 22nd March, 1918, this was a white crescent painted on the fuselage side behind the cockade. It is unlikely to have been used.

Individual Markings

By large white letters on the fuselage side behind the cockade and repeated on the upper starboard wing and below the lower starboard wing in black.

The O.C.'s aircraft marked A.
"A" Flight used B, C, D, E, F, G.
"B" Flight used H, J, K, L, M, N.
"C" Flight used O, P, Q, R, S, T.

These were painted on before going to France. Flight Commanders carried streamers on rear interplane struts.

No.94 Squadron R.A.F.

Went to France 31st October, 1918, equipped with the S.E.5a. Arrived too late to see action.

Squadron Marking

Allotted three white vertical bands painted behind the fuselage cockade. Due to their late arrival in France and the war ending, the squadron marking was not used, at least before the armistice.

Flight Markings

The O.C.'s aircraft had wheel covers painted as a cockade.
"A" Flight had wheel covers painted red.
"B" Flight had wheel covers painted white.
"C" Flight had wheel covers painted blue.

S.E.5a squadron lined up on departure for France.

S.E.5a squadron lined up on departure for France.

S.E.5a H'680 "D" flown by E.C. Mogridge.

S.E.5a H'680 "D" crashed by E.C. Mogridge 10.11.18.

S.E.5a F'871 "A" flown by A.J. Capel at le Hameau.

No.95 Squadron R.F.C.

Formed September 1917 but was disbanded 4th July, 1918, before becoming operational. Re-formed 1st October, 1918, it was disbanded at the armistice.

No.96 Squadron R.F.C.

Formed 28th September, 1917, but was disbanded 4th July, 1918, before becoming operational. Re-formed 28th September, 1918, before becoming non-operational at the armistice.

No.97 Squadron R.F.C.

Formed 1st December, 1917, as a training unit. Mobilized in July 1918 as a night bomber unit equipped with the Handley Page 0/400. Went to France and joined the Independent Force 9th August, 1918, and commenced night raids against targets in the Rhineland and the Saar.

Squadron Markings

None allocated.

Individual Markings

None recorded. Photographs of squadron aircraft show no markings of any kind.

H.P. 0/400 D'9689. Lost in action 16.9.18. Previously used by No.115 Sqdn.

FE2b. A'5761. Presentation aircraft. Mauritius No.15. Also previously used by No.115 Sqdn.

No.98 Squadron R.F.C.

Went to France in April, 1918 equipped with the D.H.9 and operated in the day bombing role until the armistice.

Squadron Markings

On the list of squadron markings dated 3rd December, 1917, were shown markings allocated for units expected to arrive in France before February 1918. Four squadrons of D.H.9s were expected, but due to problems with engines and crew training, none arrived before April. Markings were shown on the list but none were used. No.98 was allocated a white zig-zag behind the cockade.

D.H.9 "E" of "A" Flight.

Flight Markings

By coloured wheel discs. Sequence is unknown but "A" Flight used white.

Individual Markings

"A" Flight used A, B, C, D, E, F, painted in white on the cowling below the exhaust manifold.

"B" and "C" Flights are believed to have followed on with letters.

D.H.9 D.3051 "S" of Lt. Roberts-Taylor and Lt. Malyan; the "S" is on the cowling.

No.99 Squadron R.F.C.

Went to France at the end of April 1918 equipped with the D.H.9 in a day bombing role, joining the bomber force in the Nancy area which later became the Independant Force.

Squadron Markings

On the list of squadron markings dated 3rd December, 1917, were shown markings allocated for units expected to arrive in France before February 1918. Four squadrons of D.H.9s were expected, but due to problems with engines and crew training, none arrived before April. Markings were shown on the list but none were used. No.99 was allocated an 18-inch vertical white band completely around the rear fuselage immediately in front of the tailplane.

Individual Markings

The exact sequence is unknown. However one flight used 1, 2, 3, 4, 5, and 6, and one flight used A, B, C, D, E, and F. The letters K, T, and Y were also used. Most of the numbers and letters were amongst the D.H.9s used on the raid on the Badische Anilin and Soda Fabrik, Mannheim on 7th September, 1918. During September 1918 D.H.9as started to arrive, but the armistice occurred before re-equipment was complete.

No.100 Squadron R.F.C.

Went to France in March 1917 equipped with the F.E.2b for night bombing. In the last few months of 1918 they joined the Independant Force with 21 aircraft. In September 1918 they exchanged their F.E.2bs for Handley Page 0/400s. Night bombing was still their job but now more bombs could be carried further.

Squadron Markings

None were used.

Individual Markings

None were used, but several aircraft had a skull and crossbones painted on the nacelle nose below the bomb sight bracket. (This was later used as a squadron badge between the wars). Most aircraft were painted in dark colours and many did not carry cockades.

The squadron also had the F.E.2c and 2d on strength fitted with an assortment of weapons which they used during harassing missions. In September 1918 the long-promised 0/400s started to arrive and built up to a strength of ten, organized in two flights of five. Again no squadron marking was used but individual markings were used. The 0/400s were marked with a large white number in front of the fuselage cockade. The sequence is unknown, but was probably "1" to "5" in one flight and "6" to "10" in the other.

D'3039 "Z" of Lt. M.J. Papenfus and Lt. A.L. Benjarmin, shot down O.O.C. 31.7.18 by *Ltn*. Tuxen, *Jasta* 6.

C'6260 "3," Sanders' Aircraft.

"4."

ABOVE: F.E.2b A'5478 presentation "Gold Coast No.10," previously with No.23 Squadron. Struck off charge 18.18.17. LEFT: D.H.9a H'3586 in a post-war photograph.

F.E.2b 7027 originally with No.11 Squadron R.F.C. in October 1916. In April 1917 went to No.100 Squadron until 9.5.1,7 when it was struck off charge. Presented by "The Government of Johore No.3."

H.P. 0/400 "4."

No.101 Squadron R.F.C.

Formed 12th July, 1917 as a night bomber unit equipped with the F.E.2b, moving to France two weeks later. It operated in the night bomber role until the armistice.

Squadron Markings

None were allocated. No other markings are known.

No.102 Squadron R.F.C.

Formed in August 1917 as a night bomber unit equipped with the F.E.2b, moving to France in September. Operated in the night bomber role until the armistice.

Squadron Markings

None were allocated. No other markings are known.

No.103 Squadron R.A.F.

Went to France in May 1918 equipped with the D.H.9 and operated in a day bombing role until the armistice.

Squadron Markings

On the list of squadron markings dated 3rd December, 1917, were shown markings allocated for units expected to arrive in France before February 1918. Four squadrons of D.H.9s were expected, but due to problems with engines and crew training, none arrived before April. Markings were shown on the list but none were used. No.103 Squadron was allo-

F.E.2c with pilot in front.

B.E.2e A'1855 used for short range harassing attacks.

F.E.2b 4957.

A'6562.

cated two sloping white bars, one either side of the fuselage cockade. A proviso on the list stated bars should not be less than 9 inches wide and not more than 24 inches.

Individual Markings

By white letters painted on the side of the nose:
"A" Flight used A, B, C, D, E, F, Spare G.
"B" Flight used H, J, K, L, M, N, Spare O.
"C" Flight used P, Q, R, S, T, U, Spare V.

No.104 Squadron R.A.F.

Went to France in May, 1918 equipped with the D.H.9 and joined the Independant Force in a day bombing role, mainly on targets in the Saar Valley area. The squadron was due to re-equip with the D.H.10 but the armistice occurred first.

Squadron Markings

On the list of squadron markings dated 3rd December, 1917, were shown markings allocated for units expected to arrive in France before February 1918. Four squadrons of D.H.9s were expected, but due to problems with engines and crew training, none arrived before April. Markings were shown on the list but none were used. No.104 was allocated three vertical white bars behind the fuselage cockade.

Flight Markings

By coloured wheel discs, sequence unknown but probably red, white, and blue.

Individual Markings

By large white letters painted on the nose panels, in front of the leading edge of lower wing. Sequence is unknown.

Squadron Markings

During August, several Squadrons approached H.Q. R.A.F. with a view to painting on a squadron marking as a sense of unit pride. The answer was "Yes, as long as it was painted quite small." No.104 painted on a small white rectangle mid-way between the cockade and the tailplane.

D.H.9 D'2931 Forced down 12.8.18 at Buhl by *Ltn.* Monnington, *Jasta* 18.

D.H.9 D'550 "Z" of Capt. R. Jackson and 2/Lt. E.A. Slater. It crashed 6.1.19 at Ronchn Aerodrome.

D.H.9 "R" captured. On show at War Booty Exhibition, Munich, in aid of the German Red Cross.

D.H.9 "U" capturod. On chow at War Booty Exhibition, Munich, in aid of tho Cor man Red Cross.

RIGHT: D.H.9 D'2931 Forced down 12.8.18 at Buhl by *Ltn.* Monnington, *Jasta* 18.

No.105 Squadron R.A.F.

Formed 14th September, 1917, as a day bomber unit for service in France. In April 1918 it was ordered to mobilize as a corps-reconnaissance squadron equipped with R.E.8s. In May it went to Omagh, Co. Tyrone and was still there at the armistice. It was due to re-equip with Bristol Fighters but these did not arrive until December, 1918.

Squadron Markings

None are known. No other markings are known.

No.106 Squadron R.A.F.

Formed 30th September, 1917, as a corps-reconnaisance unit equipped with the R.E.8. In May 1918 it moved to Ireland where served until the armistice.

Squadron Markings

None are known. No other markings are known.

No.107 Squadron R.A.F.

Went to France in June 1918 equipped with the D.H.9 in a day bombing role until the armistice.

Squadron Markings

None issued.

Individual Markings

"A" is unknown.
"B" Flight used Roman numerals I to VI painted black on a cream background behind the fuselage cockade.
"C" Flight is unknown.

Formation Leaders were marked with a Red, Yellow, and Blue streamer fixed to the rear outer strut on each wing. Deputy Leaders had one streamer fixed on the same outer rear strut, either right or left according to his position in the formation.

Armament Note

Ex-members state they had a Lewis gun which fired downwards and backwards through the floor of the rear cockpit. This was known as the "Wind Up Gun"! This may have been a squadron modification that was unrecorded.

No.108 Squadron R.A.F.

Went to France 22nd July, 1918, equipped with the D.H.9 in the day bombing role until the armistice. It operated against targets in N.W. Belgium.

Squadron Markings

None issued.

Individual Markings

By large white letters painted on the fuselage side behind the cockade:
"A" Flight used A, B, C, D, E, F.
"B" Flight used G, H, J, K, L, M.
"C" Flight used N, O, P, Q, R, S.
Flight Commanders usually flew in A, G, and N and carried streamers on the outer rear struts.

D.H.9 D'3084 "V" forced down 12.8.18 by *Kest* 1b.

RE8 over Omagh, County Tyrone, towards the end of the war.

D.H.9 D'1733 "G" of Capt. W.R. Harrison and 2Lt. C. Thomas. Shot down in Holland 16.9.18 by I.M.F.J.

No.109 Squadron R.A.F.

Formed in 1918 as a bomber training unit but was non-operational and was disbanded.

No.110 Squadron R.A.F.

Went to France and joined the Independant Force on 31st August, 1918, equipped with the D.H.9a. The original 18 aircraft were presented by the Nizam of Hyderabad and all carried, painted on the nose panel below the exhaust pipe, the inscription "Presented by His Exalted Highness the Nizam of Hyderabad" followed by "Hyderabad No.1 to 18." No.13 was not used; 12A was substituted instead. As the D.H.9as became casualities and were either "missing" or returned to Depot for repair, the replacements were not marked by an inscription as they were not presentation aircraft.

Squadron Markings

None was allotted.

Individual Markings

By white letters painted behind the inscription on the nose panels:
"A" Flight used A, B, C, D, E, F.
"B" Flight used G, H, J, K, L, M.
"C" Flight used N, O, P, Q, R, S.

D.H.9a F'1000 "B" Presentation "Hyderabad No.7" shot down 25.9.18, to 3 A S D for repair.

D.H.9a F'977 "Hyderabad No.18."

No.111 Squadron R.A.F.

Formed at Deir-el-Belah, Palestine, on 1st August, 1917, from a flight of No.14 Squadron. It was originally equipped with whatever aircraft were available, for example Bristol Monoplanes, D.H.2s, Vickers F.B.19s, Nieuport Scouts, and Bristol Fighters. It commenced fighter patrols in September.

It was intended that the squadron would become a single-seater fighter unit and early in 1918 only the Nieuports remained until they started to be replaced by S.E.5as in June 1918. By the 19th September it was fully equipped with 16 on strength.

The squadron carried out Fighting patrols and ground strafing against the combined Turkish/German forces.

Squadron Markings

None were allocated.

Flight Markings

Probably by coloured wheel covers.

Individual Markings

There was no standard pattern. A Nieuport 24 was marked with four dark bands and named *Demoiselle*. S.E.5as were seen with a variety of white band designs on fuselage sides and top decking.

Nieuport B'1552 longside a Bristol Monoplane.

RIGHT: Nieuport 24 B'3592 *Demoiselle* used by Reg Grobby.

S.E.5a D'6139 with bombs on board.

SE5a. B27. Appears to have damaged under carriage.

No.112 Squadron R.A.F.

Formed at Bekesbourne on 30th July, 1917 as a Home Defence unit for the defence of the London area, retaining this role until the armistice.

Equipment

Sopwith Scout and Sopwith Camel.

Squadron Markings

None were allocated.

Flight and Individual Markings

For some unknown reason the Sopwith Scouts were not allowed to fly by night and therefore, as daylight raids had finished before the squadron was formed, no Scouts flew operationally.

"B" Flight in late 1917 was marked with numbers in white, midway between the fuselage cockade and the tailplane, and repeated on the upper centre section. Personal names were also used.

Sopwith Camels flew operationally in March, 1918. Personal markings such as *Pixie 11* and *Tootsie* were very popular as were good luck symbols.

Sopwith Scout *Madge* with Capt. Newton and Lt. Davies.

Sopwith Camel with Lt. Irwin and dogs.

Camel D'6473 with more dogs!

RIGHT: Camel *Tootsie* with Capt. Baker and A/c Turner, filling up.

Camel *Twinkle*.

Sopwith Scouts at Throwley "B" Flight.

No.113 Squadron R.A.F.

Formed at Ismailia, Egypt, on 1st August, 1917, as an army co-operation unit. Mainly equipped with the B.E.2e, it operated in Palestine, working with General Allenby's forces, who cleared the Turks from the area.

In 1918 it re-equipped with the R.E.8. By September 1918, 16 R.E.8s and five Nieuport Scouts were on strength. The Nieuports were used for fast reconnaissance duties. It remained in Palestine until the armistice. No markings are known.

Nieuport 24 bis at Sarona used for fast reconnaissance.

No.114 Squadron R.A.F.

Was formed at Lahore, India, from a flight from No.31 Squadron in September 1917 equipped with the B.E.2c and B.E.2e. It was used on air police duties on the N.W. Frontier with half flights in various locations, including Aden. It remained in India until the armistice. No markings are known.

Henri Farman in India with the squadron, or on detached service to Aden.

No.115 Squadron R.A.F.

Formed at Catterick 1st December, 1917, as a training unit. At the end of August 1918 it received Handley Page 0/400s and joined the Independant Force in France in September, operating in the night bombing role until the armistice.

Squadron Markings

None were allocated. No other markings are known; probably none were used.

No.116 Squadron R.A.F.

Formed 31st March, 1918, to become a night bomber unit. It was non-operational and was disbanded in November 1918.

No.117 Squadron R.A.F.

Formed 1st January, 1918, but was non-operational. Disbanded June, 1918, it reformed in September, but disbanded again 6th October, 1918.

RIGHT: 115 Sqdn. With the Independent Force, September 1918 to Armistice.

D.H.9 C'1357 "A" September/October, 1918.

No.118 Squadron R.A.F.

Formed 1st January, 1918, as a night bomer unit to have Handley Page 0/400s, it was non-operational. It disbanded November 1918 due to shortage of aircraft and crews.

No.119 Squadron R.A.F.

Formed 1st January, 1918, as a night bomber unit. It was non-operational and was disbanded in November 1918.

No.120 Squadron R.A.F.

Formed 1st January, 1918 as a night bomber unit to have D.H.9a's and join the Independant Force but the armistice stopped them going overseas.

In May, 1919 they received D.H.10's and operated between the U.K. and France as a Communications squadron carrying mail etc. Disbanded October, 1919.

No.121 Squadron R.A.F.

Formed 1st January, 1918, as a night bomber unit. It was non-operational and was disbanded in August 1918.

No.122 Squadron R.A.F.

Formed 1st January, 1918, as a night bomber unit. It was non-operational and was disbanded in August 1918.

No.123 Squadron R.A.F.

Formed 1st March, 1918, to become a day bomber unit equipped with the D.H.9. Due to pilots and observers being drafted to France as replacements for active squadrons, the unit did not become operational and was disbanded 14th October, 1918. It was formed again with the D.H.9 on 3rd November, 1918, but the armistice intervened before it reached active service.

No.124 Squadron R.A.F.

Formed 1st March, 1918, as a day bomber unit to be equipped with the D.H.4/D.H.9. It was non-operational and was disbanded 17th August, 1918.

No.125 Squadron R.A.F.

Formed 1st February, 1918, as a day bomber unit to be equipped with the D.H.4/D.H.9. It was non-operational and was disbanded 17th August, 1918.

No.126 Squadron R.A.F.

Formed 1st March, 1918, as a day bomber unit to be equipped with the D.H.4/D.H.9. It was non-operational and was disbanded 17th March, 1918.

No.127 Squadron R.A.F.

Formed January, 1918, as a day bomber unit to be equipped with the D.H.4/D.H.9. It was non-operational and was disbanded 4th July, 1918.

No.128 Squadron R.A.F.

Formed 1st February, 1918, as a day bomber unit to be equipped with the D.H.4/D.H.9. It was non-operational and was disbanded 4th July, 1918, to supply replacements.

No.129 Squadron R.A.F.
Formed 1st March, 1918, as a day bomber unit to be equipped with the D.H.4/D.H.9. It was non-operational and was disbanded 4th July, 1918, to supply replacements.

No.130 Squadron R.A.F.
Formed 1st March, 1918. It was non-operational and disbanded 4th July, 1918.

No.131 Squadron R.A.F.
Formed 1st March, 1918, as a proposed bomber unit. Did not become operational. Disbanded 17th August, 1918.

No.132 Squadron R.A.F.
Formed 1st March, 1918, as a proposed night bomber unit. It was non-operational and disbanded at the armistice.

No.133 Squadron R.A.F.
Formed 1st March, 1918, as a proposed night bomber unit. It was non-operational and disbanded 4th July, 1918.

No.134 Squadron R.A.F.
Formed 1st March, 1918, as a proposed night bomber unit. It was non-operational and disbanded 4th July, 1918.

No.135 Squadron R.A.F.
Formed 1st April, 1918. It was non-operational and disbanded 4th July, 1918.

No.136 Squadron R.A.F.
Formed 1st April, 1918. It was non-operational and disbanded 4th July, 1918.

No.137 Squadron R.A.F.
Formed 1st April, 1918, as a day bomber unit to use the D.H.9. It did not become operational and disbanded 4th July, 1918.

No.138 Squadron R.A.F.
Formed 1st May, 1918, but formation was suspended due to need for replacements in France. Disbanded 4th July, 1918. It was reformed 30th September as a fighter-reconnaissance squadron equipped with Bristol Fighters, but became non-operational due to the armistice. Disbanded February 1919.

No.139 Squadron R.A.F.
In the spring of 1918 a flight of Bristol Fighters arrived in Italy from England. Attached firstly to No.28 and then No.34 Squadrons, they were known as "Z" Flight. When a second flight was attached in June 1918 it was named No.139 Squadron. This was at Villaverla. Bristols were in short supply in Italy and elsewhere, so a third flight was never added.

Squadron Markings
Although probably unofficial, from the beginning a squadron marking was in use with various additions. First was two white vertical bands around the fuselage behind the cockade, and in some cases a black band

B.F.2b "K."

B.F.2b "A" of Capt. L.F. Hursthouse and Lt. W.W. Smith.

B.F.2b "Z" of Lt. Geyton and Lt. Dowse.

was inside the two white bands. In time the number of white bands increased. Some aircraft carried 4, 10, 12, or 13 bands, the number of which would seem to be crew's choice. At least one Bristol had the two white bands span-wise on the top wing from cockade to cockade.

Individual Markings

By white letters in front of the cockade. To disguise the fact there were only two flights these letters were a random selection, but those known to have been used were A, D, G, K, L, M, S, X, and Z. Some aircraft also had the letter on the top wing.

B.F.2b D'8075 "L" of Lt. Gwyger and Lt. Hilton, MIA 22.8.18.

LEFT: B.F.2b D'7966 "A" of Lt. C.E. Gill and Lt. T. Newey, P.O.W. 23.8.18.

BELOW: B.F.2b E'2285 "A" of Capt. L.F. Hursthouse and Capt. P. Wilson, a visitor from No.28 Squadron.

No.140 Squadron R.A.F.

Formed 1st May, 1918, as a fighter unit for the defence of London with Bristol Fighters. It was disbanded 4th July, 1918, to provide replacements for other squadrons.

No.141 Squadron R.A.F.

Formed at Rochford on 1st January, 1918, as a home defence unit for the London area until the armistice.

Equipment

B.E.12, B.E.12a, B.E.12b, Bristol Fighter, and Sopwith Dolphin.

Squadron Markings

None was allocated.

Flight and Individual Markings

None known to be carried on any aircraft until the squadron won the "Cock" trophy on 22nd September, 1918, when a "fighting cock" was painted on the fin of the C.O's Bristol Fighter and one other aircraft was seen with it painted on the fuselage.

The squadron was expected to be re-equipped with Sopwith Dolphins starting January 1918 and, in fact, received six or seven at intervals over two months. Several crashed and the programme was abandoned when the C.O., Major Babington, reported that the Dolphin was "too tricky to fly by night." This report was dated 17th March.

After winning "Cock" trophy, Suttons Farm, 22.9.18.

RIGHT: After winning "Cock" trophy, Major B.E. Baker and "decorated fin" of E'2604.

Bristol F.2b with experimental night camouflage.

No.142 Squadron R.A.F.

Formed at Ismailia, Egypt on 13th February, 1918, as a reconnaissance and artillery spotting unit to serve the armies in Egypt and Palestine. It carried out this duty in this area until the armistice.

The first flight to be formed used the B.E.12as which came from No.1 Squadron A.F.C. As the supply situation improved, further aircraft arrived until by 19th September, 1918, the squadron had five R.E.8s and seven F.K.8s.

No details of any markings are known.

R.E.8 A'3807 crashed near Jerusalem.

No.143 Squadron R.A.F.

Formed at Throwley 1st February, 1918, as a home defence unit and was part of the London air defence until the armistice.

Equipment

F.K.8, S.E.5a, and Sopwith Camel.

Squadron Markings

None were allocated.

Flight and Individual Markings

Nothing is known while using F.K.8s, which were withdrawn April/ May 1918 and replaced with S.E.5as. Some at least had a broad white band around the fuselage just behind the headrest, and the wheel discs were painted as a cockade. In June, 1918 Camels started to replace the S.E.5as, and by the armistice the squadron was fully completed.

S.E.5a C'6401 *Punjab 15 Kashmir.*

S.E.5a C'1803 "1."

LEFT: Camel H'740 with underwing serial number.

S.E.5a C'1805 "2."

Camels line up at Detling.

One flight of Camels had the wheel discs painted as a cockade and aircraft were marked "I," "II," "III," etc., in white on the fin. Personal markings were also carried, for example *Bubbles*. Another flight had a large white centre to the wheel discs.

No.144 Squadron R.A.F.

Formed at Port Said, Egypt, on 20th March, 1918, as a day bomber unit to be equipped with D.H.9s. Joining the Palestine Brigade on 14th August, 1918, it had 13 D.H.9s by the end of the month and carried out raids on Turkish targets. In October 1918 the squadron moved to Mudros in the Aegean.

Squadron Markings

A white horizontal band along the centre line of the fuselage behind the cockade.

Individual Markings

By numbers on the fuselage mid-way along the squadron marking. These markings may have been unofficial.

D.H.9 "3" Possibly C'6293. Note the white flash.

RIGHT: D.H.9 C'6293 "3." Note the large bomb in rack.

No.145 Squadron R.A.F.

Formed in May 1918 at Aboukir as a fighter unit. When joining the Palestine Brigade in August 1918 it had six S.E.5as; it added another flight some while after. It remained in Palestine until the armistice. No markings are recorded.

No.146 Squadron R.A.F.

There is no record of this unit being formed during the war.

No.147 Squadron R.A.F.

Formed in Egypt in May, 1918 but did not become operational and was disbanded.

No.148 Squadron R.A.F.

Was formed 10th February, 1918, as a night bomber unit with the F.E.2b and F.E.2d. It went to France in April 1918 and carried out raids until the armistice. No markings were used.

No.149 Squadron R.A.F.

Formed 3rd March, 1918 as a night bomber unit with the F.E.2b. It went to France in June 1918 and carried out raids until the armistice. No markings were used.

D.H.9. Palestine Brigade, August 1918. Force landed in desert – crew waving at rescue force.

S.E.5a B'538. Capt. A.I. Fleming claimed first victory for No.111 Sqdn. 23.1.18 shooting down an Albatross DIII over Tulkeram.

F.E.2b with all markings painted out.

F.E.2b probably in training role as serial is below wing (Serial No.9163 in white).

No.150 Squadron R.A.F.

Formed 1st April, 1918, at Kirec in Macedonia from flights withdrawn from Nos.17 and 47 Squadrons. These two flights were, in fact, not transferred until the 26th April and were mainly equipped with S.E.5as and a few Bristol Monoplanes. On 7th May a third flight of Sopwith Camels was added. The squadron carried out fighter patrols, ground strafing, and light bombing on the Macedonian Front until the armistice. No markings were used but one S.E.5a had *Fifi* painted on the cowling.

"A" Flight had S.E.5as. "B" and "C" Flights had a mixture of S.E.5as and Camels. At the armistice there were nine S.E.5as, seven Camels, one B.E.12, and one Bristol Monoplane.

RIGHT ABOVE: Bristol Monoplane in Macedonia. A few of these planes remained in service with 150 Sqdn. to the Armistice, amongst Camels and S.E.5as.

RIGHT: S.E.5a D'3495, Capt. G.G. Bell (Cdn.), Macedonia.

No.151 Squadron R.A.F.

Formed 12th June, 1918, from flights transferred from Nos.44, 78, and 112 Home Defence Squadrons and moved to France within a few days. Equipped with Sopwith Camels, it was the first night-fighter unit on the Western Front. It helped counter the extensive night bombing carried out by German night bombers against allied bases and areas behind the lines. This had increased considerably since the night bombing of England had stopped.

Squadron Markings

A long, narrow band in white along the centre line of the side of the fuselage, broken by the cockade. This may not have been used until after the armistice.

Individual Markings

Believed to have been dark numbers on the fuselage sides.

No.152 Squadron R.A.F.

Formed in June/July 1918 as a night-fighter squadron equipped with Sopwith Camels. It went to France on 18th October but saw no action as by then night bombing by the enemy had ceased. No markings have been recorded.

No.153 Squadron R.A.F.

Formed November 1918. Non-operational. Disbanded.

No.154 Squadron R.A.F.

Formed October 1918. Non-operational. Disbanded.

No.155 Squadron R.A.F.

Formed 14th September, 1918, as a night fighter unit to be equipped with Sopwith Camels. Non-operational and disbanded 7th December, 1918.

No.156 Squadron R.A.F.

Formed 12th October, 1918. Non-operational. Disbanded.

No.157 Squadron R.A.F.

Formed in September 1918, it was expected to be the first unit to be equipped with Sopwith Salamanders, but the armistice intervened before it was fully equipped.

No.158 Squadron R.A.F.

Formed 4th September, 1918. Non-operational. Disbanded.

No.159 Squadron R.A.F.

Formed 1st June, 1918. However, the personnel were used as reinforcements to squadrons in France. Formation was suspended and the squadron disbanded 4th July, 1918.

No.160 Squadron R.A.F.

Formed June 1918. However, the personnel were used as reinforcements to squadrons in France. Formation was suspended and the squadron disbanded 4th July, 1918.

S.E.5a, B.692, Lt. L. Hamilton, Macedonia. Note camouflaged B.E. in background.

Camel, unconfirmed from No.151 Sqdn.

Salamander F'6504 at Upper Heywood.

Salamander F'6518 at Upper Heywood.

No.161 Squadron R.A.F.

Formed 1st June, 1918. However, the personnel were used as reinforcements to squadrons in France. Formation was suspended and the squadron disbanded 4th July, 1918.

No.162 Squadron R.A.F.

Formed 1st June, 1918. However, the personnel were used as reinforcements to squadrons in France. Formation was suspended and the squadron disbanded 4th July, 1918.

No.163 Squadron R.A.F.

Formed June, 1918. Disbanded 4th July, 1918.

No.164 Squadron R.A.F.

Formed June, 1918. Disbanded 4th July, 1918.

No.165 Squadron R.A.F.

Formed June, 1918. Disbanded 4th July, 1918.

No.166 Squadron R.A.F.

Formed 13th June, 1918, at Bircham Newton as a night bombing unit. After delays it received three Handley Page V/1500 bombers and was expected to bomb Berlin, but the armistice intervened and the squadron disbanded.

No.167 Squadron R.A.F.

Formed November, 1918 at Bircham Newton as a night bombing unit. It was expected to bomb Berlin using Handley Page V/1500 bombers but it received no aircraft before being disbanded in May, 1919.

No.168 Squadron R.A.F.

Was not formed.

No.169 Squadron R.A.F.

Was not formed.

No.170 Squadron R.A.F.

Was not formed.

No.171 Squadron R.A.F.

Was not formed.

No.172 Squadron R.A.F.

Was not formed.

No.173 Squadron R.A.F.

Was not formed.

No.174 Squadron R.A.F.

Was not formed.

No.175 Squadron R.A.F.

Was not formed.

No.176 Squadron R.A.F.

Was not formed.

No.177 Squadron R.A.F.

Was not formed.

No.178 Squadron R.A.F.

Was not formed.

No.179 Squadron R.A.F.

Was not formed.

No.180 Squadron R.A.F.

Was not formed.

No.181 Squadron R.A.F.

Was not formed.

No.182 Squadron R.A.F.

Was not formed.

No.183 Squadron R.A.F.

Was not formed.

Handley Page V/1500 heavy bomber. The Armistice arrived before any could be used.

No.184 Squadron R.A.F.

Was not formed.

No.185 Squadron R.A.F.

Was formed 21st October, 1918, at East Fortune as a Torpedo Bomber Unit equipped with the Sopwith Cuckoo. These were to be embarked on the carrier H.M.S. Argus, intending to attack the German High Seas Fleet in its bases as it had not put to sea after Jutland with serious intent. The war finished before this attack was mounted and the squadron was disbanded in April, 1919, although many experiments were carried out with H.M.S. Argus.

Squadron Markings

None were allocated. No other markings are known.

Sopwith "Cuckoo" N'7157 at Marske, in transit to the squadron. Presentation aircraft "Whitechurch."

"Cuckoo" N'6952 and N'6954 en route to No.185 Sqdn at East Fortune, end october 1918.

No.186 Squadron R.A.F.

Was formed at Throwley on 1st April, 1918, as a night training unit equipped with Avro 504Ks until the armistice.

Squadron Markings

None were allocated. No other markings are known.

No.187 Squadron R.A.F.

Formed 1st April, 1918, as a night training unit equipped with Avro 504Ks, Sopwith Scouts, and Camels until the armistice. No markings are known.

"Cuckoo" N'6954 during practice drop at "Torpedo Aeroplane School", East Fortune.

No.188 Squadron R.A.F.

Was formed in December 1917 as a night training unit for pilots expecting to join the home defence units flying Camels. It was in this role until the armistice, providing trained pilots for the operational home defence units and those planned to form. No markings are known.

No.189 Squadron R.A.F.

Formed in December 1917 as a night training unit for Camel pilots, remained at Suttons Farm until the armistice providing trained pilots for home defence units. No markings are known.

No.190 Squadron R.A.F.

Formed 24th October, 1917, as a night training unit but was non-operational.

No.191 Squadron R.A.F.

Formed November, 1917 as a night training unit but was non-operational.

No.192 Squadron R.A.F.

Formed 5th September, 1917, as a night training unit, retaining this role until the armistice using F.E.2bs.

No.193 Squadron R.A.F.

Was not formed.

RIGHT: HMS Furious, 1.11.18. "Cuckoo"s at rest in the nest! Note folded wings.

No.194 Squadron R.A.F.
Was not formed.

No.195 Squadron R.A.F.
Was not formed.

No.196 Squadron R.A.F.
Was not formed.

No.197 Squadron R.A.F.
Was not formed.

No.198 Squadron R.A.F.
Formed at Rochford 1st June, 1917, as a night training unit with Camels, retaining this role until the armistice. No markings are known.

No.199 Squadron R.A.F.
Formed 1st June, 1917, as a night training unit equipped with F.E.2bs. It retained this role until the armistice. Farmans and F.E.2bs were seen with a white elongated "M" around the nose.

No.200 Squadron R.A.F.
Formed 1st July as a night training unit equipped with F.E.2bs, retained this role until the armistice. No markings are known.

No.201 Squadron R.A.F.
Originally formed as No.1 Squadron R.N.A.S. with a mixed collection of aircraft. In June 1915, while at Dunkerque, the squadron was renumbered No.1 Wing R.N.A.S. Shortly after, three flights were combined and known as "A" Squadron. On 3rd December, 1916, this was re-numbered No.1 Squadron R.N.A.S. Equipped with Nieuport two-seaters and Moranes, the squadron received its first Sopwith Triplane in June 1916 and became fully equipped in January 1917. It later returned to England to re-equip with Camels, returning to France in February, 1918.

Individual Markings on Sopwith Triplanes
By large white numbers painted on the fuselage side behind the cockade, the numbers going from 1 to 18.

Squadron Markings on Sopwith Triplanes
Allotted on 26th August, 1917, these were two white vertical bars on the fuselage side behind the cockade. They were painted quite small.

Individual Markings on Sopwith Triplanes
With the introduction of squadron markings, the cockade was painted out and the individual marking painted in its position. The number sequence remained the same.

These markings remained until the squadron was withdrawn in November 1917 before returning to England in December for re-equipment with Sopwith Camels. It returned to France at end of February 1918 fully equipped with Camels. The Camels carried on the large individual numbers on the fuselage.

M.F. "Shorthorn."

F.E.2bs.

Sopwith Triplane *15 Peggy* No.16 is N'5425.

RIGHT: Sopwith Triplane N'5377 "4" of F/S.Lt. M.J. Watson, P.O.W. 3.10.17.

Squadron Marking on Sopwith Camels

Allotted 22nd March, 1918, this was one white vertical bar painted on the fuselage side behind the cockade. In or about August some aircraft had the bar painted in front of the tailplane; this is understood to have been a "painter's error." The Camels were also "painted up," but never in the same way as other Naval Squadrons. These served as individual markings.

Flight Markings

"A" Flight used red wheel covers and fin.
"B" Flight used white wheel covers and fin.
"C" Flight used blue wheel covers and fin.

Individual Markings

"A" Flight used A, B, C, D, E, F in white on the red fin.
"B" Flight used S, T, U, V, W, X in white on fuselage by cockpit.
"C" Flight used 1, 2, 3, 4, 5, 6 in white on fuselage by cockpit.

Flight Commanders' Markings

"A" Flight used two streamers from rudder.
"B" Flight used two streamers, one from each elevator.
"C" Flight used two streamers, one from each interplane strut.

No.201 was one squadron which removed "X" from its markings and used "Z" in its place.

Camels; early issue still carry large numbers as on Triplanes.

Camel, possibly B'6418, flown December 1917 to May 1918 by Capt. C.B. Ridley. The ring on top decking above squadron markings may be a Lieutenant's Curl.

Sopwith Triplane line up 28.10.17 with pilots.

Sopwith Triplane N'5429 "2" of F/S.Lt. J.R. Wilford. P.O.W. 13.9.17 by *Ltn.* Kurt Wusthof, *Jasta* 4.

Camel "S" at Bertangles, August 1918.

RIGHT: Camel "V" of Lt. Sehl.

Camel "B" and "C" Flights lined up.

ABOVE AND TWO BELOW: Shown here is Capt. W. Barker's Camel B'6313, in Italy – the number of stripes varied. At the end of his tour he returned to the UK 30.9.18. then asked to go to France and eventually took a Sopwith Snipe E'810 attached to No.201 Sqdn. for two weeks. On 27.10.18 he made what was to be his last patrol and engaged a large number of Fokker DVIIs single-handed, destoyig four and being wounded three or four times – he then crashed behind British lines. His Snipe was recovered and sent back to Canada on show. He received his Victoria Cross on 30.11.18.

No.202 Squadron R.A.F.

The original No.2 Squadron R.N.A.S. was formed in October 1914 and by the end of the year was at Ostende. The equipment was varied B.E. types, Nieuport Two-Seaters, and later Sopwith Two-Seaters. The squadron's main duties were coastal patrols along the Belgian coast, attacks on coastal installations and German shipping, and artillery spotting for the Royal Navy bombarding targets ashore.

No details are known definitely for this period but probably the Sopwiths were marked with flight letters and individual numbers as were other R.N.A.S. units.

D.H.4s arrived in 1917 and by about July the squadron was fully equipped and carried on the duties as before. No squadron markings are known but it is possible that they used two vertical white bars side by side behind the cockade, and if so it may or may not have been official.

In 1918 the squadron changed its role and each flight had a special role to perform. "A" Flight were known as the "Photography Flight." They had wheel covers half white, half red. Aircraft were marked with large white letters below the exhaust manifold. Known to have been used were: A, B, D, I, O, S, T.

"B" Flight were responsible for wireless work, that is, spotting for naval guns. They usually had white wheel covers, marked with large white letters below the exhaust manifold. Known to have been used were: E, K, L, M; others were probably used also.

"C" Flight were known as the "Escort Flight" and escorted the other two flights. They had blue wheel covers and used large white letters below the exhaust manifold. Known to have been used were: J, R, Z; others were probably used also.

Individual Markings

A number of aircraft were painted with various designs, some on the fins, some on the nose. Designs seen on fins included a crescent moon, a crocodile, and a red devil with fingers to nose. Designs seen on noses included a blue bird and a "lightning" flash along the fuselage. The coloured wheel covers were not strictly adhered to.

The Escort Flight are reputed to have two Vickers on the cowling, two Lewis guns on the upper centre section, and two Lewis guns for the observer. This is not confirmed. The Photography Flight had a camera box on the underside of the fuselage below the observer's cockpit.

D.H.4 "A," "A" Flight aircraft.

D.H.4 "D," "A" Flight aircraft of Lt. Pendred running up.

D.H.4 "I," "A" Flight aircraft.

D.H.4 "T," "A" Flight aircraft airborne.

D.H.4 "O" and "S," "A" Flight aircraft.

D.H.4 "R," "C" Flight aircraft.

No.203 Squadron R.A.F.

The original 3 Squadron R.N.A.S. served in the Dardanelles and was disbanded at the end of 1915. It was reformed from units at Dunkerque in June 1916, flying various aircraft. At the beginning of 1917 it was equipped with Sopwith Scouts, moved up to the Somme, and attached to the R.F.C.

Squadron Markings

None allotted initially. On 22nd March, 1918, a squadron marking, consisting of a white ring painted on the side of the fuselage mid-way between the tail and the cockade, was allotted.

Flight Markings

"A" Flight had blue cowlings.
"B" Flight had red cowlings.
"C" Flight had black cowlings.

After 22nd March, 1918, cowlings were painted in the same method as during the earlier period, but this was discontinued about September.

Individual Markings

Most aircraft were marked with the first letter of the pilot's surname or nickname. In addition, most carried a name which contained the flight colour, for example, all of "C" Flight:

F/Cmdr Mack	F.SL. Pierce	F.SL. Rochford
N'6172	N'6171	N'6207
"M"	"P"	"R"
"Black Tulip"	"Black Arrow"	"Black Bess"

D.H.4 "M," "B" Flight aircraft.

These were painted quite small roughly below the cockpit. Artistic license was taken with painting the arrow and the horse.

Members of "A" and "B" Flights used similar methods of indentification but names, when used, did not always contain the flight colour.

In July 1917 the squadron re-equipped with Sopwith Camels which were painted up in the same way as the Scouts. No squadron marking was used and no trace of one being allotted has been found. These markings remained until the squadron was withdrawn in November 1917 to Walmer for a rest.

Sopwith Scout N'6183 *Mildred H.*

While in the U.K., most of the Camels were very brightly painted with stripes, bands, and many other devices. These were still on when they returned to Bray Dunes in January 1918. When they replaced Naval Eight on the 1st March, 1918, on attachment to the R.F.C., they exchanged their Camels for the Bentley-engined Camels of Naval Eight. They flew these Camels, still with the white disc squadron marking and individual letters of their previous owners, as new markings were to be issued in about a fortnight.

After 22nd March, 1918, individual markings were roughly in the earlier fashion but were more subdued. "A" Flight used Roman numerals within two narrow white bands between the cockade and squadron marking. "C" Flight used pilot's initial on fuselage side and an eagle badge below the cockpit similar to an R.N.A.S. pilot's "wings."

In later 1918 cowlings and side panels were painted white.

Sopwith Scout N'6171 "P" *Black Arrow* of F/S/Lt. Pierce, blown over by wind at Marieux.

Sopwith Scout. N'6464 "D" of F/S/Lt J.B. Daniells, P.O.W. 11.5.17 by *Vzfw*. Rissinger of *Jasta* 12.

Sopwith Scout. N'6172 "M" *Black Tulip* of Flight/Cmdr. Mack, P.O.W. 12.4.17, shot down by *Hptm*. von Osterroht of *Jasta* 12.

Camel B'7230 "T" of F/S/Lt K.D. Campbell, P.O.W.

Camels in squadron line up February 1918 at Middle Aerodrome.

LEFT: Camel B'6401 of Sqn/Cmdr. L.S. Breadner at Middle Aerodrome, Bray Dunes, February 1918.

Camel *Fidelity* of F/Lt. G.B. Anderson.

Camel B'7275 "P" of "C" Flight at Liettres.

Camel B'3858. The stripes are possibly red, white, and blue. A "Tudor Rose" is on four wings.

Camel *Nibs* of "A" Flight.

Camel D'9638 shot down in the British lines 2.10.18.

Camels in squadron line up with pilots.

RIGHT: Camel F'3961.

No.204 Squadron R.A.F.

The original was No.4 Squadron R.N.A.S. which became No.4 Wing R.N.A.S. The new No.4 Squadron R.N.A.S. was formed 31st December, 1916, from "A" Squadron, 5th Wing R.N.A.S. at Coudekerque. Equipped with Sopwith two-seaters, it was to be a bomber unit. However, in March 1917 it was re-equipped with Sopwith Scouts as a fighter unit mainly to escort bombers and fly protection patrols for the fleet.

In June, 1917 it started to re-equip with Sopwith Camels and mainly operated on the French and Belgian coasts. It remained in the fighter role until the armistice.

Squadron Markings

None were issued for the two-seaters or Sopwith Scouts. After changing to Camels, no markings appear to have been issued for the squadron and they are not on the lists for either the 26th August or 3rd December, 1917. Squadron markings were finally allocated 22nd March, 1918; two white bars painted immediately in front of the tailplane sloping inwards at the top. Precise details are missing, but some of these markings were possibly painted in a flight colour and were also repeated on the top decking. These squadron markings should have been used until the armistice, but when No.148 American Squadron left the R.A.F. on attachment to the U.S.A.S. on 28th October, 1918, their markings were issued to No.204 Squadron R.A.F. to disguise the fact of their withdrawal. This last was a white triangle behind the fuselage cockade.

Individual Markings

Some Sopwith Scouts were marked with names on the sides, roughly between the cockade and cockpit, in ornate style, for example: *Anzac*, *Bobs*, and *DoDo*, while others were completely unmarked. Initially, Camel markings were probably in the same pattern as on the Sopwith Scouts. Later, these appear to have been pilot's choice with names and mottoes, but some time in this period white numbers "1" – "24" painted in front of the cockade were used:

"A" Flight used 1–8.
"B" Flight used 9–16.
"C" Flight used 17–24.

This existed to the armistice and later.

Sopwith Scout *Bobs*.

Camel N'6346 flown by Flt,/Cmdr, G.M. Rouse in mid-1917. It was one of the first Camels in service.

RIGHT: Camel B'5243 flown by F.C. Tonks later in 1917.

Sopwith Scout N'6185 *Anzac* with *DoDo* and others.

Camel B'7234 *Laura* of Lt. Wilson. Taken at Strenght, 25.5.18.

Camel. Jenner-Parsons in the flood.

Camel. Flown by Lt. R.M. Gordon, D.F.C. mid-1918. The "Stag & Crown" is the badge of the Gordon Highlanders and "By Dand" their motto.

Camel. The motto is Lowland Scots, not Gaelic "Watchfulness."

Camel B'5642 "7" *Mabs* on 3.11.18.

RIGHT: Camel F'3222 "9" *Stars* of Lt. Hopson on 1.11.18.

Camel F'6037 "16" *Thumbs Up* of Lt. Chisam on 4.11.18.

No.205 Squadron R.A.F.

The original No.5 Squadron R.N.A.S. formed at Coudekerque on the last day of 1916 and was previously known as "B" Squadron of No.5 Wing R.N.A.S. Equipped with Sopwith two-seaters, it was a day bomber unit operating against coastal targets and aerodromes.

Squadron Markings

None were allocated.

Flight Markings

The flight letter was painted behind the fuselage cockade in white.

Individual Markings

By numbers 1-6 painted behind the flight letter. In addition, a small "5" was painted by the top of the letter or figure, although this was sometimes omitted.

By August, 1917 the squadron was fully equipped with D.H.4s. No squadron markings were allocated at that time, and flight and individual markings were as before.

On the 1st April, 1918, the squadron was renumbered No.205 Squadron R.A.F., still with D.H.4s although a few D.H.9as arrived shortly before the armistice. The markings changed – flight markings were discontinued and individual letters were painted behind the cockade on the fuselage. Letters were used on both the D.H.4s and D.H.9as.

D.H.4 "B1."

D.H.4 N'5978 "B3."

D.H.4 "A3."

LEFT: D.H.4 "B5."

D.H.9a F'1001 "L."

D.H.9a F'1048 "T."

D.H.9a E'9707 "A."

D.H.9a E'1108 "G" of Capt. A.R. McAfee and Lt. S.J. Furze.

No.206 Squadron R.A.F.

The original No.6 Squadron R.N.A.S. was formed in December, 1916 at Dunkerque as a fighter unit equipped with Nieuport Scouts of various types, changing to Sopwith Camels in July 1917.

Due to shortage of pilots, the squadron disbanded at the end of August, 1917. It re-formed in February 1918 as a day bomber unit equipped with D.H.9s.

Squadron Marking Using Nieuports

No squadron marking was used.

Individual Markings Using Nieuports

By large black numbers on the fuselage sides.

Squadron Marking Using Sopwith Camels

Allotted 26th August, 1917 – a white square on the fuselage sides behind the cockade. It is unlikely that this marking was ever used, due to the disbandment.

Individual Markings Using Sopwith Camels

By white letters on fuselage sides.

Squadron Marking Using D.H.9s

None was allotted.

Individual Markings Using D.H.9s

By large white letters on fuselage side behind the cockade:

"A" Flight used A, B, C, D, E, F.

"B" Flight used J, K, L, M, N, O (approximately).

"C" Flight used U, V, W, X, Y, Z.

RIGHT: Nieuport Scout with F/Lt. E.W. Norton D.S.C.

Nieuport Scout N'3200.

D.H.9 "C."

No.207 Squadron R.A.F.

Originally "B" Squadron 4 Wing R.N.A.S. formed 1st November, 1916, it was retitled No.207 Squadron R.A.F. on amalgamation 1st April, 1918. Formed as a heavy bombing unit and commenced using Handley Page 0/100s in April 1917.

Day operations were undertaken against enemy naval vessels but after 3115 was shot down by a German seaplane fighter on 26.4.17 off Nieuport, day operations were abandoned in favour of night bombing.

Squadron Markings

None were used.

Individual Markings

As far as is known, no markings were used in the early period but in late 1918 a flight letter and individual number was seen on some aircraft. There were either painted on the nose or on the fuselage side either side of the cockade in white.

Allocations of H.P. 0/100 and 0/400 Bombers

The usual number of aircraft was ten machines per squadron, varying due to losses and replacements being delayed. Many aircraft were re-paired, overhauled, re-built at base workshops, and then re-issued to squadrons needing them. This meant a large number served in several squadrons but due to the often obscured serial number on the end of the fuselage (usually hidden by the fin and rudder,) it is not possible to identify all aircraft amongst the squadrons.

D.H.9 "B."

D.H.9 "F."

D.H.9 "J."

RIGHT: H.P. 0/400 D'5422 with "3" on nose.

H.P. 0/400 D'5429 visiting Detling.

Arrival of the first 0/100, No.3116, at Coudekerque 4.3.17.

No.208 Squadron R.A.F.

Originally formed as No.8 Squadron R.N.A.S. by drawing a flight from the three Naval Wings then at Dunkerque. No.1 Wing provided six Sopwith Scouts, No.4 Wing six Nieuports, and No.5 Wing six Sopwith Two-seaters. No.8 formed at St. Pol on 25th October, 1916.

By mid-November the Nieuports and Sopwith Two-seaters were replaced by Scouts. These, in turn, were replaced by Sopwith Triplanes commencing in March 1917, which in turn were replaced by Sopwith Camels commencing early in July, but this was not completed until 6th September. In October 1918 Sopwith Snipes arrived but the armistice occurred before the squadron had the chance to use them very much, if at all.

Sopwith Scout A'626 of F/S.Lt. J. Croft, POW 4.1.17.

Squadron Markings

None used before 26th August, 1917, at least officially. Allocated on 26th August, 1917, this was a white disc on fuselage side behind the cockade. These were painted on the remaining Triplanes as well as the Camels. New squadron markings were allocated on 22nd March, 1918; these were two white bars sloping in at the top behind the cockade.

Flight Markings

None were used.

Individual Markings

May have been used on the Sopwith Scouts in the fashion of names but only one or two details have been recorded. Most of the Sopwith Triplanes had names on the side, usually below the cockpit, for example: *Pip, Joan, Tiki, Angel, Gwen, Maud, Blimp, Binky III, High Jinks, Hilda, Veda, Dusty, Lily.*

Individual Markings were introduced late in 1917 with white letters behind the white disc. Originally these were: "A" Flight A–F, "B" Flight G–L, "C" Flight M–R. When extra Camels arrived they took letters from "R" onwards. Eventually aircraft were marked to indicate the pilot's name in many cases.

After 22 March, 1918, individual markings were as before, but were now painted in front of the cockade, roughly below the cockpit. The squadron and individual markings were repeated on the Sopwith Snipes.

RIGHT: Sopwith Scout *Binky II* of Lt. G.G. Simpson.

Sopwith Triplane N'5468 *Angel* of S.F.Lt. Jenner Parsons.

Sopwith Triplane Has "8N's" marking but could be from another squadron.

Camels after letters were introduced.

Camel crashed on allied side of the lines near Cherisy on 4.9.18 by 2/Lt. E. Munro.

Sopwith Triplane N'5482 *Maud* of F/Lt. C.D. Booker.

Camels during winter 1917/18 before letters were used.

Camel D'1845 "C" crashed.

Sopwith Snipe E'8132 "D" post war.

Sopwith Snipe E'8270 "V" post war.

No.209 Squadron R.A.F.

Originally formed as No.9 Squadron R.N.A.S. on 1st February, 1917, at St. Pol from a nucleus from Naval Eight, also taking over their Sopwith Scouts and Nieuports when they converted to Sopwith Triplanes.

Its duties were to provide cover for the fleet and to combat enemy bombing raids on coastal towns in France and England. In June they were attached to the R.F.C. flying Sopwith Scouts and Triplanes, and in July 1917 re-equipped with Sopwith Camels until the armistice. No markings known on the period before Camels, possibly individual letters or numbers were used.

Squadron Markings

Allocated 26th August, 1917, this was a white crescent on fuselage side behind the cockade. Early Camels carried this marking but in September the squadron indulged in a heavy "painting up" period. There seems to have been no system in this. A new squadron marking was allocated 22nd March, 1918, which was three white vertical bars, one in front of the fuselage cockade and two behind it, although many aircraft did not use it.

Individual Markings

During the decorative period the Camels were decorated with coloured bands, circles and other designs on the fuselage, tailplane and centre section. Colours seem to have been blue and white and red and white. When these were discontinued is uncertain but in April 1918 there was still some decoration used. Later, from photographs it seems as though pilots chose their own markings for fuselage and wings. Many aircraft also painted out the fuselage cockade.

At the end of the war or just after, two squadron Camels were photographed with correct squadron markings; one, Serial No.H.7000, has "3" on the fin, the other has "2" on the fin with an unreadable serial number prefixed with "F." These may have been a late war style of marking, but details are lacking.

Camel N'6358 of F/S/Lt. N. Black shot down by three German aircraft at Zarren on 11.10.17; Black was KIA. Black was in "C" Flight who did not "paint up" as did "B" Flight.

Camel at Middle Aerodrome, Bray Dunes, decorated.

RIGHT: Camel B'3884 decorated.

Camel decorated.

Camel B'6230 of Flt./Cmdr. Banbury.

Camel B'3881 of F/S/Lt. Pierce at Leffrinkhouche, September 1917.

Camel F'6030 used by Major Gerrard from 3.9.18. Later it was used by other pilots.

Camel, probably B'7270 of Capt. A.R. Brown.

Camels showing a variety of markings or none.

No.210 Squadron R.A.F.

Originally formed as No.10 Squadron R.N.A.S. at St. Pol on 12th February, 1917 as a fighter unit flying protection patrols over the Fleet and escorts to bomber and reconnaissance units. In May it joined 11th Wing on attachment to R.F.C.

It was equipped with Nieuport Scouts and Two-seaters and a few Sopwith Triplanes. The Nieuports were withdrawn and they were fully equipped with Triplanes, using them until 26th August, 1917, when Sopwith Camels were on strength and remained until the armistice.

Markings on the Nieuports are unknown and probably none were used.

Squadron Markings Using Sopwith Triplanes

None were allocated but on the "proposed" list issued 15th August, 1917, it was suggested that two white vertical bars behind the cockade should be used. However, when the amended list was issued, markings were not shown for Triplanes but amended for Camels.

Flight Markings Using Sopwith Triplanes

"A" Flight used red cowlings and wheel covers.
"B" Flight used black cowlings and wheel covers.
"C" Flight used blue cowlings and wheel covers.

This was intended to help the mechanics to recognize their own aircraft if they landed at the end of the aerodrome and needed pushing into the hangars. "B" Flight also painted the metal panels behind the cowling black and "A" and "C" may have done likewise.

Individual Markings Using Sopwith Triplanes

There was no standard style at this time. The usual method was by the pilot's initial, usually painted behind the cockade, and photographs show that Flight Commander Collishaw also had it painted on the tailplane, at least on the starboard side. Probably other pilots used their own ideas of markings. Known couplings were Collishaw "C," Sharman "S," Page "P," Kent "K."

Additional to these type of markings "B" Flight also painted names in 3-inch letters below the cockpit – *Black Maria* was Collishaw, *Black Sheep* was F/S/Lt. G.E. Nash, *Black Roger* was F/S/Lt. E.V. Reid, *Black Death* was F/S/Lt. J.E. Sharman, *Black Prince* was F/S/Lt. W.M. Alexander. It is unknown whether the other flights used names.

Squadron Marking Using Sopwith Camels

Allocated 26th August, 1917, these were two white vertical bars on the fuselage sides, one in front of the cockade and one midway between the tailplane and cockade. A new marking was allocated 22nd March, 1918; this was a white disc behind the cockade. When the two American Camel squadrons left the R.A.F. on attachment to the U.S.A.S. on 28th October, 1918, their markings were issued to R.A.F. units to disguise the fact they had been withdrawn. Markings of 17th American went to No.210 Squadron R.A.F.; this was a white dumbell painted behind the cockade. Letters were used as before. After the armistice some letters were converted to monograms.

Flight Markings Using Sopwith Camels

Flight letter "A," "B," or "C" on fuselage sides immediately in front of the first bar of the squadron marking in large white letters.

Individual Markings Using Sopwith Camels

These were confined to the wheel covers and were in flight colours and white. Some examples – black and white checks, three black bars, two black rings, black star. Similar markings in red and blue for other flights.

About the end of December 1917 there was more painting up. The cowling and side panels back to the rear of the cockpit were painted in the flight colour and three horizontal white bands were superimposed. This was almost immediately ordered by the Brigade Commander to be removed. This style of decoration was considered wasting materials and was strictly forbidden. However, the order was not strictly obeyed but as aircraft were lost the replacements were not painted up.

These markings were finally finished when the Bentley engined Camels arrived at the beginning of February, 1918.

During this "striped" period, the flight colours were changed. "A" was now black, "B" was red, "C" was blue. When the Bentley Camels arrived, the Flight letters were discontinued and individual letters replaced them – the sequence is uncertain but probably "A" Flight A–H, "B" Flight J–Q, "C" Flight R–Z.

Sopwith Triplane "Q;" the serial is hidden but could be N'5368 of Lt. C.R. Pegler, KIA 12.7.17, or N'5478 of Lt. J.A. Page, KIA 22.7.17, both from Naval 10.

Sopwith Triplane N'5357 "K" of F/S/Lt. Kent, POW 17.6.17.

Camel B'6289 of "A" Flight flown by F/S/Lt. D.L. Nelson.

Camels of "A" Flight; the nearest aircraft was flown by Capt. A.W. Carter.

Camel of "C" Flight used by Capt. Coombes.

Camels of "B" and "C" Flights; B'6299 was used by F/Cmdr. N.M. Macgregor.

Camel B'5658 of "B" Flight flown by F/S.Lt. F. Booth, missing 3.1.18.

Camel B'7227 "G" of 2/Lt. R.G. Carr, MIA 21.6.18.

ABOVE: Camel "S;" no details are known. BELOW: Camels. F'5914 "S" of Capt. H.T. Mellings, "B" Flight Commander, MIA 20.7.18. B'7153 "V" was used by L.P. Coombes, I.E. Sanderson, and S.C. Joseph.

No.211 Squadron R.A.F.

The original 11 Squadron R.N.A.S. was formed in March 1917 as a fighter squadron at Dunkerque. Due to shortage of pilots and aircraft it remained basically a training and holding unit until being disbanded at the end of August. It was re-formed as a bomber squadron in March 1918 at Petite Snythe equipped with D.H.9s in the day bombing and reconnaissance role.

Squadron Markings

None were allotted.

Flight Markings

"A" and "C" Flights had plain wheel covers. "B" Flight had white covers with a coloured spiral painted on.

Individual Markings

By white letter in various styles painted roughly below the pilot's cockpit:

"A" Flight used A, B, C, D, E, F.

"B" Flight used G, H, J, K, L, M.

"C" Flight used N, O, P, Q, R, S.

Any extra aircraft carried on from these.

Formation Leaders

A very frequent target was the Docks at Bruges, Ostende, and Zeebrugge, all of which were heavily defended by A.A. guns as well as fighters. It was found that this caused the formations to spread out and straggle. The formation leader carried easily seen markings to enable the other members to join up much easier.

D.H.9 B'7623 "L" of Lt. D.R. Harris (U.S.A.S.) and 2/Lt. J. Munro. Lost 16.8.18 bombing Bruges.

D.H.9 D'7204 "J" of Lt. J.A. Dear and 2/Lt. J.F. Peters; on 24.8.18 it was hit over Bruges, landed in Holland, and was interned.

Another view of D.H.9 D'7204, "J".

D.H.9 B'7661 "E" of Lt. H.E. Tansley and 2/Lt. N.B. Harris, lost 21.5.18 bombing near Varssenaere. It was shot down by *Flugmeister* Wagner, M.J.I.

ABOVE: D.H.9 D'2781 "M" of Sgt. Good and Sgt. Partridge. Hit over Zeebrugge on 25.7.18, it landed in Holland and was interned. The observer was badly wounded and later died.
RIGHT: D.H.9 "A" *Acme*.

No.212 Squadron R.A.F.

Originally No.12 Squadron R.N.A.S. formed in 1917 at Petite Snythe near Dunkerque, as a holding unit for pilots who would go to replace losses in the R.N.A.S. units in the field. The only duty involved was to maintain a high patrol over Dunkerque to drive away German high photographic machines which would try and photograph results of raids and other activities in the area. The enemy usually flew too high to be intercepted but the exercise was good training.

Various types of aircraft were used, mainly ones that the squadrons had finished with.

Squadron Markings

None were allocated, probably as the squadron was a holding unit with no permanent members; no kind of individual markings were used.

No.213 Squadron R.A.F.

In June, 1917 the "Seaplane Defence Flight" was formed at Dunkerque from naval pilots in the depot. Its duties were as escorts to seaplanes working along the Flanders coast. Initially equipped with Sopwith Scouts and Seaplanes, it exchanged these for Camels starting in September 1917.

In mid-January 1918 it became No.13 Squadron R.N.A.S. stationed at St. Pol. On 1st April, 1918 it became No.213 Squadron R.A.F., still on protection duties up to the armistice.

Squadron Markings

None were allotted during the war.

Individual Markings

On Sopwith Scouts and Seaplanes in usual naval fashion of this period – names, initials, coloured bands, and designs. These carried on to the Camels but began to disappear shortly after the amalgamation. A fairly standard method commenced around June/July 1918 although exact details are lacking – all fuselage cockades were painted out.

Flight Markings

By designs on wheel covers.

Flight Commanders

By bands of colours around the fuselage – red, white, blue – red, white, red – black, white –blue, white, blue – no numbers were used.

Individual Markings

By white numbers 1 to 5 painted on the fuselage sides in a variety of

Sopwith Scout N'6203 *Mina* of F/Lt. L.H. Slatter.

Sopwith Triplane No.2 Sqdn. RNAS crashed by F./S./L. Daly, Serial N'5369 at Petite-Synthe – Daly was unhurt.

Camel N'6625. This is a "2FI" (one) – probably a visitor.

D.H.9a F'955 – probably another visitor.

Sopwith Scout N'6203 *Mina* of F/Lt. L.H. Slatter.

colours and designs. During October 1918 "A" and "C" Flights seem to have had a change, that is:
"A" Flight painted a fancy "A" onthe fin in a dark colour and a light band around the fuselage with the individual number in white on it.
"C" Flight Commander painted a distorted lightning flash in white on fuselage sides while flight members had thick block letters.

It would seem as though it was a personal choice and not a sequence.

The squadron seems to have never conformed to R.A.F. regulations after the amalgamation, probably because its duties were almost confined to working with the navy. Pilots seem to have used markings of choice and it seemed that when a pilot left the squadron his replacement adopted his own markings.

Sopwith Baby *Phyllis*.

Camels of "A" Flight circa May 1918. The Camel with black and white stripes was flown by Capt. Horstman as Flight Commander. L–R: Hancocks, Talbot, Pinder, Capt. Horstman, Gray, Taylor.

Camels of "B" Flight, spring 1918. L–R: Greene, Capt. Slatter, Mackay.

Camels of "C" Flight, spring 1918.

Camel, "C" Flight/Commander's aircraft, B'7175.

Camel B'3782 of F/L.J.W. Paynter, June/July 1918.

Camel C'200 "B" flown by Capt. Swanston at war's end.

No.214 Squadron R.A.F.

Originally formed as No.7A Squadron R.N.A.S. at Coudekeque 23.7.17 with eight Handley Page 0/100s from No.7 Squadron R.N.A.S., it was re-titled No.14 Squadron R.N.A.S. on 9.12.17 and re-titled again as No.214 Squadron R.A.F. on amalgamation 1.4.18. It continued in the night bombing role as before and remained in this role until the armistice.

Squadron Markings

None were used.

Flight and Individual Markings

During the period before amalgamation, a flight letter and individual number were used painted on the fuselage sides either side of the cockade, usually in a colour outlined white. This appears to have died out later in 1918. When the squadron flew to Egypt in mid-1919 most aircraft were marked with letters. See note on No.207 Squadron R.A.F. allocation to units.

H.P. 0/400 C'9648 forced down in Holland by German fighter from *Schlasta* 16, S.E. of Wulpen, 30.6.17. The crew was Lt. J.D. Vance, 2/Lt. S.B. Potter, and Sgt. R. Kimberley.

H.P. 0/100 3122 "?4" night bombing St. Denis-Westrem Aerodrome near Ghent. Lost 26th/27th October, 1917, with F/S/Lt. G. Andrews (P.O.W.), 2/Lt. W.W. Kent (K.I.A.), Gunlayer G.A. Kent (P.O.W.). Squadron was then No.7A R.N.A.S.

H.P. 0/100 3123, September 1917 at Redcar, resting from operations. Squadron was No.7A at this date. Was lost 31.10.17 when flown by Lt. Sieveking and A/Ms Brooks and Dodds. Aircraft marked "D'3."

No.215 Squadron R.A.F.

Formed at Coudekerque 10.3.18 from elements of No.7 and No.14 Squadron R.N.A.S. as No.15 Squadron R.N.A.S, re-titled No.215 Squadron R.A.F. on amalgamation. It became part of the Independant Force in August as a night bombing unit.

Squadron Markings

None were used.

Flight and Individual Markings

As far as is known, none were used. See No.207 Squadron R.A.F. for notes on allocation to units.

H.P. 0/400 C'9685; this also served with No.216 Squadron R.A.F. There was a white outline to stripes on fin.

H.P. 0/100 3121,"A'3" return from raid on Bruges 11–12.12.17, F/Lt. C.H. Darley, W/Cdr. T.A.Cull D.S.O, F/Lt. G. Gilmor. Squadron was then No.14 R.N.A.S.

No.216 Squadron R.A.F.

Originally formed by detaching a flight from No.7 Naval Squadron in September 1917, it was re-titled "A" Squadron R.N.A.S. from 5.10.17 on moving to France. Re-titled No.16 Squadron R.N.A.S. from 8.1.18 and on amalgamation became No.216 Squadron R.A.F. It performed night bombing until the armistice.

Squadron Markings

None were used.

Flight and Individual Markings

By flight letter and individual number on fuselage side either side of the cockade. One flight used red outlined white and another flight used blue outlined white. See note on No.207 Squadron R.A.F. for allocation to units.

H.P. 0/100 3134, shot down by flak at Kroppen 22–23.5.18 with 2/Lt. H.L. Leroy, 2/Lt. R.W. Peat, and Pte. W.J. Trite, on raid to Saarbrucken.

Another view of H.P. 0/100 3134.

H.P. 0/100 3135, crashed on return from bombing raid on the Bosch Works at Stuttgart, the crew was Lt. A.C. Kilburn, Lt. R.W. Heine, and Sgt. R. Adair.

No.217 Squadron R.A.F.

Formed originally as No.17 R.N.A.S., 13th January, 1918 as an anti-submarine patrol group with D.H.4s. They also bombed coastal targets.

Squadron Markings

None were allocated.

Flight Markings

All the flights were marked but not identified; that is:

One flight had red wheel covers with white outline.

One flight had red wheel covers with white outline and a white segment from the axle nut to the air valve. Radiator grille marked in white squares to form a checkerboard pattern.

One flight had white wheel covers with an uneven red circle, and a red centre spot. Radiator grille had six diagonal white lines across.

One D.H.4 had a "2" on the fin, while another had "B" on fuselage side. These may have been a personal marking or a previous squadron's marking.

D.H.4 A'7935 "2" of Lt. G. Brenton and Lt. J. Fountain. When bombing Zeebrugge it landed in Holland 17.6.18.

D.H.4 Flight line up.

No.218 Squadron R.A.F.

Formed 24th April, 1918, and in June went to France as a day bomber unit equipped with D.H.9s. Joined the Dover-Dunkerque Naval Command and operated mainly against targets in Belgium and coastal targets in Northern France.

Squadron Markings

None were allocated.

Individual Markings

One flight was marked in Roman pattern figures painted white behind the cockade – I, II, III, IV, V, VI – other aircraft had no markings other than cockades.

D.H.9 C'1211 "VI" of Lt. W.F. Purvis and Sgt. Locke. It was hit by A.A. fire on 29.6.18, landed in Holland, and was interned.

D.H.9 D'1708 "VI" crashed in Holland and interned.

D.H.9 D'3271 of Capt. J.F. Chisholm D.S.C., D.F.C., and Sgt. Williams. While bombing Bruges on 26.9.18 the radiator was holed by A.A. fire. Fired on by Dutch A.A. over Flushing, it landed on the beach in front of The Grand Hotel.

No.219 Squadron R.A.F.

A small detachment of Short Type 184 seaplanes operating from Westgate on anti-submarine patrols covering the approaches to the Thames Estuary was re-named No.219 Squadron R.A.F. on 1st April, 1918. No markings are known.

ABOVE: Sopwith Baby N'1019 used for short-range patrols form Westgate and Dunkerque.

LEFT: Fairey IIIB. N'2245 sunk down in the sand at Westgate.

No.220 Squadron R.A.F.

Originated as "C" Flight R.N.A.S. at Mudros early in 1916. In January re-named "C" Squadron until the formation of the R.A.F. Carried out reconnaissance, bombing, and anti-submarine patrols in the Aegean Sea using Sopwith Two-seaters, Nieuport Two-seaters, and others, until receiving D.H.4s, D.H.9s, and Sopwith Camels as escorts. No markings are known and probably none were used.

No.221 Squadron R.A.F.

Originated as "D" Flight R.N.A.S, then "D" Squadron until formation of R.A.F. It used D.H.4s, D.H.9s, and Camels as escorts. No markings are known and probably none were used. It carried out reconnaissance, bombing, and anti-submarine patrols in the Aegean Sea.

No.222 Squadron R.A.F.

Originated as "A" Flight R.N.A.S. then became "A" Squadron until formation of R.A.F. Used D.H.4s, D.H.9s, and Camels as escorts. No markings are known and probably none were used. It carried out reconnaissance, bombing, and anti-submarine patrols in the Aegean Sea.

No.223 Squadron R.A.F.

Originated as "B" Flight R.N.A.S. then became "B" Squadron. Formed at Mitylene in the Aegean as a general duties unit. It became No.223 Squadron R.A.F. on 1st April, 1918, but was disbanded in July and the seaplane unit at Otranto became No.223, remaining as a mobile unit until the armistice.

It was equipped with D.H.4s, D.H.9s, and Camels as escorts and Sopwith Baby, Sopwith Schneider, and Short Type 184 floatplanes. There are no details of markings and probably none were used.

No.224 Squadron R.A.F.

On 1st April, 1918, the No.66 Wing at Otranto, Southern Italy, became No.224 Squadron R.A.F. comprising Nos. 496, 497, and 498 flights with Camels, D.H.4, D.H.9, and Short Seaplanes. No squadron markings were issued.

D.H.4 B2137 being assembled at Chimino Aerodrome, Taranto, Italy.

No.225 Squadron R.A.F.

No.225 Squadron with Nos. 481, 482, and 483 Flights formed on 1st April, 1918, based at Otranto with some Sopwith Two-seaters, floatplanes of varying types, and some Sopwith Camels. No squadron markings were issued.

No.226 Squadron R.A.F.

On 1st April, 1918, the No.67 Wing at Taranto, Southern Italy, became No.226 Squadron R.A.F. comprising Nos. 472, 473, and 474 Flights equipped with D.H.4, D.H.9s, and some Camels for escort duties. It bombed targets along the Adriatic Coast; their principle raids were on submarine bases and later, after moving to Mudros, raids on Constantinople were undertaken.

No squadron markings were issued but some aircraft had personal markings, often on wheel covers.

LEFT: D.H.9s ready to raid Cattaro 1.7.18.

D.H.9 D.2803 crashed at Petrovsk, North Russia, January 1919. Note tail markings.

Camel B'3769 running repairs at Mudros.

D.H.9 D'3007 at Mudros Oct.-Dec. 1918.

Camels and pilots at Chimino Aerodrome, Taranto.

No.227 Squadron R.A.F.

Formed on 1st April, 1918, with Nos. 499, 550, and 551 Flights at Taranto, equipped with Caproni Ca42, D.H.4, and D.H.9 aircraft but did not become operational and was disbanded at the armistice.

No.228 Squadron R.A.F.

Formed at Great Yarmouth on 20th August, 1918, comprising Nos. 324, 325, and 326 Flights that had been flying patrols over the North Sea as far as the Dutch coast. The patrols were for various reasons – anti-submarine, anti-shipping – always looking to see if the German High Seas Fleet had ventured out, and as fighter patrols to combat the German naval fighters operating from their coastal bases.

It was equipped originally with a variety of seaplanes and eventually Felixstowe F.2a Flying Boats. No squadron markings were issued but the F.2as usually had hulls painted in bright patterns in colours using red, blue, black, and white.

F.2a N'4283 the first painted boat from Great Yarmouth, probably black and white. Art work by Bob Leckie and Gerry Livock, "2" on rudder.

F.2a, possibly N'4304 flown by Bob Leckie from Great Yarmouth. Stripes were probably red and white.

F.2a N'4512 flown by Gerry Livock from Great Yarmouth, probably red and white.

RIGHT: F.2a used at Great Yarmouth by Bob Leckie. It was probably red and white, struts the same colours, "4" on wing.

Caproni Ca42, N'527 one of six, N'526–N'531, used January to March 1918 by Nos. 499, 550, or 551 Flights in the Otranto area, Southern Italy. Crest is uncertain – appears to be a legendary bird. All six aircraft are reported as having a design on the nose. Recorded are the Medusa and a bulldog.

F.2a, serial unknown, at Great Yarmouth. Diamonds were red on a white hull. A Sopwith Baby is in the background with black and white striped cowling.

No.229 Squadron R.A.F.

Formed at Great Yarmouth with Nos. 428, 429, 454, and 455 Flights on 20th August, 1918, equipped with Sopwith, Short, and Fairey Seaplanes for short range coastal patrols. No squadron markings were issued.

No.230 Squadron R.A.F.

Formed at Felixstowe 20th August, 1918, with Nos. 327, 328, and 487 Flights, equipped with various Seaplanes and Curtiss H.16 and F.2a and F.3 flying boats. It shared the same duties as No.228 Squadron and also painted hulls in the same fashion. No squadron markings were issued.

Camel modified. F3128 for lighter trials.

Camel as above with jettisonable undercarriage.

No.231 Squadron R.A.F.

Formed at Felixstowe 20th August, 1918, with Nos. 329 and 330 Flights. It was equipped with various Seaplanes and Curtiss H.16 and F.2a and F.3 flying boats, and flew anti-submarine and anti-shipping patrols over the North Sea as far as the Dutch coast. The patrols were also as fighter patrols to combat the German naval fighters operating from their coastal bases.

F.2A N'4513 on its first war patrol 28.8.18.

Sopwith Baby N'2071, Blackburn built. Red and white checks on cowling, white "K" Blackburn logo on fin. It had two Lewis guns a 65 lb bomb, and a 130 hp Clerget. It was at Killingholme in January 1918 and with No.455 Flight, Great Yarmouth, later in 1918.

F2A N'4545. 10.10.18. Red and white from Felixstowe.

Probably N'4060 and is an H'16. Note balanced rudder and ailerons. Red and white.

No.232 Squadron R.A.F.

Formed at Felixstowe 20th August, 1918 with Nos. 333, 334, and 335 Flights. It was equipped with various Seaplanes and Curtiss H.16 and F.2a and F.3 flying boats, and flew anti-submarine and anti-shipping patrols over the North Sea as far as the Dutch coast. The patrols were also as fighter patrols to combat the German naval fighters operating from their coastal bases.

D.H.9 B'9369 at Guston Road.

No.233 Squadron R.A.F.

Formed at Dover, 31st August, 1918 with Nos. 407, 471, and 491 Flights, equipped with Short 184s and D.H.9s for short range coastal patrols, and a flight of Camels which were detached to Walmer. No squadron markings issued.

No.234 Squadron R.A.F.

Formed August 1918 at Trescoe, Isles of Scilly, with Nos. 350, 351, 352, and 353 Flights. It was equipped with various seaplanes, Short 184, etc., later with F.2a and F.3 flying boats to cover the Western Approaches. No squadron markings were issued.

F3 N"4415 at Tresco, Isles of Scilly.

No.235 Squadron R.A.F.

Was formed August, 1918 at Newlyn with Nos. 424 and 425 Flights equipped with Short 184s for Coastal patrols.

No squadron markings were issued but many of the Shorts were marked with "N," some on the fin or fuselage and some on the floats.

Short 184 N'1604 "9" on the slipway.

Short 184 N'1601 at Newlyn. Note rails and rail track.

No.236 Squadron R.A.F.

Formed in August 1918 with Nos. 493, 515, and 516 Flights at Mullion, Cornwall, to cover the South West approaches of the English Channel, equipped with D.H.6 and D.H.9 aircraft. No squadron markings were issued.

RIGHT: D.H.6 C'7847 at Mullion, Cornwall, 1918. Note difference in uniforms.

No.237 Squadron R.A.F.

Formed in August 1918 with Nos. 420, 421, 422, and 423 Flights at Cattewater, Plymouth, equipped mainly with Short 184 Seaplanes for coastal patrols.

No squadron markings were issued. Aircraft were identified by a flight letter and an individual number on the fuselage behind the cockade.

RIGHT: Short 184 "A7" over The Channel.

BELOW: Short 184s on the Mole at Cattewater.

Short 184s; the steam crane lifts the aircraft from the Mole into the water and back again. The crane runs on rails.

No.238 Squadron R.A.F.

Formed 20th August, 1918, at Cattewater with Nos. 347, 348, and 349 Flights equipped with various seaplanes for coastal patrols, but later had Curtiss H.16 and Felixstowe F.2a and F.3 for longer patrols. Detachments at Holy Island and Killingholme. No squadron markings were issued.

No.239 Squadron R.A.F.

Formed August 1918 at Torquay with No.418 Flight with Short 184s. No squadron markings were issued.

Short 184 N'9074 at Torquay.

No.240 Squadron R.A.F.

Formed 20th August, 1918, at Calshot to cover the approaches to Southampton with Nos. 345, 346, 410, and 411 Flights equipped with Short 184 and 320 with a few Fairey "Campania" seaplanes, plus Curtiss H.12 and Felixstowe F.2a flying boats.

F2a N'4534 at Calshot.

No.241 Squadron R.A.F.

Formed August 1918 with Nos. 416, 417, and 513 Flights at Portland. It used Short 184, "Campania," and Wight Converted Seaplanes, plus D.H.6s. No squadron markings were issued but aircraft were marked "P."

Short 184 N'1612 at Catte Water.

Short 184 N'1754 at Catte Water.

Curtiss H.12 on patrol; the front gunner has moved back into the cockpit.

ABOVE: Fairey Campania N'2363. Rolls-Royce "Eagle."

LEFT: Short 184 on the beach. This aircraft appears to be damaged, possibly from a storm.

Wight Converted at Portland being beached.

Fairey Campania at Portland.

No.242 Squadron R.A.F.

Formed August 1918 at Newhaven with Nos. 408, 409, and 514 Flights equipped with Short 184 and "Campania" Seaplanes and with two flights of D.H.6s for short range coastal patrols, with a detachment to Telescombe Cliffs to cover part of the English Channel.

No squadron markings were issued but some seaplanes marked "N" on fins and floats.

Short 184 with modification to exhaust.

Short 184 almost beached.

RIGHT: Short 184 being manhandled off the beach.

Short 184 N'1685 on dry land.

No.243 Squadron R.A.F.

Formed in August,1918 with Nos. 414 and 415 Flights at Cherbourg, France, to cover the approaches to the South Western Ports, equipped with Short 184 and Wight Converted Seaplanes. No squadron markings were issued but some Seaplanes had "CH" on fuselage sides.

Short 184 from Cherbourg.

Short 184 in trouble.

No.244 Squadron R.A.F.

Formed 25th July, 1918, at Bangor, North Wales, with Nos. 521, 522, and 530 Flights, equipped with D.H.6s for anti-submarine patrols covering the middle of the Irish Sea with detachments at Luce Bay and Tallaght. No squadron markings were issued.

No.245 Squadron R.A.F.

Formed at Fishguard in August 1918 with Nos. 426 and 427 Flights with Short 184s to fly coastal patrols over the Irish Sea. No squadron markings were issued.

No.246 Squadron R.A.F.

Formed August 1918 at Seaton Carew with Nos. 402, 403, 451, 452, and 495 Flights. Operated to cover the Teeside Ports with patrols over the North Sea. Early equipment was Short 184 and Sopwith Seaplanes

Short 184 on the crane like a bird with a broken wing.

Short 184 N'2998, Newlyn. Built by J.S. White, East Cowes.

Short 184 N'9858 at Cherbourg.

D.H.6 C'7863.

Short 184 N'1086 at Fishguard.

Short 184 bombed up.

Short 184 bombed up. Improved version with 240 hp Renault engine.

Hamble Baby at Fishguard.

and F.E.2bs, later receiving Blackburn Kangaroos for anti-submarine patrols. The Kangaroos had a good bomb load but only 11 were received by the armistice. No squadron markings were issued.

No.247 Squadron R.A.F.

Formed 20th August, 1918, at Felixstowe with Nos. 336, 337, and 338 Flights with various Seaplanes, later receiving F.2a and F.3 flying boats for patrols across the North Sea. No squadron markings were issued but flying boat hulls were painted as with other Felixstowe based F.2a and F.3.

F.2a N'4296 being loaded on to a lighter at Felixstowe. Colors were red and white stripes with the remainder in P.C.10.

Blackburn "Kangaroo" B'9987 at Seaton Carew 1918.

Blackburn "Kangaroo" at Seaton Carew after the snowstorm.

No.248 Squadron R.A.F.

Formed August 1918 at Hornsea with Nos. 404, 405, and 453 Flights equipped with flights of D.H.6 aircraft for anti-submarine patrols, with a detachment to North Coates to cover approaches to Grimsby. No squadron markings were issued.

No.249 Squadron R.A.F.

Formed 18th August, 1918 at Dundee with Nos. 400, 401, 419, and 450 Flights equipped with Sopwith Baby Seaplanes, Short 184s, and D.H.6s. It flew anti-submarine patrols off the Scottish Coast. No squadron markings were issued.

Hamble Baby N'1197 at Dundee. Built by Parnell & Sons, Bristol. 110 hp Clerget.

No.250 Squadron R.A.F.

Formed May 1918 at Padstow with detachments to Westward Ho and North Devon with Nos. 494, 500, 501, 502, and 503 Flights. It was equipped with D.H.6 and D.H.9s for short range coastal anti-submarine patrols to cover the approach to the Bristol Channel. No squadron markings were issued.

D.H.6 C'5194 at Padstone. Built by Kingsbury Aviation. A former RFC trainer.

No.251 Squadron R.A.F.

Formed May 1918 at Hornsea with Nos. 504, 505, 506, and 510 Flights equipped with D.H.6s; just before the armistice it received a few D.H.9s. Detachments were stationed along the Yorkshire Coast to cover East Coast convoy routes. No squadron markings issued.

No.252 Squadron R.A.F.

Formed May 1918 at Tynemouth with Nos. 495, 507, 508, 509, and 510 Flights equipped with D.H.6s to cover approaches to the Tyne and ports in the area. It was scheduled to have had Blackburn Kangaroos, but delays in production and the armistice stopped this. No squadron markings were issued.

Sopwith Baby N'1418 was originally R.N.A.S. In 1917 it went to No.453 Flight and was there at the end of May 1918.

Short 184 N'1274 detached to Hornsea. Note torpedo rack.

Curtis H16 N'4072 at Dundee. To No.249 Sqdn. 20.8.18.

Blackburn "Kangaroo" B'9976 – only one of this type in 252 Sqdn.

No.253 Squadron R.A.F.

Formed June 1918 at Bembridge, Isle of Wight, with Nos. 412, 413, 511, 512, and 513 Flights with Short 184s and Fairey "Campania" Seaplanes. In August it received flights of D.H.6s for short range coastal patrols to cover approaches to Southampton. No squadron markings were issued but Short 184 carried a large white "B" on the fin.

Fairey F.17 "Campania" with one of the R.N.A.S. Flights at Bembridge, Isle of Wight.

No.254 Squadron R.A.F.

Formed May 1918 at Prawle Point, South Devon, with Nos. 492, 515, 516, 517, and 518 Flights with D.H.6s and D.H.9s for short range coastal patrols to cover the approaches to Plymouth. No squadron markings were issued.

No.255 Squadron R.A.F.

Formed July 1918 at Pembroke with Nos. 519, 520, 521, 522, and 524 Flights, equipped with D.H.6s mainly to cover approaches to Pembroke Docks. No squadron marking were issued.

No.256 Squadron R.A.F.

Formed June 1918 at Sea-Houses, close to Holy Island and the Tweed Estuary as a close range anti-submarine unit, with Nos. 495, 525, 526, 527, and 528 Flights, equipped with D.H.6s and proposed Blackburn Kangaroos which never arrived. No squadron marking was issued.

D.H.6 B'3098 ex-RFC. "Having a paddle!"

Sopwith Baby N'2111 built by Blackburn.

D.H.6 B'2903 at Prawlcpoint. Ex RFC also used by 255 Sqd.

D.H.6 B'2903 while at Isle of Grain testing Depot, 19.10.18.

D.H.6 B'2917 ex-RFC. Became G-EAHE on civil register.

No.257 Squadron R.A.F.

Formed at Dundee in August 1918 with Nos. 318 and 319 Flights with Short 184s. It was planned to re-equip with F.2a flying boats but only a few were received before the armistice. No.squadron markings were issued.

No.258 Squadron R.A.F.

Formed at Luce Bay in July 1918 with Nos. 523, 524, and 529 Flights with D.H.6s for coastal patrols over the Northern Irish Sea and Western Scottish coast. No squadron markings were issued.

No.259 Squadron R.A.F.

Should have formed in August 1918 at Felixstowe with F.2a flying boats but there is no record of its ever forming.

No.260 Squadron R.A.F.

Formed August 1918 at Westward Ho, North Devon, with Nos. 502 and 503 Flights with D.H.6s for coastal patrols. No markings were issued.

No.261 Squadron R.A.F.

Should have formed in August 1918 at Felixstowe with F.2a flying boats but there is no record of its ever forming.

No.262 Squadron R.A.F.

There is no record of its ever forming.

No.263 Squadron R.A.F.

Formed 27th September, 1918, at Otranto, Southern Italy, Nos. 359, 435, 436, and 441 Flights with Sopwith Baby, Short 184, and Short 320 seaplanes and a few Felixstowe F.2a flying boats. It had a detachment to Santa Maria di Leucoa. It flew Italian coastal patrols and covered the Otranto Barrage patrol warships. No squadron markings were issued.

No.264 Squadron R.A.F.

Formed 27th September, 1918, at Suda Bay, Crete, Nos. 339 and 340 Flights with Short 184s covered the Southern Aegean Sea and Eastern Mediterranean. No squadron markings were issued.

No.265 Squadron R.A.F.

Should have formed at Gibralter with Nos. 364, 365, and 366 Flights equipped with Short 184s and Felixstowe F.3s. There is no record of it ever forming.

No.266 Squadron R.A.F.

Formed at Mudros at the end of September 1918 with Nos. 437 and 488 Flights with Short 184 and Short 320. No squadron markings were issued.

Short 184 N'9085 Petrovsk, June-July 1919 being lowered to the sea.

Curtiss H.16 N'4072 at Dundee with diamond markings on P.C.10 covering the aircraft. The rear aircraft has a zigzag marking.

Short 184 N'2813 Mudros, December 1918.

Short 184 N'9078 Petrovsk, 1919, being lifted from HMS Orlionoch.

No.267 Squadron R.A.F.

Formed at Kalafrana, Malta, on 27th September, 1918, with Nos. 360, 361, 362, and 363 Flights with Short 184 and a few Felixstowe F.2a and F.3 to cover approaches to Malta and surrounding sea areas. No squadron markings were issued.

No.268 Squadron R.A.F.

Formed at Kalafrana, Malta, in August 1918 with Nos. 433 and 434 Flights with Short 184 and Short 320 to cover approaches to Malta and surrounding sea areas. No squadron markings were issued.

Short 320 N'1367 at Kalafrana, probably post-war.

No.269 Squadron R.A.F.

Formed at Port Said in October 1918 with Nos. 431 and 432 Flights equipped with B.E.2e, Short 184, and D.H.9 aircraft for duties in the Suez Canal area. No squadron markings were issued.

Short 184 N'1091 off Port Said. 240 hp Renault engine.

No.270 Squadron R.A.F.

Was planned to form at Alexandria but was delayed until April, 1919.

No.271 Squadron R.A.F.

Formed at Taranto at the end of September 1918 with Nos. 357, 358, 359, and 367 Flights with Short 184 and Felixstowe F.3. No squadron markings were issued.

No.272 Squadron R.A.F.

Formed at Machrihanish on the Mull of Kintyre, Western Scotland, end of July 1918 with Nos. 531, 532, and 533 Flights, equipped with D.H.6s and a small number of Fairey 111a and 111b used as short range coastal patrol and mine spotting aircraft covering the Clyde approaches. No squadron markings were issued.

F2a N'4490 at Kalafrana, probably post-war.

Short 184 N'9164 at Kalafrana, probably post-war.

Short 184 N'2812. British built at Port Said. 260 hp Sunbeam engine. Nov. 1918.

B.E.2c 6802, 269 Sqdn. (anti-submarine flight). Presentation aircraft, "Associated Commercial Travellers Association of Australia," January 1919. Was in No.14 Sqdn. 4th Naval Wing.

No.273 Squadron R.A.F.

Formed August 1918 at Burgh Castle with Nos. 474, 485, 486, and 534 Flights to cover the approaches to the Wash and East Coast convoy routes. Equipped with D.H.4, D.H.9, and Sopwith Camels. No squadron markings were used.

No.274 Squadron R.A.F.

Was planned to form at Seaton Carew in November 1918 and to fly Vickers Vimy aircraft on anti-submarine patrols over the North Sea. The armistice occurred before formation.

No.306 Flight R.N.A.S.

This was the only R.N.A.S. Flight which escaped the amalgamation with the R.F.C. in 1918, remaining independant until demobilized in March 1919. Houton Bay was an uninhabited area northwest of Scapa Flow and the unit had F.2a, F.3, and some seaplanes and would have flown patrols to cover the naval base, sea areas around the base, and the southern part of the Northern Patrol areas. No squadron markings are recorded and were probably by signs and names.

H.P V/1500 E'8293 built by Wm. Beardmore and Co. at Dalmur, Bircham Newton, 1919. Post-war photograph.

No.17 (American Squadron) Attached to R.A.F.

Formed from American personnel trained in England, it went to France in July 1918 equipped with Sopwith Camels until 28th October, 1918, when they joined the U.S.A.S.

Squadron Marking

Allotted on 29th June, 1918, this was a white dumbell painted on the fuselage side behind the cockade.

Flight Markings

"A" Flight used red wheel covers.
"B" Flight used white wheel covers.
"C" Flight used blue wheel covers.

Individual Markings

By large white letters painted on the fuselage side in front of the cockade, repeated on the top wing on the starboard side:
"A" Flight used B, C, D, E, F, G.
"B" Flight used H, J, K, L, M, N.
"C" Flight used O, P, Q, R, S, T.
The O.C. used "A."

F.3 Flying Boat N'4403 *Houton Bay* on 25.5.18.

Sopwith Camel D'9495 from "A" Flight.

No.148 (American Squadron) Attached to R.A.F.

Formed from American pilots and ground crews who had been trained in England and had been attached to various squadrons in France for experience and training. It went to France at the beginning of July 1918 attached to the 10th Brigade until 28th October when they were withdrawn to join the U.S.A.S. It was equipped with Sopwith Camels.

Squadron Marking

Allotted on 29 June, 1918, this was a white triangle painted on the fuselage side behind the cockade.

Flight Markings

"A" Flight used red wheel covers.
"B" Flight used white wheel covers.
"C" Flight used blue wheel covers.

RIGHT: Sopwith Camel C'8337 used by Lt. J.A. Myers and Lt. Snoke.

Individual Markings

By large white letters painted in front of the fuselage cockade:
The C.O. flew "A."
"A" Flight used B, C, D, E, F, G.
"B" Flight used H, J, K, L, M, N.
"C" Flight used O, P, Q, R, S, T.
Later, when the strength was increased, letters were used that carried on from "T."

Flight Commanders' Markings

"A" Flight Commander flew "B" (Lt. Oliver).
"B" Flight Commander flew "N" (Lt. Springs).
"C" Flight Commander flew "S" (Lt. Clay).

Sopwith Camel of "C" Flight.

The Long Range Spotting Flights

Five flights of six Bristol Fighters were established in 1918 to engage in artillery spotting further over the lines to take advantage of heavier guns with a longer range. The purpose was also to ease the burden on the R.E.8 squadrons who were programmed to receive Bristols as replacements, firstly in April then September, 1918. This was due to the failure of the Sunbeam Arab and Hispano-Suiza engine programmes. In fact, the Bristols never did arrive, except one or two per squadron for "special jobs."

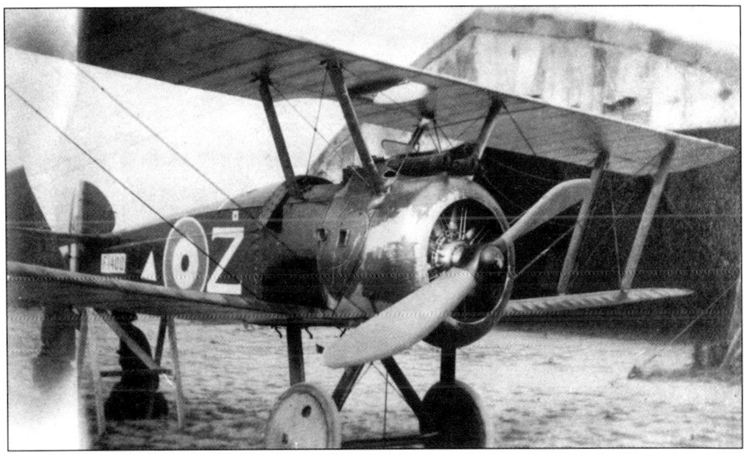

Sopwith Camel F'1400 "Z" used by Lt. Errol Zistel, August 1918.

The Five Flights Were:

"L" Flight went to France in July 1918. No squadron markings were used; the aircraft were marked A, B, C, D, E, F.
"M" Flight went to France 6th October, 1918. No squadron markings were used. One Bristol was marked "U;" there are no other details.
"N" Flight went to France in September 1918; there are no details.
"O" Flight went to France 1st November, 1918; there are no details.
"P" Flight went to France in October 1918; there are no details.

Bristol F2b D'7938 "D."

Bristol F2b, F'5812 "A" of Capt. B.E. Catchpole and 2/Lt A.J. Findley, A.M. Morris at Bruay, autumn 1918. Written off 24.10.18 near Monchy-le-Preux.

ABOVE: Bristol F2b F'4306 presented by Burgate 1st Wing at Aubuay post-war.

LEFT: Bristol F2b D'7938 "D" with crew and ground crew.

Special Duty Flight R.F.C.

This was a small unit with various types of aircraft formed to carry out duties that did not fall within the compass of normal squadrons of the line. Its original duty was to land agents behind the enemy lines and to pick them up again. Later agents were dropped by parachute. Bombing raids were also made on specific targets at night, usually by single aircraft.

No markings, other than standard cockades and rudder stripes, were used. Often the white was blanked out in these.

Bristol F2b F'4857 "U."

No.1 Wing R.N.A.S.

The system of titling units within the R.N.A.S. was completely different to within the R.F.C. The term wing roughly corresponds to squadron in the R.F.C. whereas a squadron usually of six pilots corresponds to a flight in the R.F.C.

By March 1916 No.1 Wing had moved across to Dunkerque and was carrying out coastal reconnaissance and bombing on German bases at Ostende and Zeebrugge as well as attempting to intercept Zeppelins raiding British and French towns. For this they had a varied selection of aircraft.

No.1 Wing replaced No.2 Wing R.N.A.S. on their move to cover the Dardanelles campaign. In March/April 1916 No.1 Wing provided personnel to form No.5 Wing R.N.A.S. that was planned to form at Coudekerque. No.1 Wing also provided personnel for "A" Flight which was re-titled No.1 Squadron R.N.A.S. in December 1916.

Shortly after this, the Wing became the supply and administration body for the squadrons in it and had to no aircraft of its own to use operationally.

B.E.12 6547, Lt. C.A. Bean left on a night bombing raid 10.8.18 and failed to return. Note the exhaust pipe turns outwards and down instead of up.

R.E.P. Parasol 8460 of F/S/Lt. J.E.D. Errol-Boyd on 3.10.15. During Royal Navy and R.N.A.S. operations against "Zeebrugge Sheds" the R.E.P. was hit by naval gunfire; it landed in Holland and was interned. It was bought by the Dutch in February 1916 and serialed L.A.23.

Sopwith Scout N'6161 of F/S/Lt. G.L. Elliott. Captured 2.2.17 near Blankenberghe, it was painted in German colours.

No.2 Wing R.N.A.S.

Originally it was in the Dunkerque area operating coastal patrols and bombing German bases on the French Coast. Equipment was varied as were the duties.

In June 1915 the Wing was withdrawn from Dunkerque and despatched by sea to cover the campaign at the Dardanelles. It operated from Imbros and other Islands. When the Dardanelles campaign ended and the military forces were withdrawn, No.2 Wing was also disbanded and served as re-inforcements to other units in the area. No markings are known to be recorded. Possibly some personal names were used.

Maurice Farman, possibly 113, at Imbros.

Maurice Farman, close up of 113? Showing offensive armament of twin Lewis guns.

B.E.2c at Imbros.

B.E.2c and Nieuport in the wing.

Nieuport 10, one of nine that went to the Aegean area. It is in French markings as delivered with a cockade on its rudder.

Henry Farman "ready to bomb the enemy."

No.3 Wing R.N.A.S.

Formed at Manston early in 1916 with Sopwith two-seaters. By July enough aircraft had become available to start moving across to France using Luxeuil-les-Bains as a base. The Wing was formed for the express purpose of strategic bombing. Targets were factories, etc., within the Saar Basin and in Lorraine.

Originally it was supposed to have 100 aircraft, but due to losses by squadrons in the Somme Battles the Wing never achieved this number. In August there were only 22 and in December only 47. The Wing was disbanded in April 1917 and had no connection with No.3 Squadron R.N.A.S. other than several pilots were posted to it.

The Wing comprised two squadrons, known as "Red" and "Blue" and had bombers (single seat) and fighters (two seaters).

Sopwith two-seater 9722 "19."

Squadron Markings

None were allotted

Individual Markings

By white numbers painted on the fuselage sides just forward of the tailplane. These numbers ran from 1 to at least 43.

Sopwith two-seater line up from "Red Squadron."

Pilots' Individual Markings

"Red Squadron" used square markings of a red and white geometric pattern immediately behind the fuselage cockade and on either side of the top of the tailplane.

"Blue Squadron" was as "Red Squadron" but in blue and white using the same, or similar, patterns.

It is probable that these markings had died out by the time of disbandment.

ABOVE: Sopwith single seater bomber N'5116 "43" with the bomb bay doors open.

LEFT: Sopwith single seater bomber 9660 "1" shot down in Germany 12.10.16 on the Oberndorf raid. F/S/Lt. C.H.S. Butterworth became P.O.W.

No.4 Wing R.N.A.S.

Originally was at Eastchurch with four squadrons of six pilots, carrying out coastal patrols and bombing. It also carried out some experimental work. In the early days it also served as an Acceptance Aircraft park and testing assembled aircraft. In view of this the photographs shown could have been taken when with other R.N.A.S. units and at various stations.

The appointment of W/Cmdr. C.L. Lambe in August 1915 gave him control of the bases at Dover and Dunkerque. Later in the year he decided that with some re-organization and re-inforcements it should be possible in the spring of 1916 to become more offensive minded from the Dunkerque bases.

To further this he had new aerodromes built at Coudekerque and Petite Synthe and when these were ready he moved No.4 Wing and its four squadrons to Petit Synthe where they undertook offensive patrols. Later in 1916 units were re-organized and the Wing became the administration and supply for squadrons in it.

Avro 504 1012 showing R.N.A.S. early pattern cockade.

RIGHT: R.E.P. Parasol 8454, French-built with Le Rhône engine at Eastchurch 30.8.15.

Bleriot Parasol 1548 of French-built batch 1538–1549 with 80 hp Gnome. All were used at Eastchurch in 1916.

R.E.P. Parasol crashed at Dunkerque.

Caudron GIV built in France.

R.E.P. Parasol 8457, French-built with Le Rhône engine. Photograph shows later marking than 8454.

R.E.P. Parasol 8554. French built 30.8.15.

R.E.P. Parasol. 4th Naval Wing. French built.

Caudron GIV, probably 3334 built by the British Caudron Co., batch 3333 to 3344.

Caudron GIV 3334 from the rear.

Caudron GIV, probably 3334.

4th Wing RNAS Nieuport 10/12, 3165 or 3163.l

BELOW: 4th Wing RNAS Nieuport 10/12 3184. 80 hp Le Rhone engine.

4th Wing RNAS Nieuport 10, 3967. Purchased in France. 80 hp Le Rhone engine.

No.5 Wing R.N.A.S.

At the beginning of March 1916 the Wing was formed at Dover from personnel of No.1 Wing R.N.A.S. and moved to Coudekerque equipped with one flight of Sopwith two-seaters, Caudron twin-engined bombers, and Breguet bombers. These were divided into "A" and "B" Squadrons until 31st December, 1916, when they were divided and henceforth became known as No.4 and No.5 Squadrons R.N.A.S. No.4 eventually became a fighter unit while No.5 became a bomber unit.

By October 1916 the Breguets had been replaced by Nieuport two-seaters and the Caudrons were going, being replaced by Sopwith two-seaters. Although the official date of the formation of Naval 5 is given as 31st December, 1916, it was not really final until they moved to Petite Synthe in March 1917.

Squadron Markings

No markings were allocated.

Flight and Individual Markings

By large white letters and numbers on the fuselage side.

Sopwith two-seater N'5114 B'3. Built as single-seat bomber, it was crashed by Sqn/Cmdr. Newton-Clare on 26.2.17.

Sopwith two-seaters at Coudekerque in February 1917; A'2, A'3, A'8 have a wing-mounted Lewis gun.

Sopwith two-seater 9376 A'5 of F/Lt. D.A. Nelles, D.S.C., forced to land by engine trouble in Holland 22.4.17.

RIGHT: Sopwith two-seater B'6 in early 1917.

MARKINGS AND FINISH ON BRITISH AIRCRAFT

Illustrations by Bob Pearson

Most British aircraft had an ex-works finish of PC10 uppersurfaces, with clear-doped linen (CDL) undersurfaces. National markings usually consisted of cockades on fuselage and wings, and stripes on the rudder. Unless otherwise stated these were Blue/White/Red outermost or forward. Unit markings were mainly white geometric shapes or bands on PC10 aircraft, or black/red on CDL or "silver" aircraft.

Nieuport 27 serial unknown, Captain Wendel W Rogers, No.1 Sqdn. RFC. Overall aluminum finish with a black (or red) vertical bar. The individual aircraft marking "H" is in black. On December 12 ,1917, Captain Rogers shot down a Gotha over Paris, although not necessarily in this aircraft.

RAF SE5a B8508, Lt. ETS Kelly, No.1 Sqdn. RAF. When No.1 Sqdn. was re-equipped with SE5as in January 1918, they adopted a new marking of two inward sloping bars on either side of the fuselage cockade, this was replaced by a white circle in March 1918. B8508 was shot down by Ltn. Raesch of Jasta 43 on 13 June 1918. Kelly was taken POW and later died of his wounds.

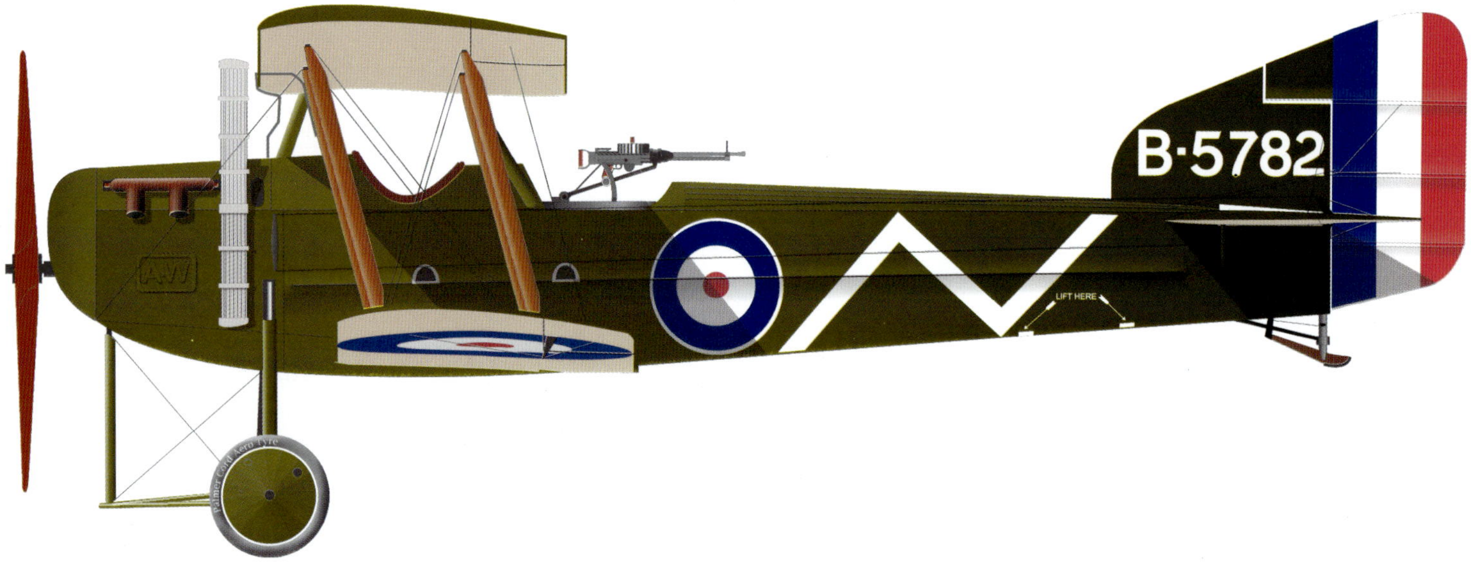

Armstrong-Whitworth FK8 B5782, No.2 Sqdn. RFC. According to Stewart Taylor, this aircraft was flown by Lt. Alan A McCleod during December 1917. The white zig-zag was carried on their aircraft until ordered removed during the German Spring offensive in 1918

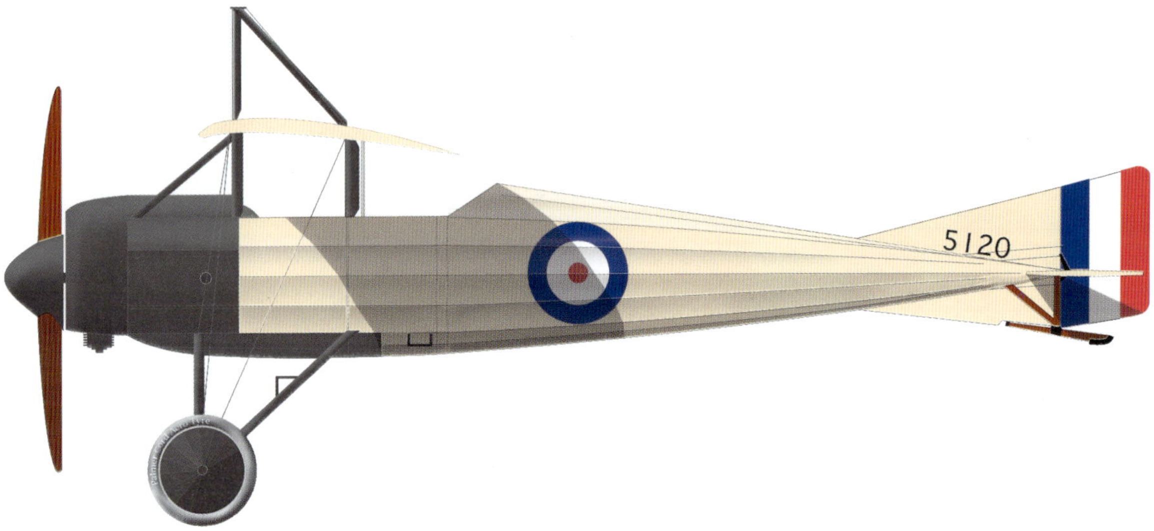

Morane-Saulnier Type LA 5120, No.3 Sqdn. RFC wears typical Morane markings for early 1916 of a black cowl and spinner.

Sopwith Camel D9443, Lt. AT Partridge, A Flight, No.3 Sqdn. RAF, August 1916. No.3 Sqdn. used two vertical bars as its marking. Even though it was directed to be changed in December 1917 (to a bar either side of cockade) and again after March 22 1918 (two bars forward of roundel), they continued to use their earlier markings until the end of the war. The overall PC10 Camel of Lt. Partridgo exhibits wear to the finish of the cowl.

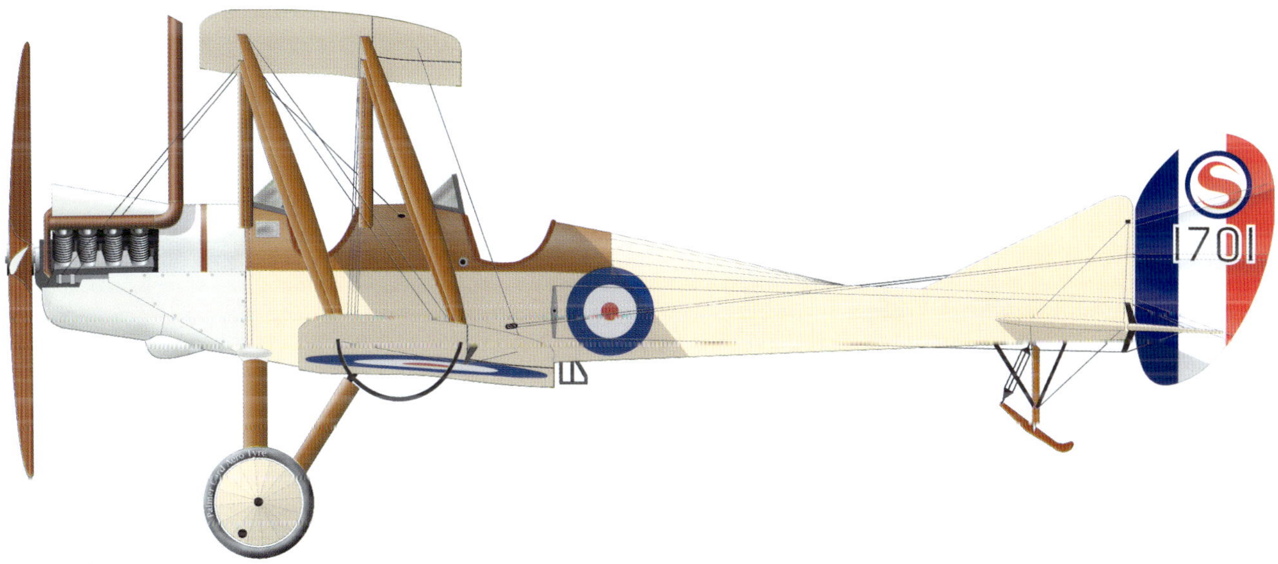

RAF BE2c 1701, No.4 Sqdn. RFC. In plain finish with the emblem of the "Britons Overseas" on the rudder.

RAF BE2f 2567, No.10 Sqdn. RFC. In overall PC10 finish. No.10 Sqdn. carried a white disc on their BE2 and FK8 aircraft.

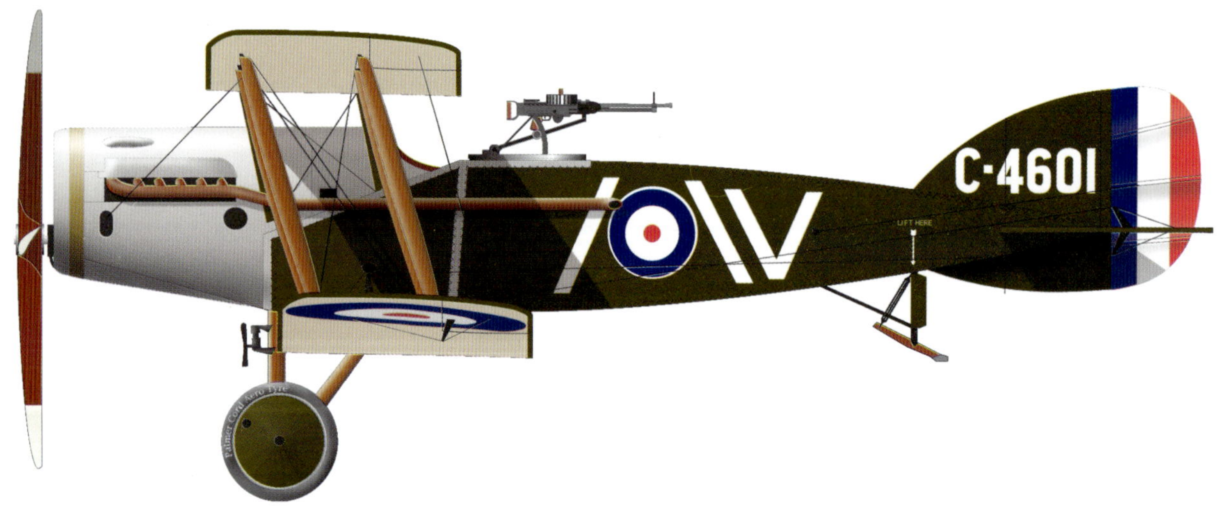

Bristol F2b C4601, No.11 Sqdn. RFC. In standard Bristol finish of PC10 fabric and battleship grey metalwork, C4601 shows the No.11 Sqdn. marking of two inward sloping bars. The exhaust pipe has been extended.

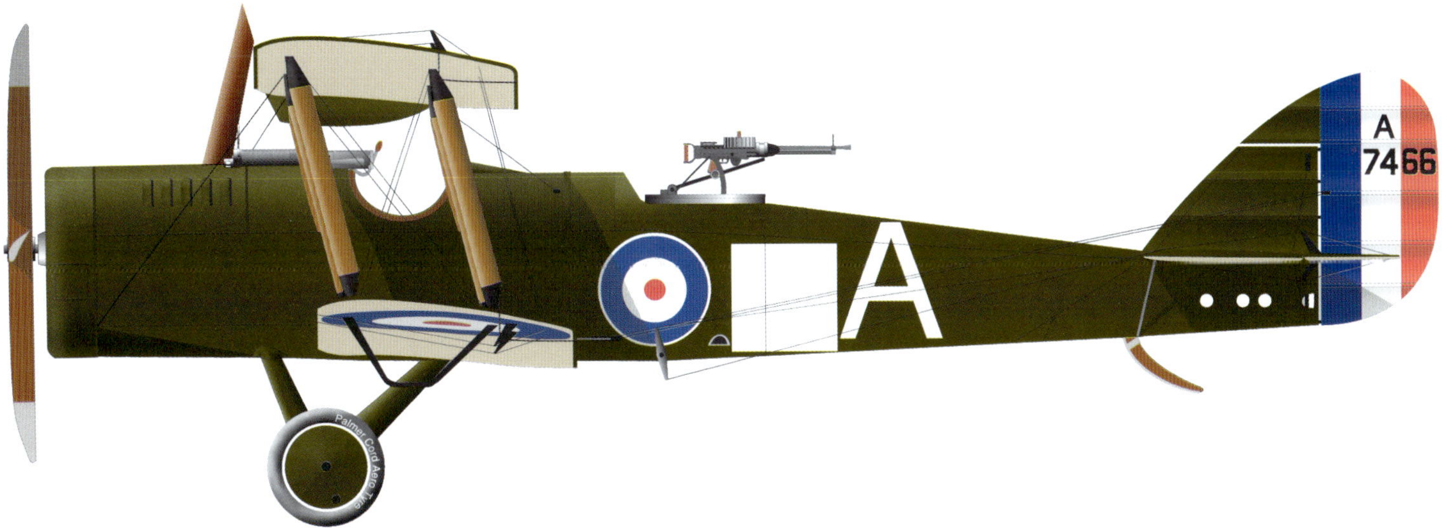

DeHavilland DH4 A7466, No.18 Sqdn. RFC. Overall PC10. Unit marking of a large white square. Individual letter "A" shows it to be the first aircraft in "A" flight.

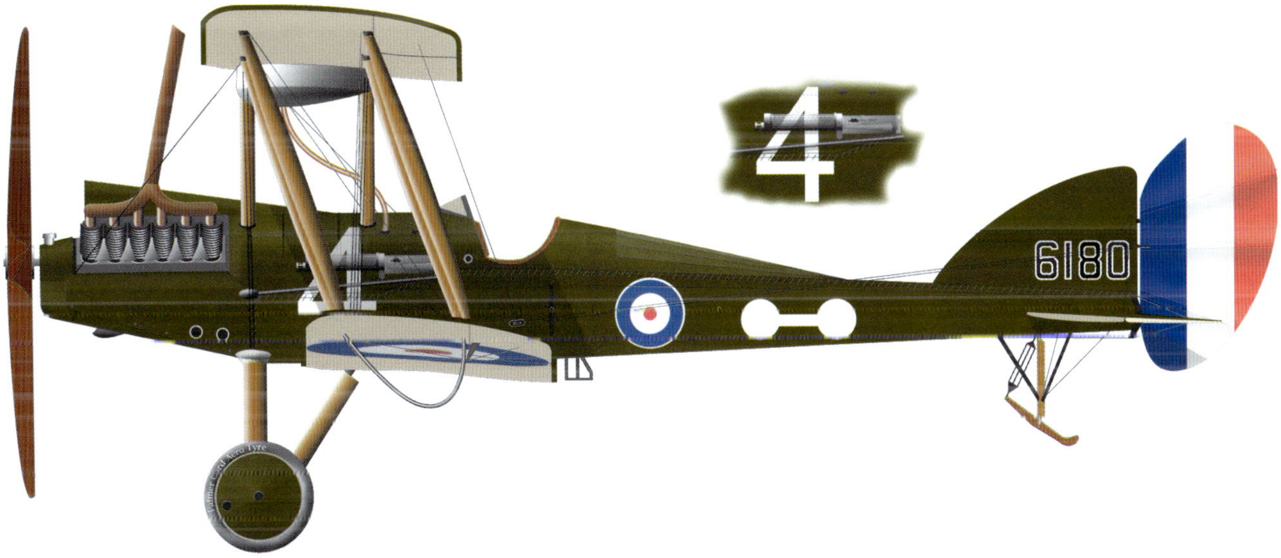

RAF BE12 6180, No.19 Sqdn. RFC. Overall PC10. The dumbbell was used by No.19 on their BEs, SPADs and Dolphins. 6180 has the number "4" painted over-top of its Vickers gun as can be seen in the detail illustration.

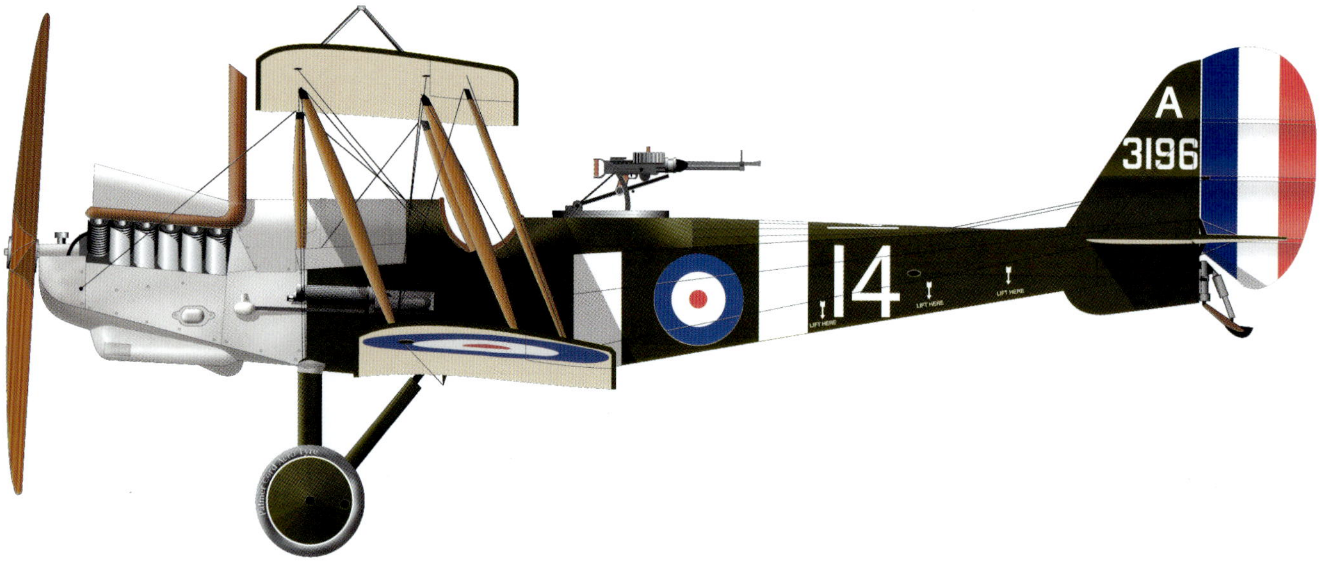

ABOVE AND OPPOSITE: RAF RE8 A3196, No.16 Sqdn. RFC. Overall PC10, with battleship gray cowl.

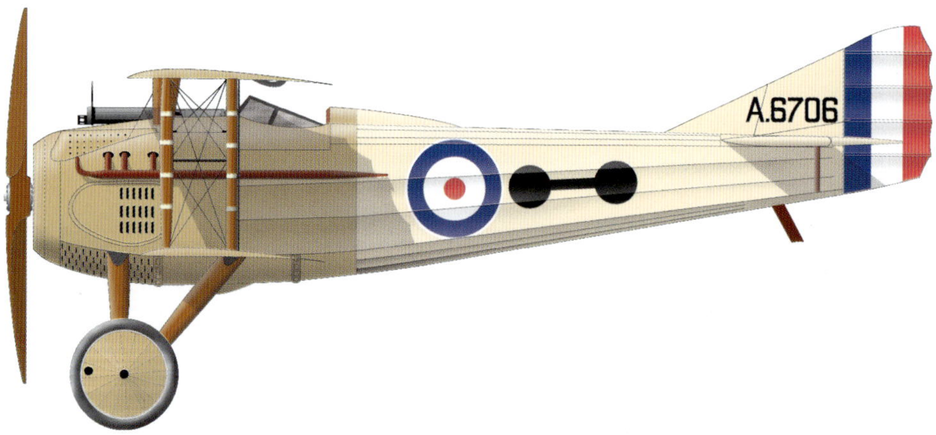

SPAD VII A6706, No.19 Sqdn. RFC. Finished in the typical French "Yellow" scheme of CDL fabric and a light yellow on all metal or wood surfaces, A6706 has the unusual feature of white outlined cockades on the fuselage. Normally, these would not be outlined, as on the next two aircraft.

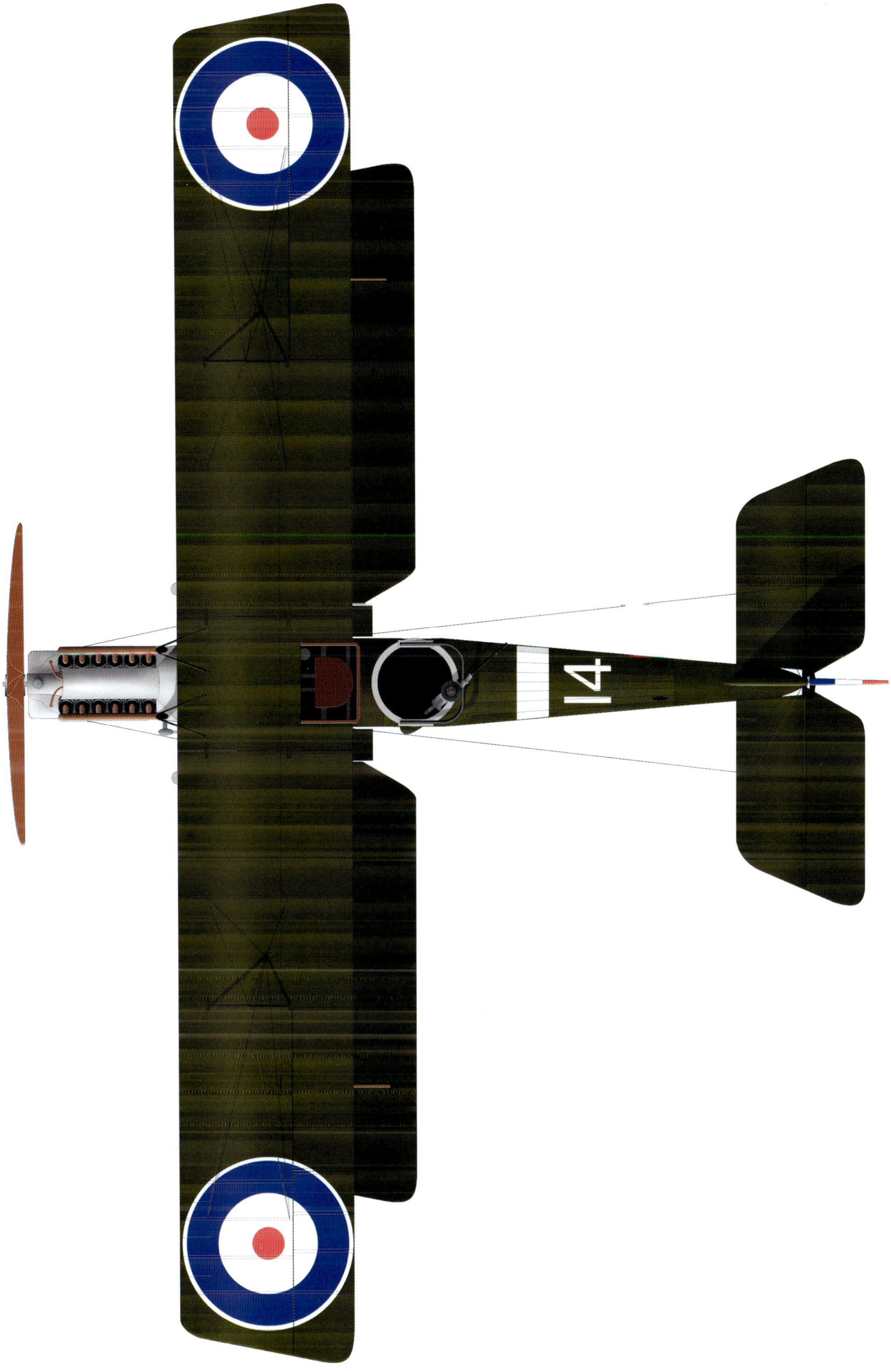
14

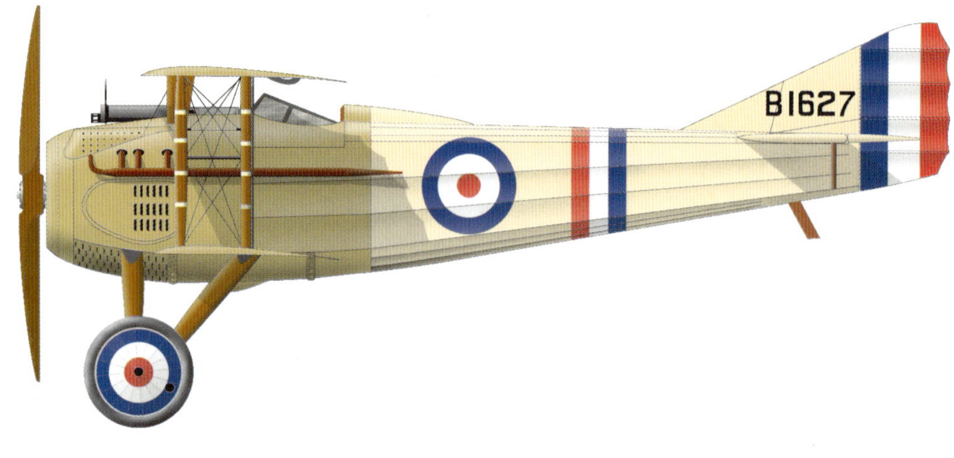

SPAD VII B1627, Lt. S.F. Allabarton, No.19 Sqdn. RFC. For a time No.19 Sqdn. dispensed with the dumbbell and used coloured bands for individual markings.

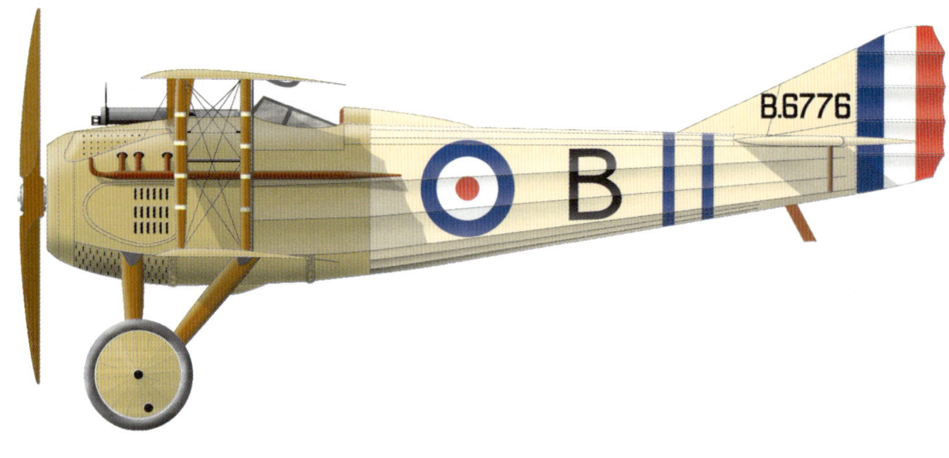

SPAD VII B6776, 2/Lt. S.L. Whitehouse, No.19 Sqdn. RFC. In French yellow finish. Colour of the letter "B" and bands are speculative.

Sopwith Dolphin B7855, No.19 Sqdn. RAF. Overall PC10. White wheel covers and dumbbell. Letter "C" is repeated on upperwing.

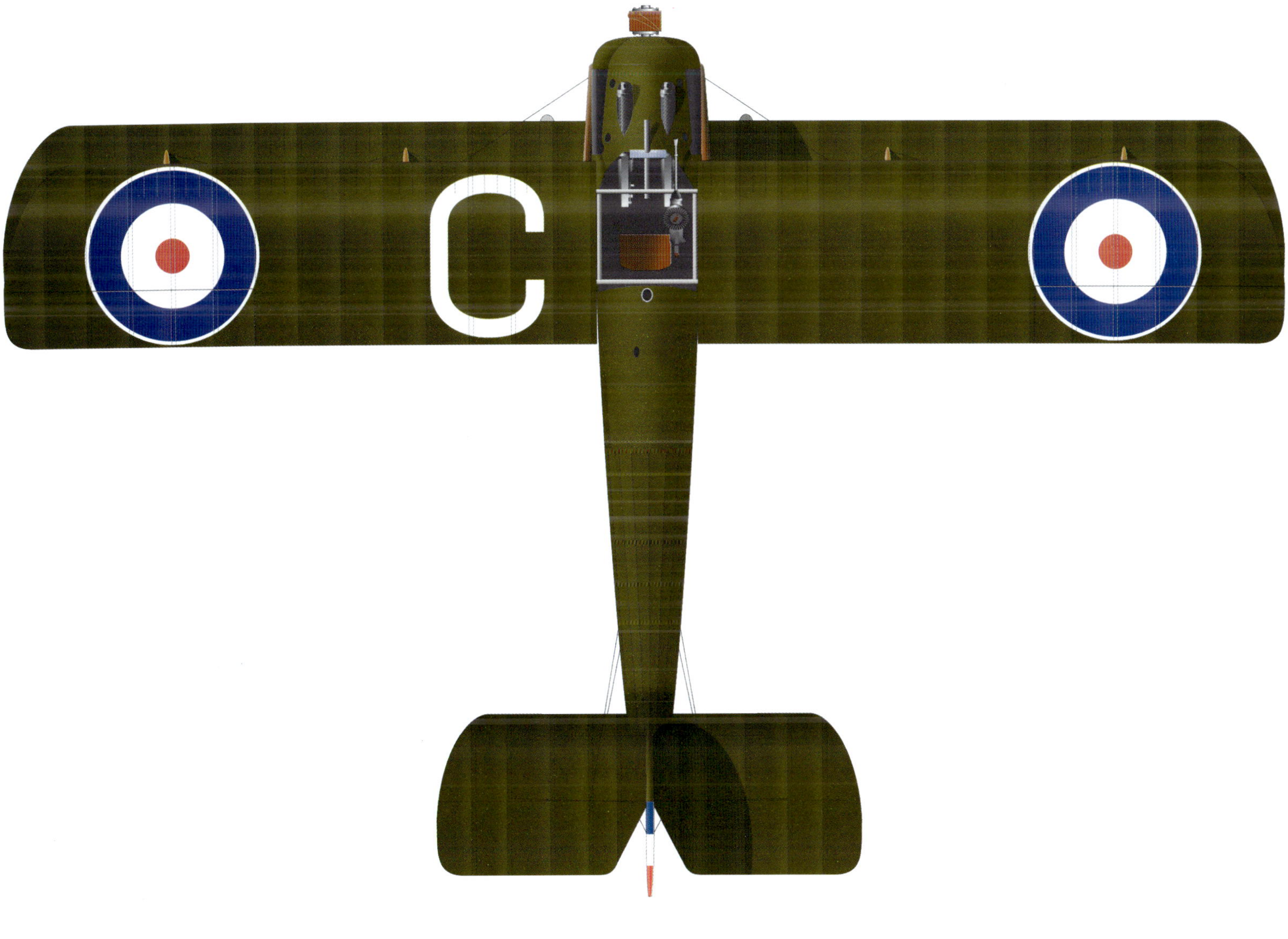

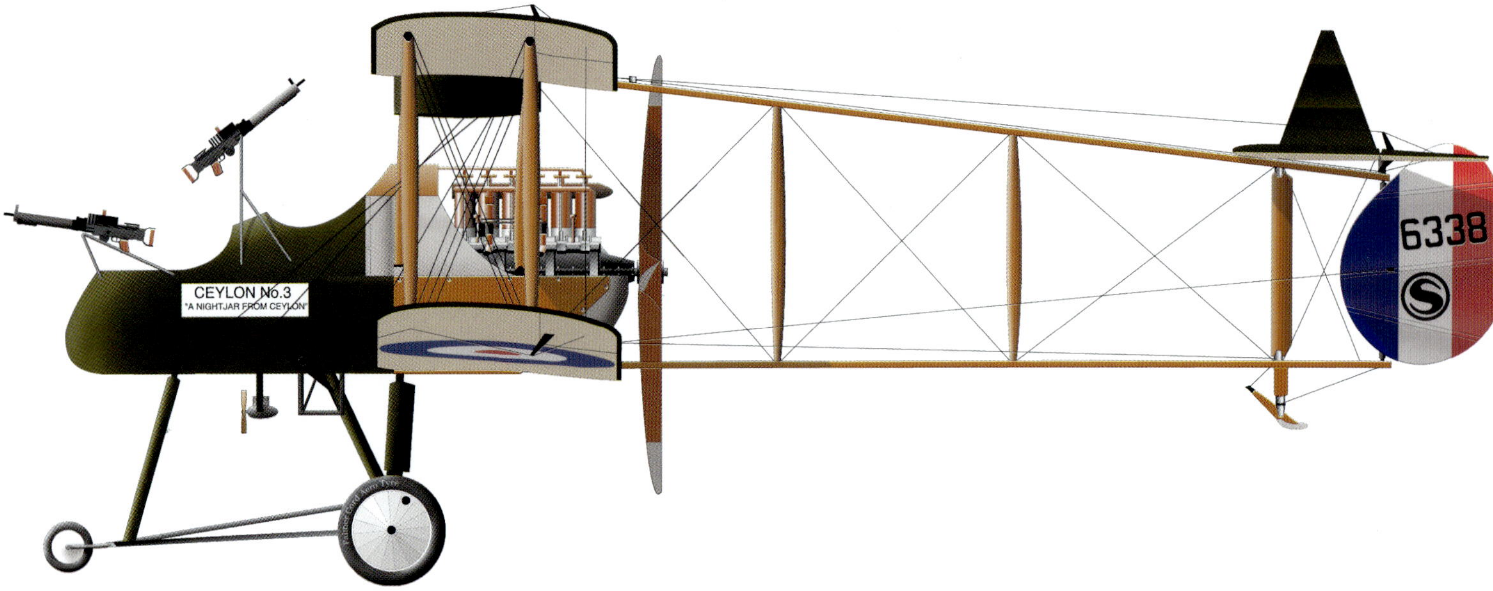

RAF FE2b 6338, 2/Lt. LA Newbold / 2/Lt. HF Champion, No.20 Sqdn. RFC, February 1916. A presentation aircraft named "CEYLON No.3: A NIGHTJAR FROM CEYLON", 6338 was finished in PC10, aluminum and varnished wood on its nacelle. Note the "goalpost" form of rear Lewis mount.

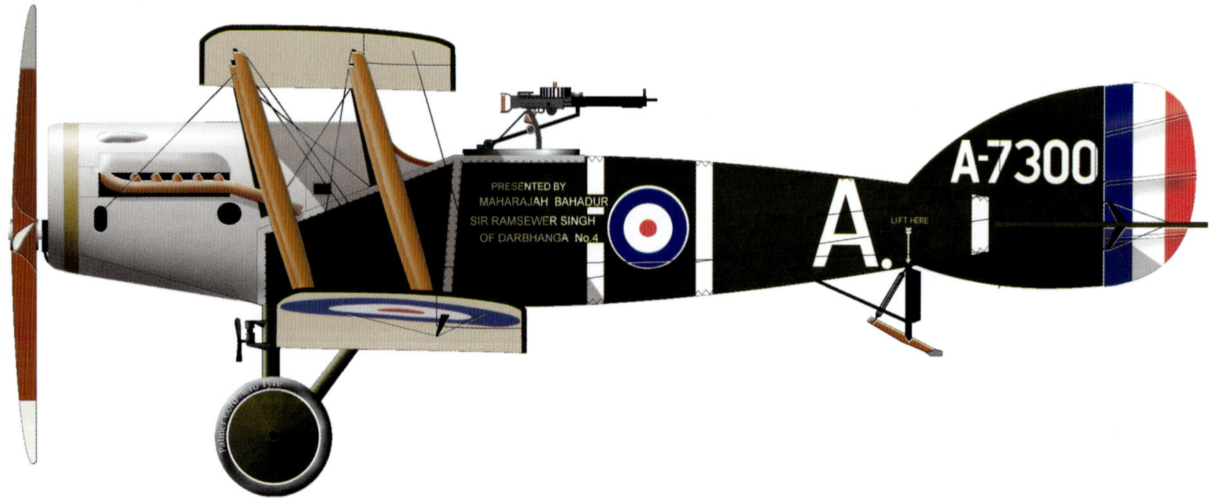

Bristol F2b A7300, No.22 Sqdn. A presentation aircraft "Presented by Mahararajah Bahadur, Sir Ramsewer Singh of Darbhanga No.4", A-7300 has the three white bands of No.22 Sqdn.

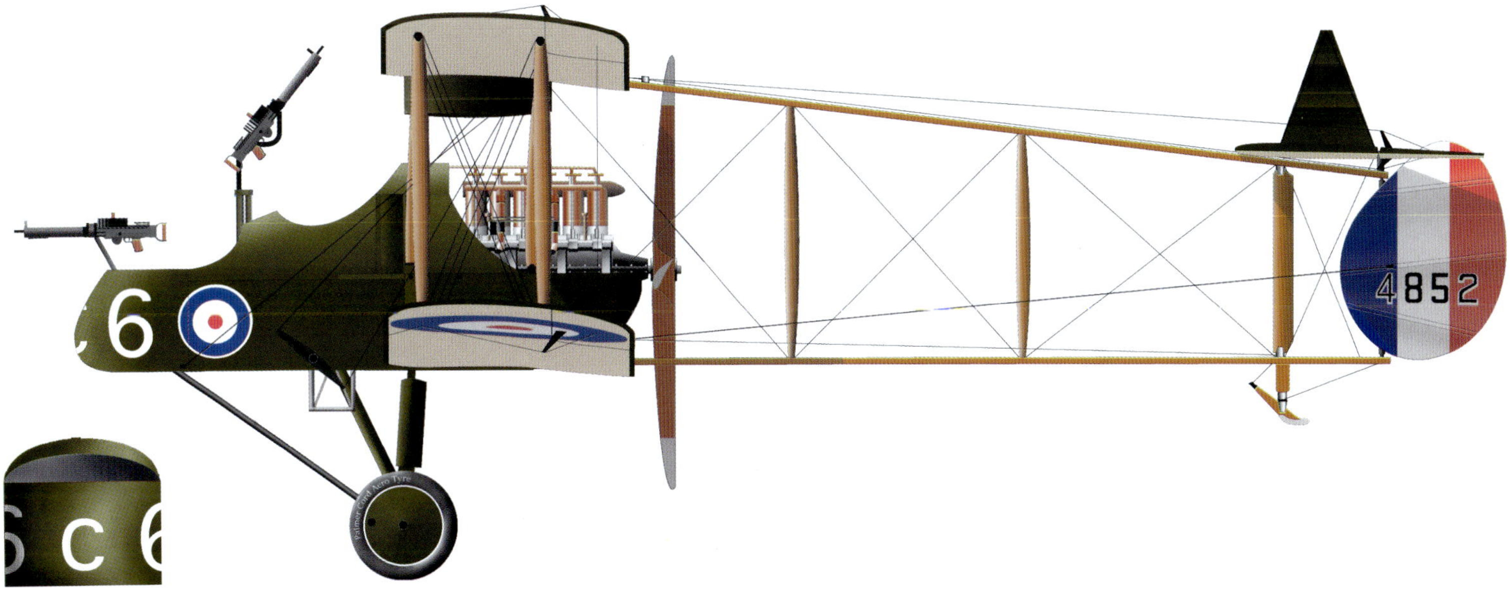

RAF FE2b 4852, Sgt B Irwin/2/Lt. FG Thiery, No.23 Sqdn. RFC, September 1916. Overall PC10, 4852 carried the flight marking "C6" on the front of the nacelle. The undercarriage has undergone the Trafford Jones modification, while the rear Lewis is on a telescopic mount.

Sopwith Dolphin C4147, No.23 Sqdn. RAF. Finished in overall PC10 with a battle-ship gray cowl and plywood panels.

Sopwith Dolphin C3824, Captain J.W. Pearson, No.23 Sqdn. RAF. Overall PC10 with a white disc. From 22 March 1918, the white disc replaced the previous marking of a white triangle, which was carried on their earlier SPADs.

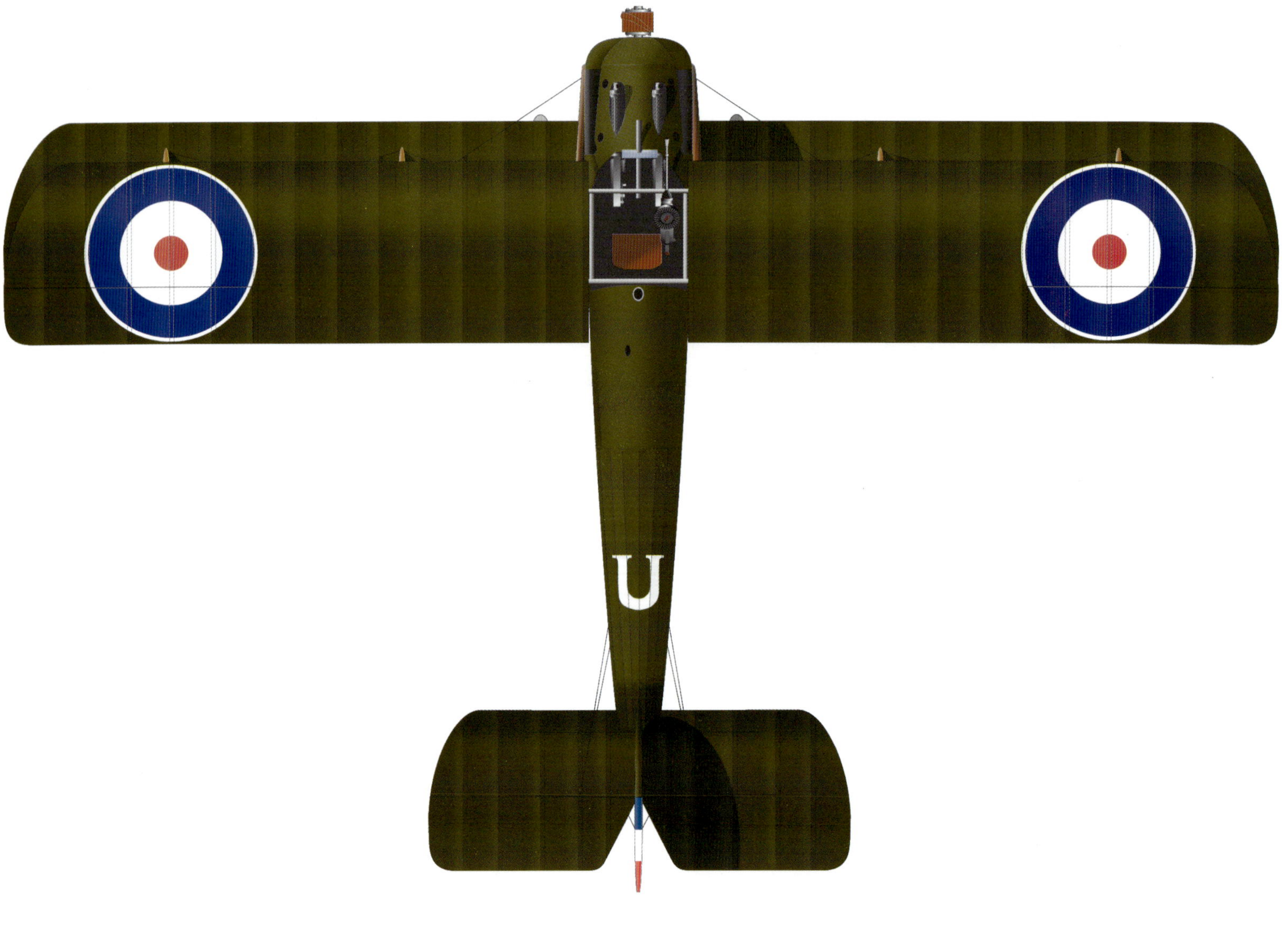

DeHavilland DH2 5998, Captain J.O. Andrews, No.24 Sqdn. RFC. PC10 fabric, gray metalwork, booms and struts. No.24 used red, blue and black/white to denote flight and individual aircraft. Each flight had its own colour, worn by each aircraft on its wheel covers, and in various combinations on the interplane struts. The underside of the nacelle carried a saw-tooth pattern in black.

RAF SE5a B891, Captain G.E.H McElroy, No.24 Sqdn. RFC. The unit marking of a white stripe in front of the cockpit signified No.24 Sqdn.

RAF SE5a D3444, Lt. F.E. Beauchamp, No.24 Sqdn. RAF. Previously the aircraft of Captain I.D.R. MacDonald in which he had claimed six victories. On 30 July 1918, part of the fabric came off the top wing and Lt. FE Beauchamp crashed, but was uninjured. Of interest is the black/white drop shadow to the serial of D3444.

DeHavilland DH4 serial unknown, No.25 Sqdn. used a white horizontal crescent as its marking.

Sopwith Camel B6313, Captain William George Barker; C Flight, No.28 Sqdn. RFC. No.28 squadron used a white square as their marking. Originally the individual flights were identified by a small flight letter and a large individual number for each aircraft. Barker"s B6313 is seen here in its original marking of "C1" and white wheel covers. The "C1" and white square were repeated on the upper wing. Also of note is the small spinner on the propeller.

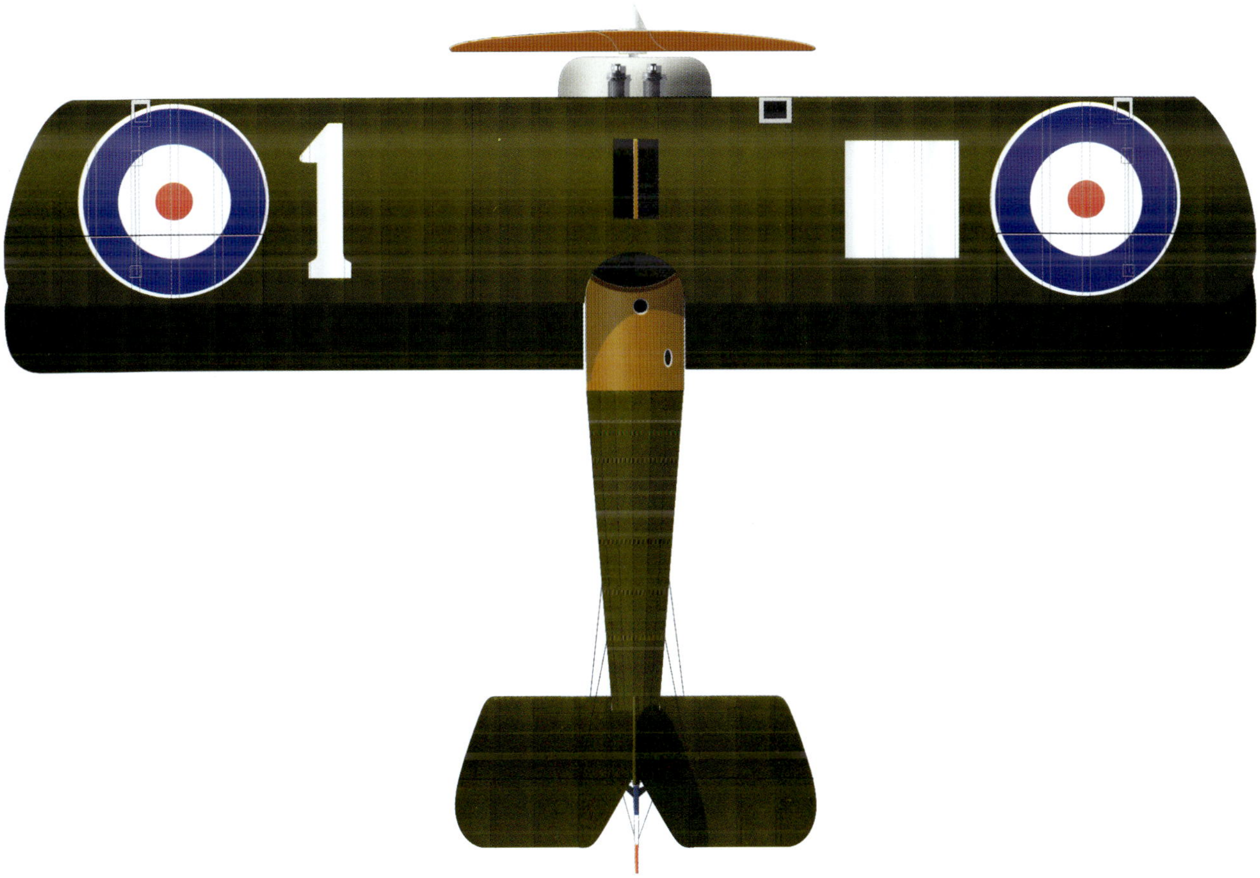

Sopwith Camel serial unknown, No.28 Sqdn. RFC, Italy. Ex-works finish of PC10, varnished ply and natural aluminum. The 28 Sqdn. white square and flight letter "J" are shown on the fuselage and repeated on the upperwing.

DeHavilland DH2 serial unknown, No.32 Sqdn. RFC. PC10 was worn on all horizontal surfaces of this aircraft, with CDL on lower and on the nacelle. There was no unit marking, beyond the flight markings worn on the wheel covers. These denoted the individual flights of No.32 Sqdn., that shown being from A Flight.

Nieuport 17 A6684, No.29 Sqdn. RFC. Overall aluminum finish. Red band around fuselage and red/white wheel covers mark this Ni.17. There is also a thin white outline to thc fusclage cockade.

RAF SE5a D6884, No.32 Sqdn. RAF. Overall PC10. Note the flight letter "A" above the leading edge of the lower wing.

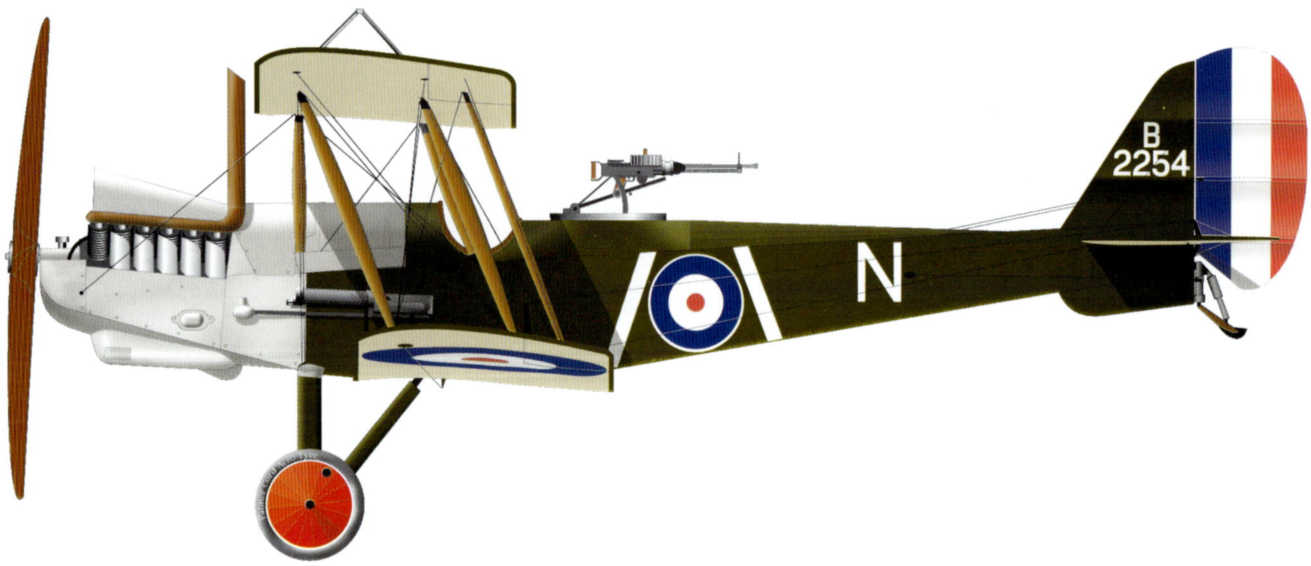

RAF RE8 B2254, No.34 Sqdn. RFC. No 34 Sqdn. used two inward sloping white bars as its marking. Red wheel covers.

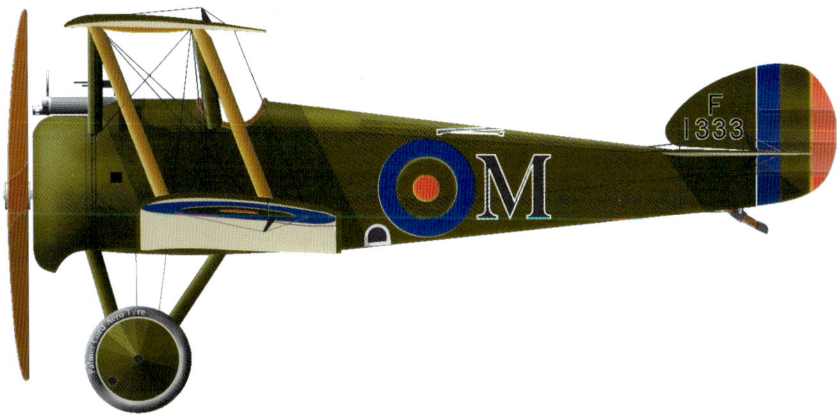

Sopwith Camel F1333, Lt. Murray, No.37(HD)Sqdn. RAF. Overall PC10 with the white of the national markings overpainted in PC10. Letter "M" was in black with a thin white outline, and was repeated on the decking behind the cockpit.

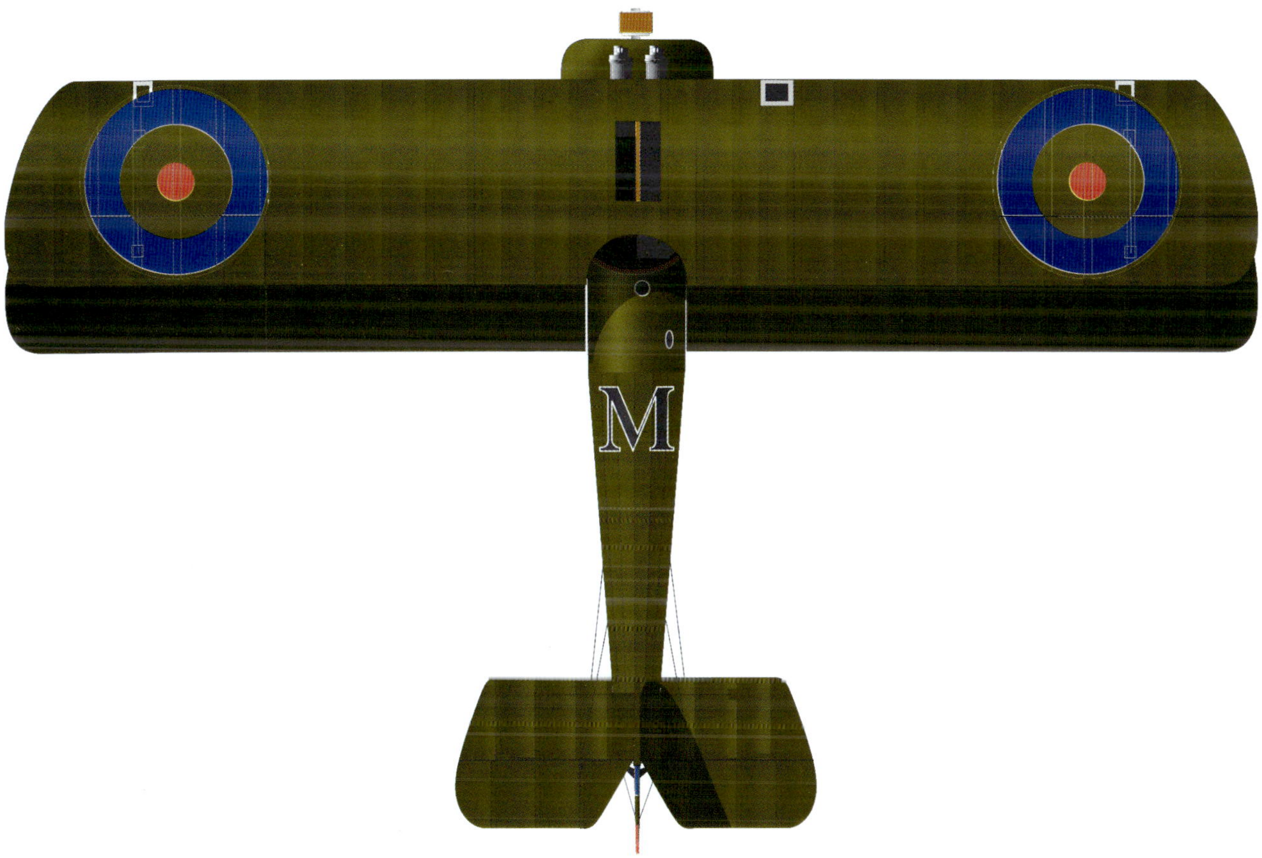

Bristol F2b C4636, No.39(HD)Sqdn. RAF. In common with other home defence aircraft, C4636 has the white of its national markings overpainted with PC10. The individual number "A6" is highlighted with a white drop shadow

Nieuport 17 B1552, No.40 Sqdn. RFC. B1552 is interesting for having a white surround to its fuselage cockade and individual number "4".

Nieuport 27 B3607, Lt. W MacLanachan, No.40 Sqdn. RFC. Three white bands were No.40 Sqdn."s markings on both their Nieuports and SE5a aircraft. Under the pseudonym of "McScotch" , MacLanachan wrote of his experiences in No.40 Sqdn. in "Fighter Pilot". B3607 carried two overwing Lewis guns.

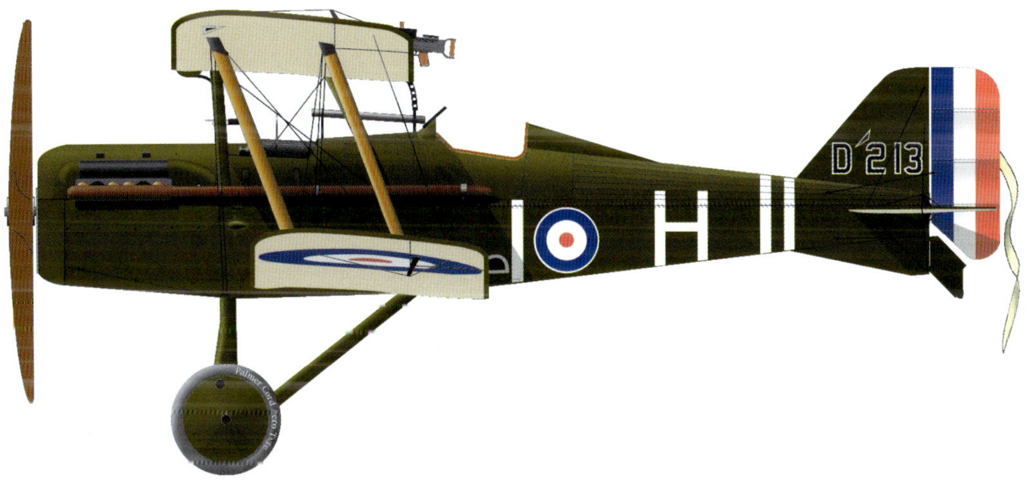

RAF SE5a D213, 2/Lt. P Learoyd, No.40 Sqdn. RFC, Spring 1918. Standard PC10 finish. Still with the unit marking of three white bands. Letter "H" repeats on port top wing.

RAF SE5a B875, No.40 Sqdn. RAF. B875 has the post March 1918 marking of a zig-zag on the rear fuselage. Wheel covers are white and the interplane struts bear a unique pattern as per other aircraft in B flight.

DeHavilland DH5 A9474, Lt. F.S. Clark, No.41 Sqdn. RFC. Overall PC10. Unit marking of two vertical bars on either side of the fuselage cockade.

RAF SE5a F5547, No.41 Sqdn. RAF. No.41 squadron changed their unit marking from the previously described bars, to both being behind the cockade in March 1918.

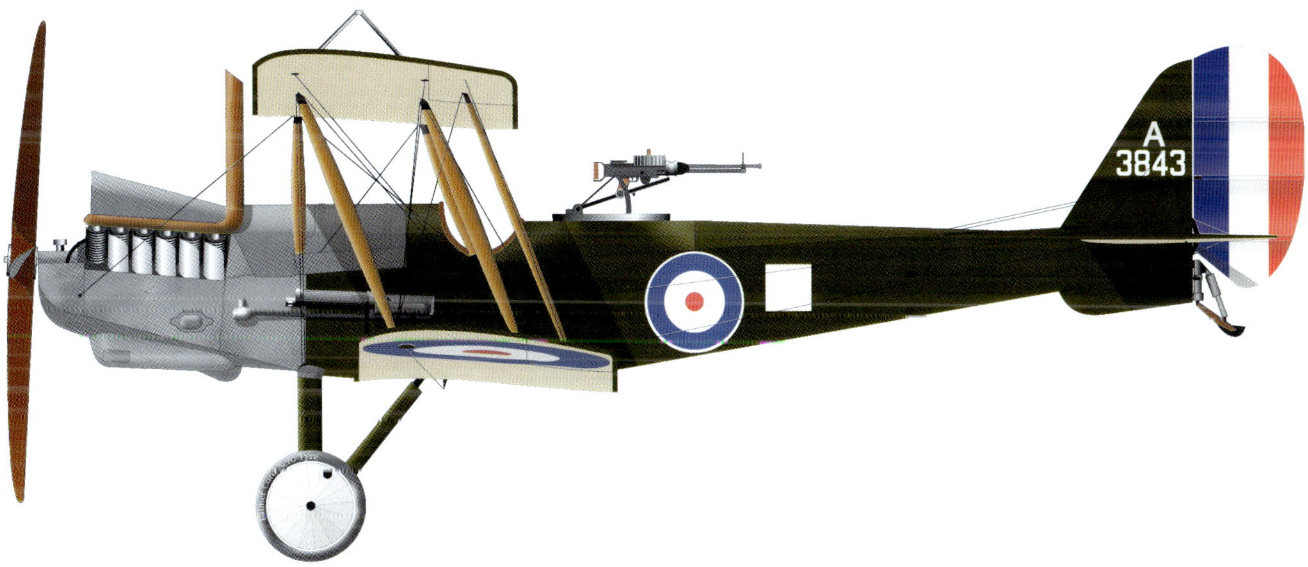

RE8 A3843, No.42 Sqdn. RFC. Overall PC10, with grey cowl and white wheel covers. No.42 used a white square as their markings.

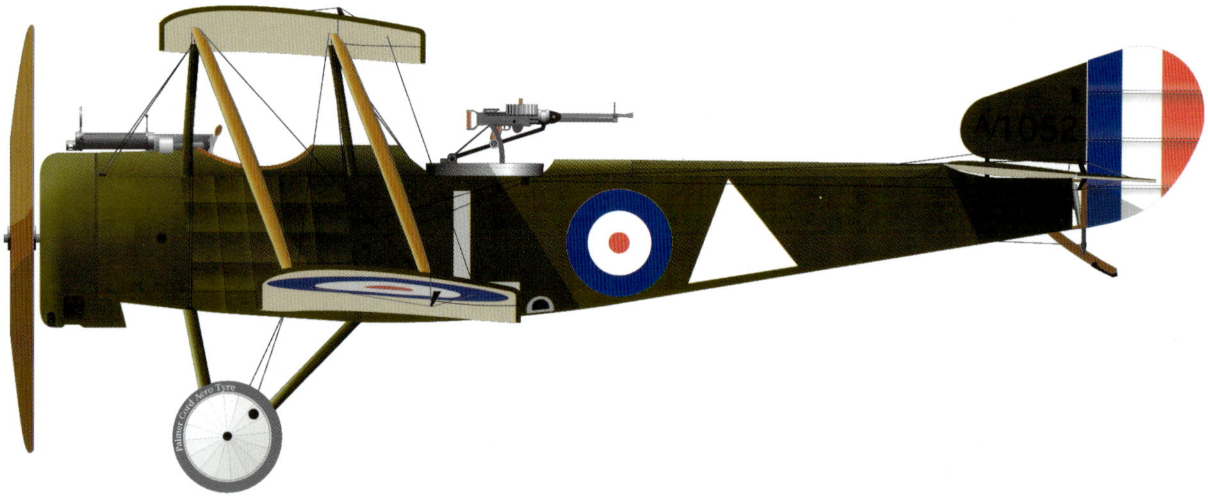

Sopwith 1 1/2 Strutter A1052 (?), No.43 Sqdn. RFC. The white triangle was carried by the Sopwith 1 1/2 Strutters and Camels of No.43 Sqdn. Strutter "L" was formerly marked as B6. Close examination of the serial appears to show it to be A1052.

Sopwith 7F.1 Snipe E8015, Lt. E. Mulcair, No.43 Sqdn. RAF. No.43 changed their marking from the white triangle to two sloping bars in March 1918. Note the partially painted cowl and flank panels.

Sopwith Pup B1777, 2/Lt. Arthur Gould Lee , No.46 Sqdn. RFC. A presentation aircraft "BRITISH GUIANA No.2", B1777 also bore the name CHIN-CHOW while No.46 Sqdn. was on home defence duties. Note the red disc above the centre-section and the different form of the wing and fuselage "4".

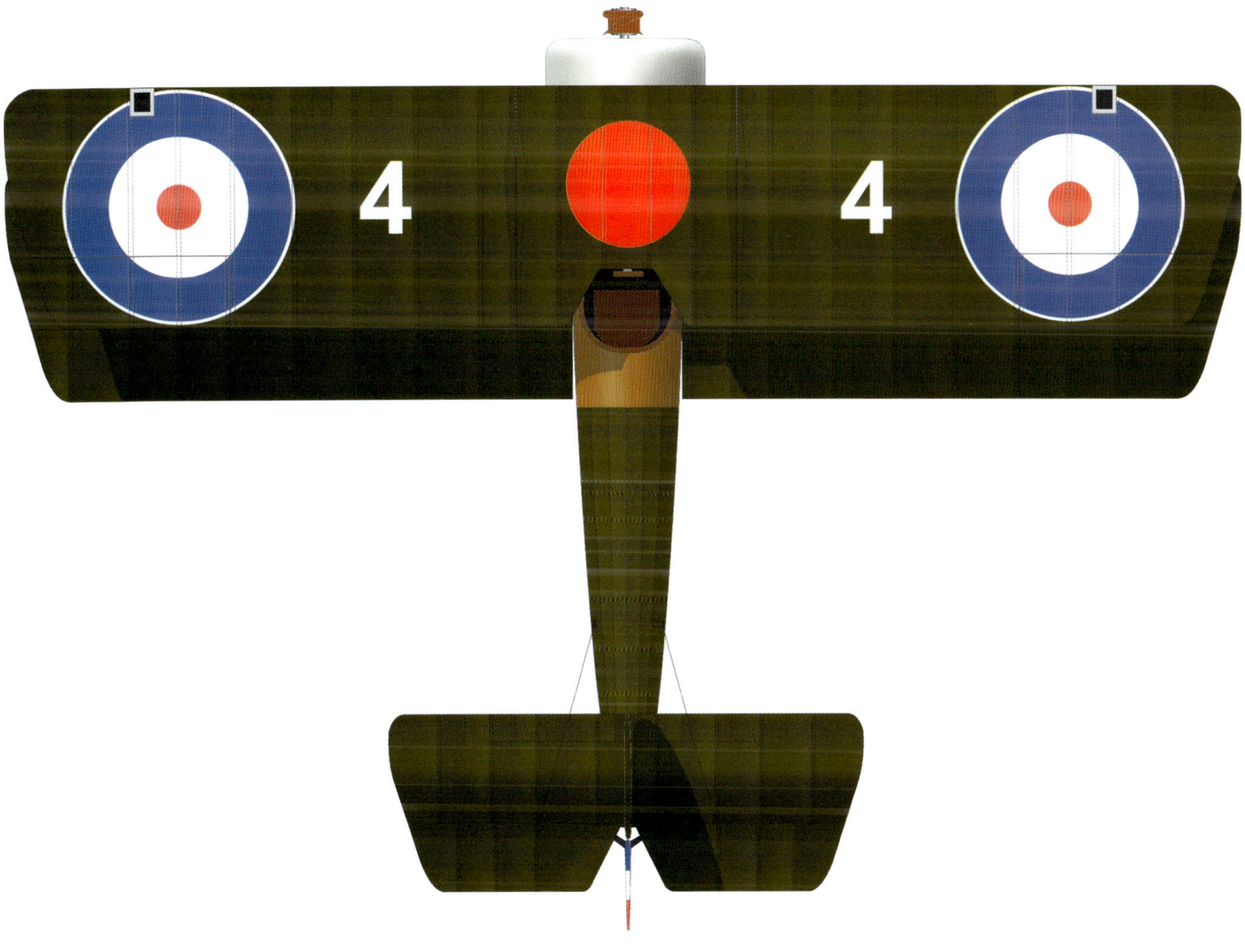

Sopwith Camel F6245, No.46 Sqdn. Ex-works finish of PC10 fabric, varnished plywood and natural metal cowl.

Sopwith Camel serial unknown, Captain C.J. Marchant, No.46 Sqdn. RFC, January 1918. The aircraft of the "A" Flight commander, possibly Captain C.J. Marchant, shows the No.46 Sqdn. marking of two thin white bands around the aft fuselage in front of the tailplane. Standard finish. Numeral "1" repeats on upper wing.

Sopwith Camel (F1955 ?), Capt S M Kinkead, No.47 Sqdn. RAF. While serving with"B" Flight of "A" Detachment of the RAF Instructional Mission to Russia at Ekaterindor in 1919. During this time he shot down two Bolshevik Nieuports. The fuselage cockade is in a form of the old Imperial Russian marking of red, blue and white. The rudder and fin has a diagonal white stripe, while the nose of the fuselage carries a horizontal stripe.

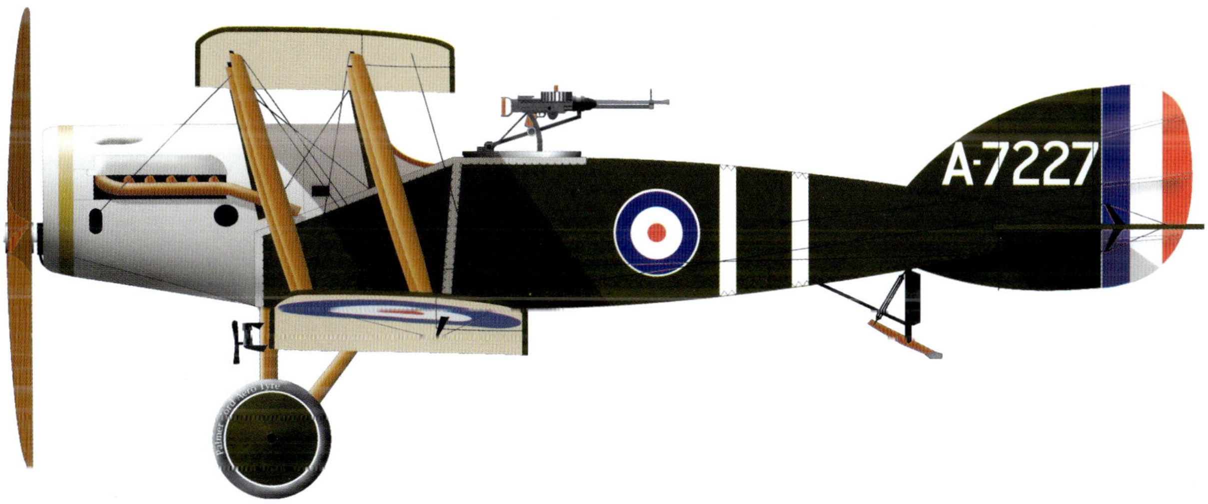

Bristol F2b A7227, Capt Keith Park, No.48 Sqdn. RFC. Two white bands were carried from the summer of 1917 until ordered removed in March 1918.

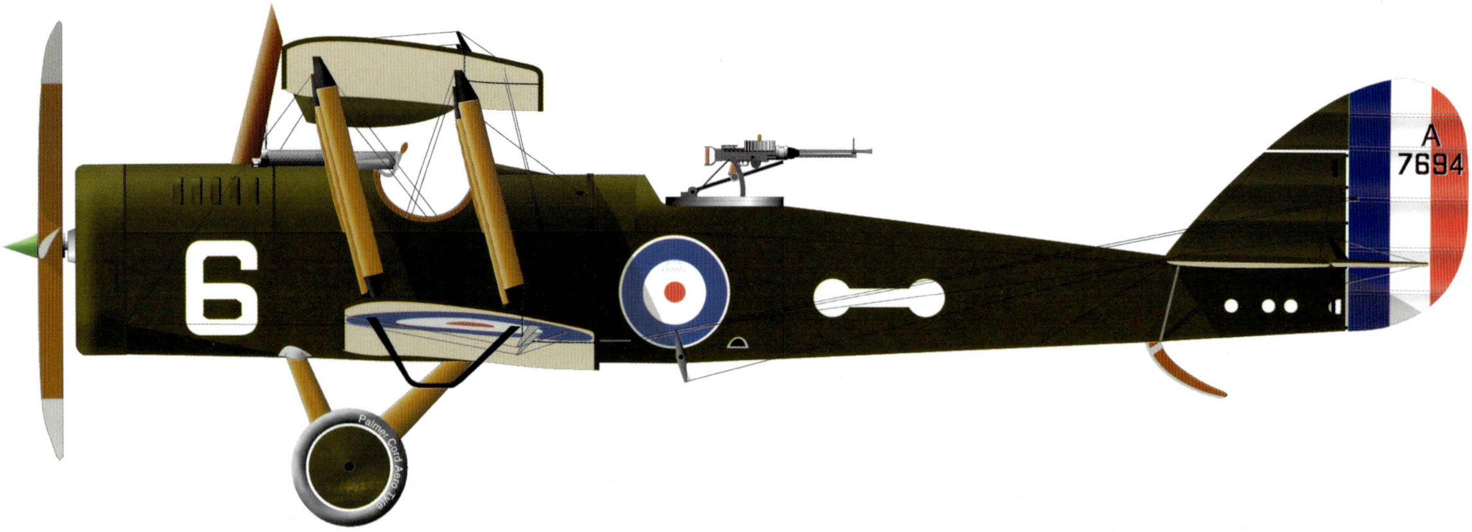

DeHavilland DH4 A7694, No.49 Sqdn. RFC. Nicknamed "Miss Greencap", A7694 was in overall PC10 and carried the 49 Sqdn. dumbbell.

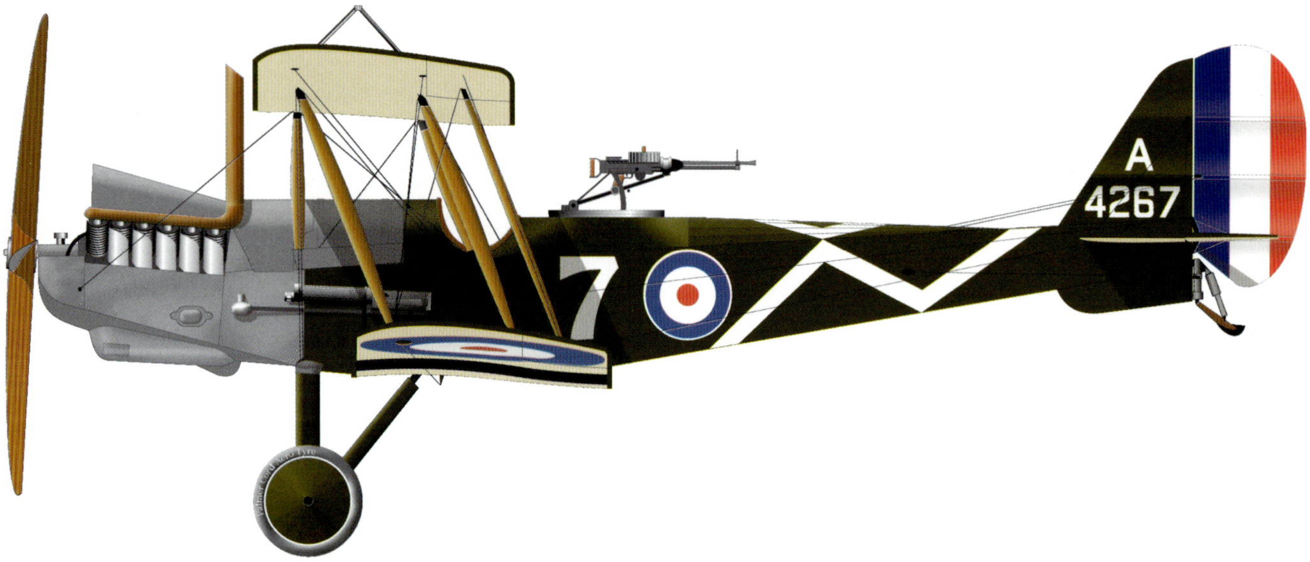

ABOVE AND OPPOSITE: RAF RE8 A4267, No.52 Sqdn. RFC. Zig-zag line on fuselage side, repeated on turtledeck. Individual number "7" is also carried on the upper wing centre-section.

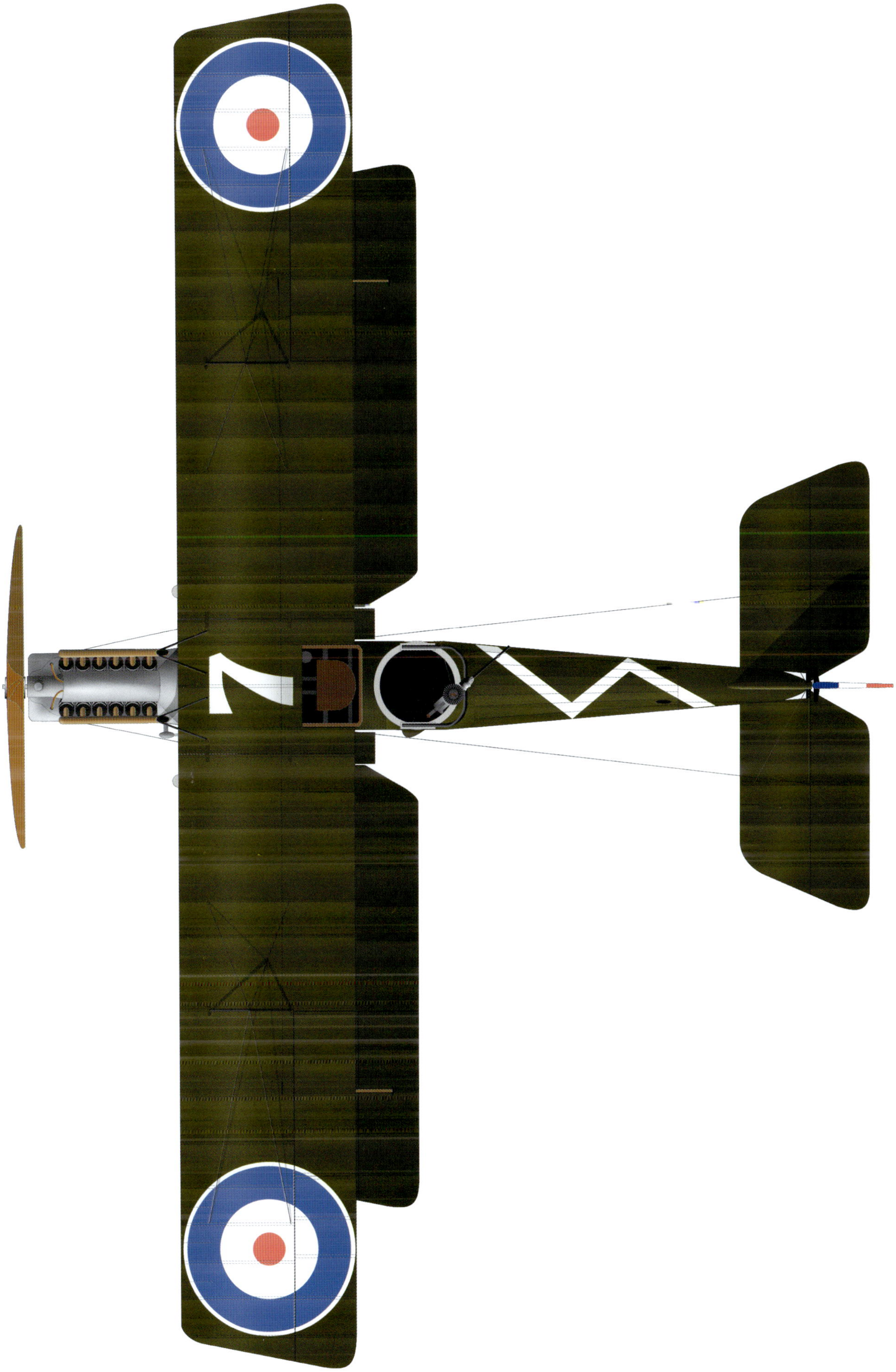

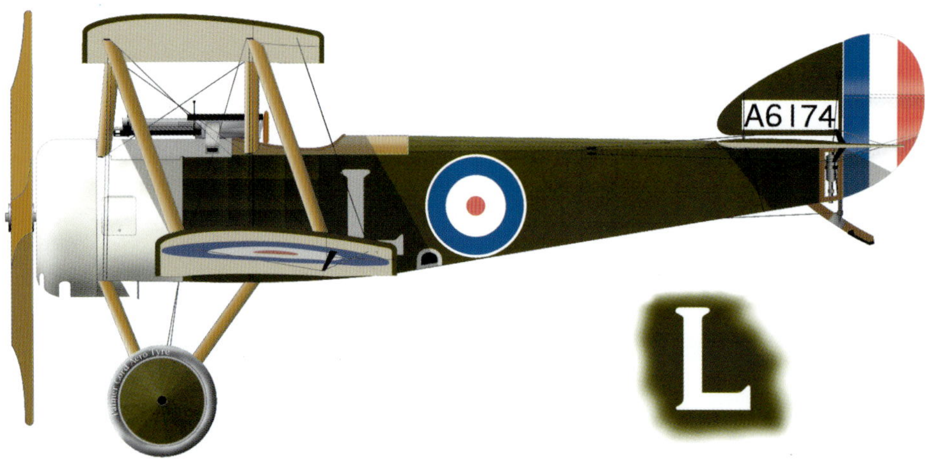

Sopwith Pup A6174, 2/Lt. Hadrill, No.54 Sqdn. RFC. The 27th victory of Ltn. Werner Voss, Hadrill"s Pup carried the name "CANADA" on the centre-section.

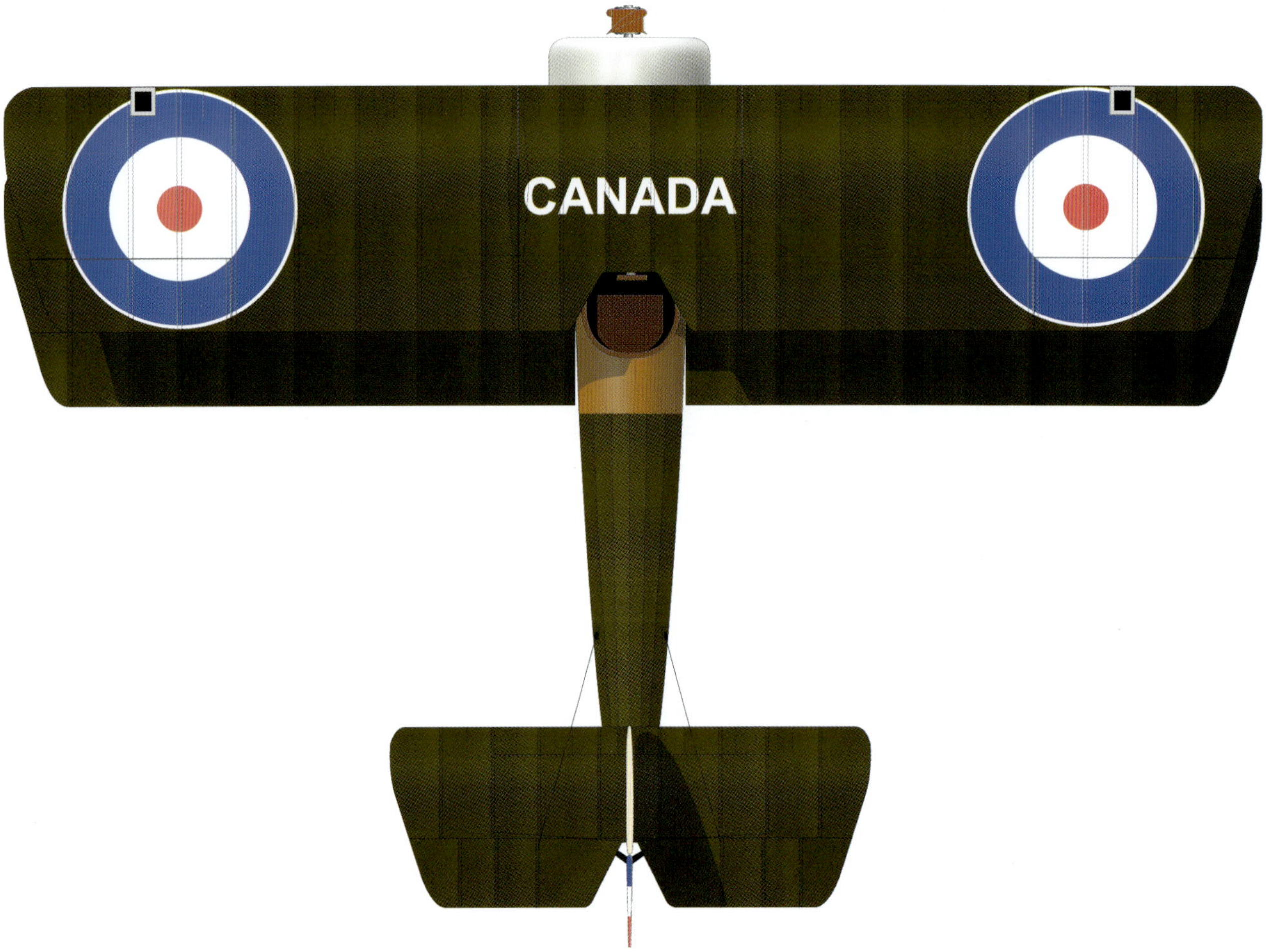

Sopwith Camel B5423, Lt. F.H. Ohrt, No.54 Sqdn. RFC. Ex works finish of PC10, varnished ply and natural metal. The original unit marking was a horizontal stripe along the upper longeron. B5423 (and Ohrt) was shot down on 19 January 1918. Ohrt, an American, was taken POW.

Sopwith Camel B5417, 2/Lt. G.A.C Manley, No.54 Sqdn. RFC. Finish as per B5423. The marking of No.54 Sqdn. was ordered changed to a vertical bar in December 1917. However, as seen above, this did not take effect until late in January 1918. B5417 shows the new marking. B5417 was shot down on 9 February 1918, with Manley becoming a POW.

DeHavilland DH4 A7624, No.55 Sqdn. RFC. Overall PC10. Unit marking of a white triangle. Letter "M" on nose.

RAF SE5 A8920, Lt. Dickinson, B Flight, No.56 Sqdn. RFC. As No.56 was originally the only SE5 squadron in France, a separate squadron marking was unnecessary, however the three flights did use coloured wheel covers to distinguish the flights. B Flight used blue and white quarters, "A" Flight used red and and "C Flight used white. The individual code "B4" may have been repeated on the rear decking.

RAF SE5a B595, Lt. M.E. Mealing, C Flight, No.56 Sqdn. RFC. The official marking for No.56 Sqdn. was originally a dumbbell in the respective flight colours, this lasted for a very brief period and was replaced with an 18" wide band around the aft fuselage in front of the tailplane., The letter "W" was repeated on the upper wing

Nieuport 23 B1575, 2/Lt. G.A.H. Parkes, No.60 Sqdn., July 1917. Aluminum finish overall. Each aircraft of No.60 Sqdn. carried a letter indicating its flight and place within same. Therefore, B1575 is aircraft "1" of B Flight. Parkes was shot down on 15 July 1917 by von Tutschek and taken prisoner.

RAF SE5a B507, Lt. J.J. Fitzgerald, No.60 Sqdn. RFC, October 1917. After engine failure forced Fitzgerald to land behind German lines, B507 was extensively photographed by the Germans. The 60 Sqdn. marking of a white disc can be seen, as can the elaborate flight letter "A", which was also carried on the upper wing centre-section.

RAF SE5a D6945, Lt. Beck, No.60 Sqdn. RAF, October 1918. In march 1918, No.60 changed their marking to two white bands around the aft fuselage just forward of the tailplane. D6945 is typical of their markings.

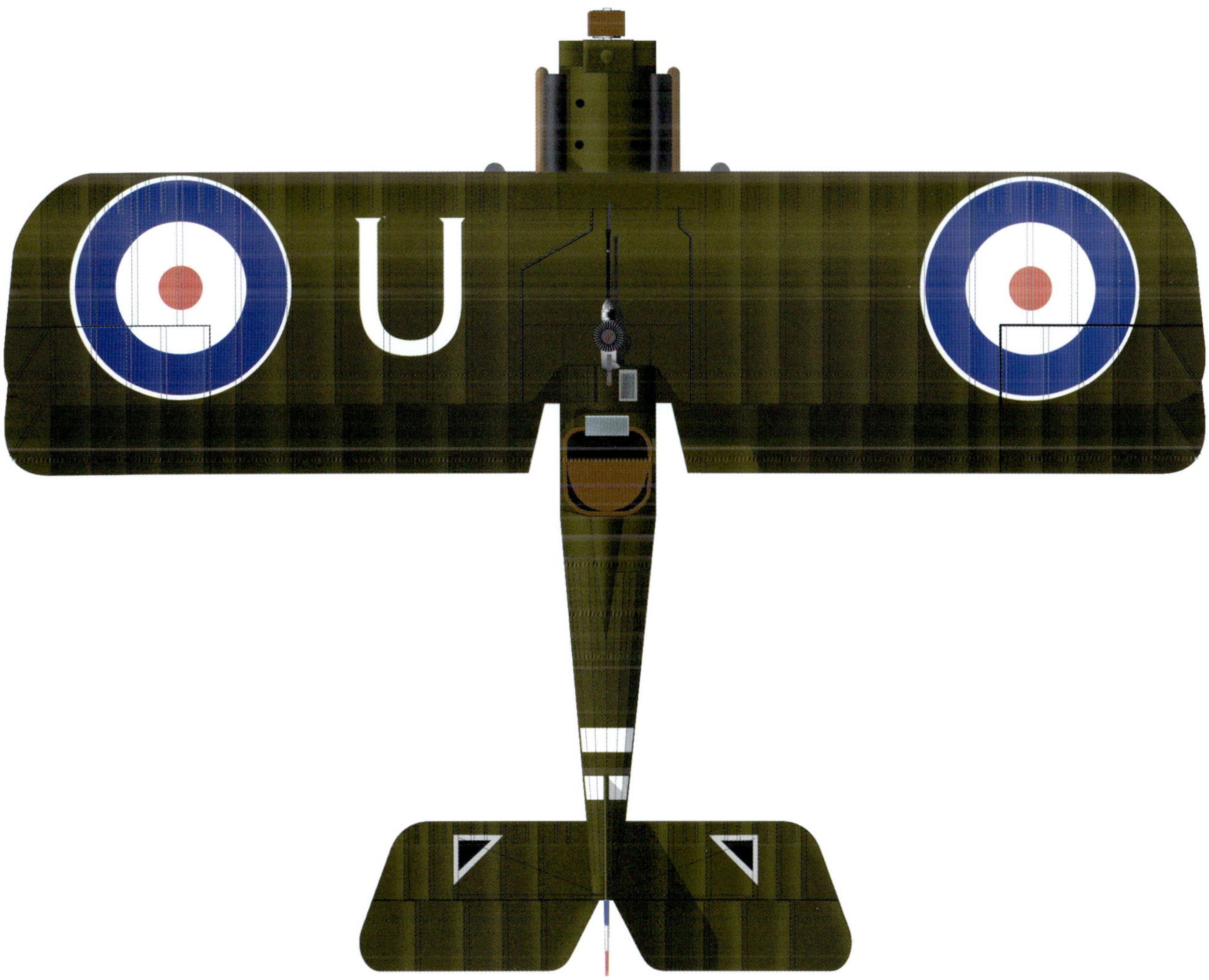

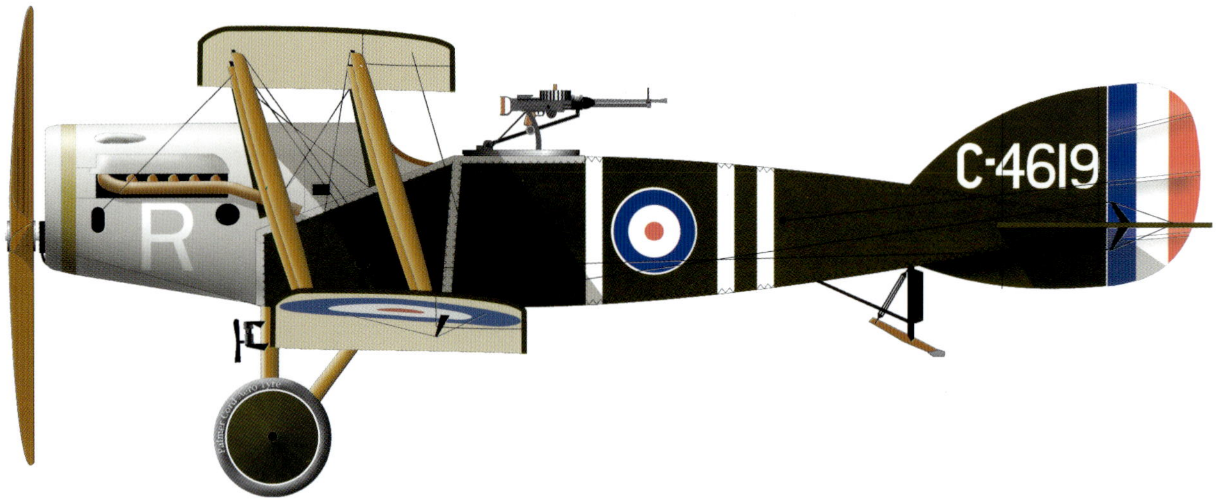

Bristol F2b C4619, Captain W.E. Stanton / Lt. J.R. Gordon, No.62 Sqdn. RFC. Three white bands are the marking of No.62 in the pre-March 1918 era. C4619 is also seen in photos after the stripes were removed.

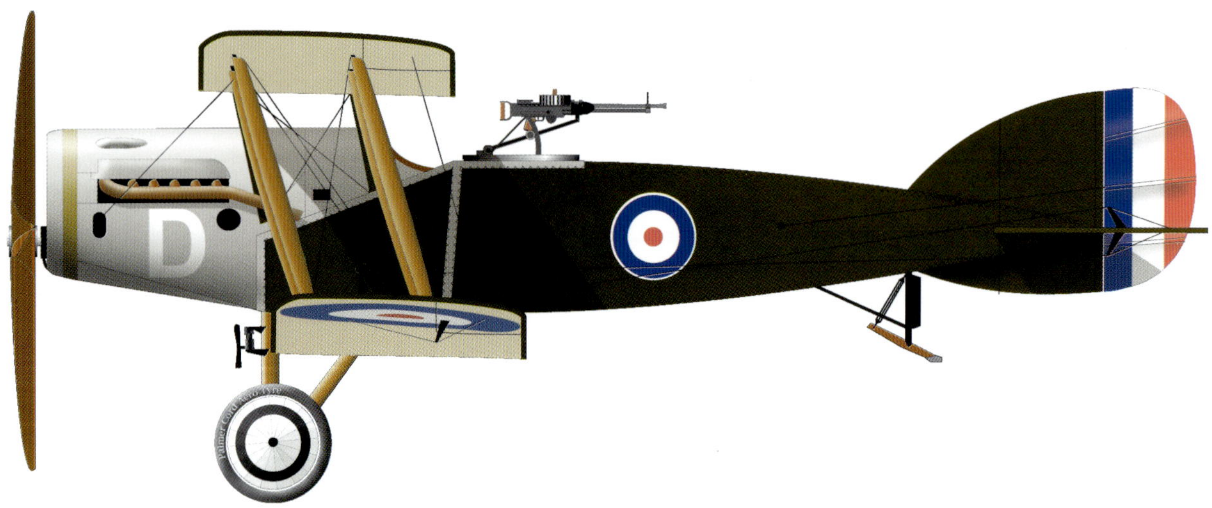

Bristol F2b serial unknown, No.62 Sqdn. RAF. In common with all other two-seater RFC units, no.62 removed their unit markings on 22 March 1918. the only distinguishing feature on this anonymous Bristol is the letter "D" on the cowl and the white and black wheel covers.

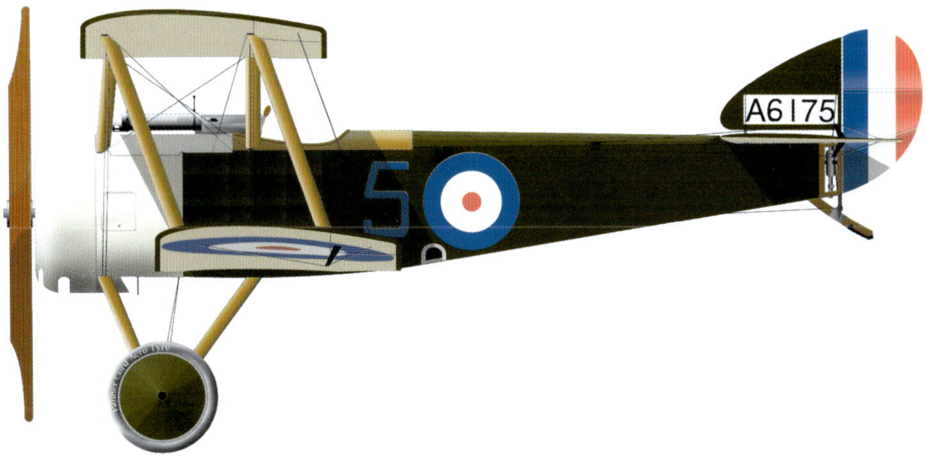

Sopwith Pup A6175, 2/Lt. R.S. Capon, No.66 Sqdn. RFC, April 1917. Ex-works finish of PC10, varnished plywood and natural metal. Flight marking of a blue number "5". Capon was shot down ad taken prisoner on 4 April 1917.

Sopwith Camel E7167, 2/Lt. J.M. Kelly, No.66 Sqdn. RAF, October 1918. When no.45 squadron was withdrawn from Italy, many 66 squadron Camels had the 45 Sqdn. dumbbell added in an attempt to hide the fact that 45 Sqdn. was gone. Kelly was shot down, captured and later escaped on 22 October 1918.

Sopwith Camel E1496(?), Captain WC Hilborn, No.66 Sqdn. RAF. No.66 Sqdn. used a horizontal stripe and a vertical bar as their unit marking on the Camel. Unlike other 66 Sqdn. aircraft I have seen, Hilborn"s Camel has its flight letter in front of the vertical bar. Also note the small spinner. Mrs Margaret Hilborn Sawyer photos via Wayne Ralph

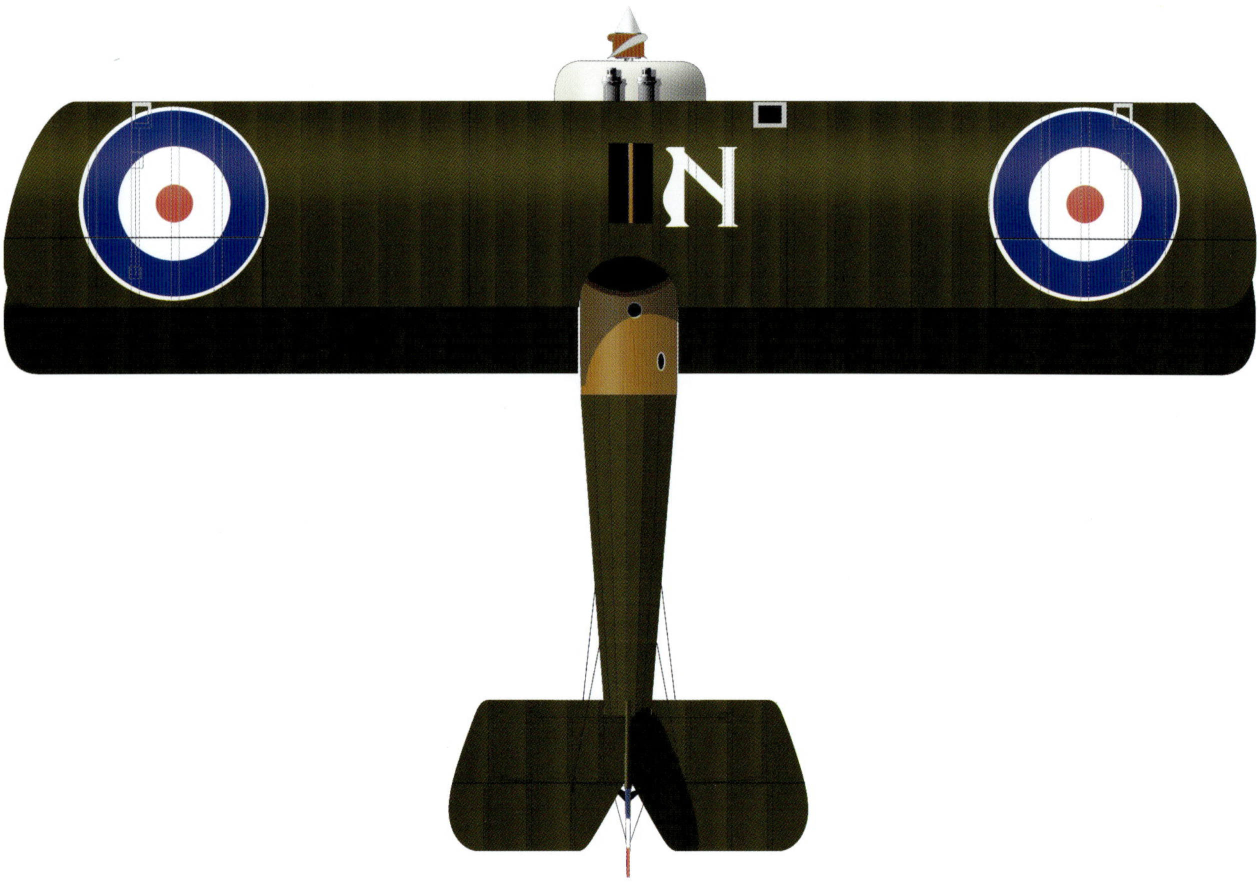

DeHavilland DH5 serial unknown, No.68(A)Sqdn. RFC/2AFC. No 68(A) Sqdn. used a white band around the rear fuselage as its marking on their DH5s.

Sopwith Camel serial unknown, No.70 Sqdn. RAF. After 23 March 1918, No.70 Squadron"s marking was changed from the zig-zag to three bands around the rear fuselage, seen here on the overall PC10 aircraft "Q".

Sopwith Camel serial unknown, No.70 Sqdn. RFC . Shown in overall PC10 with the 70 Sqdn. marking of a zig-zag on the fuselage. The individual flight marking "O" on the fuselage is repeated around the centre-section cutout.

Sopwith Camel serial unknown, Major Hubbard, No.73 Sqdn. RAF. Overall PC10, with white wheel covers can be seen on the aircraft of the No.73 Sqdn. commander. Of interest is his personal marking which is based on the nursery rhyme bearing his name – Mother Hubbard"s cupboard.

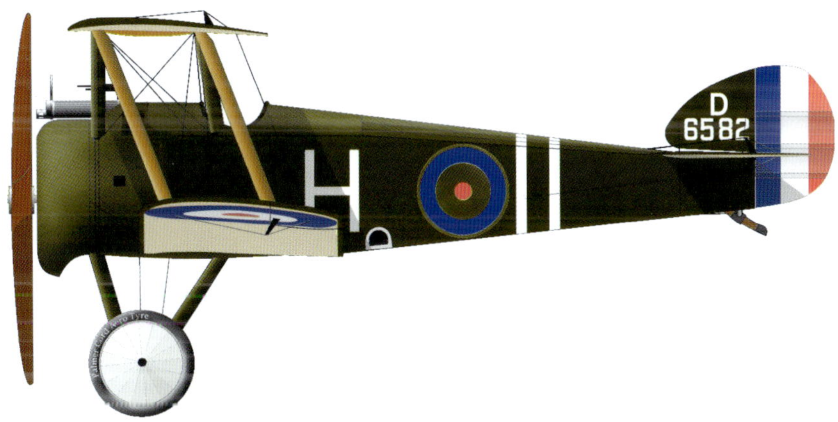

Sopwith Camel D6582, No.73 Sqdn. RAF, Summer 1918. The 73 Sqdn. marking was two thin white bands around the aft fuselage. For low level operations the national markings had the white overpainted in PC10.

Sopwith 5F.1 Dolphin D3584, No.79 Sqdn. RAF, 1919. This Dolphin is seen postwar as part of the "Army of Occupation". Overall PC10, unit marking of a small white square.

RAF SE5a D6933, Lt. J.A. Rorison, No.85.Sqdn. RAF, August 1918. "NEWPORT FIFE No.4" shows the typical No.85 Sqdn. marking of a white hexagon, which was usually repeated on the rear decking. The letter "N" is also on the upper wing.

Sopwith 5F.1 Dolphin C4131, Captain W.M. Fry, No.79 Sqdn. RAF, May 1918. This 79 Sqdn. Dolphin carries an interesting pattern of black and white checks on the docking aft of the cockpit. Otherwise it is in standard finish of PC10 and battleship gray.

Sopwith 5F.1 Dolphin C4168, Major J.C. Callaghan, No.87 Sqdn. RAF, July 1918. No87 squadron used a sideways "S" as their unit marking. However Major Callaghan decorated his Dolphin with a cloverleaf and had the "S" upright.

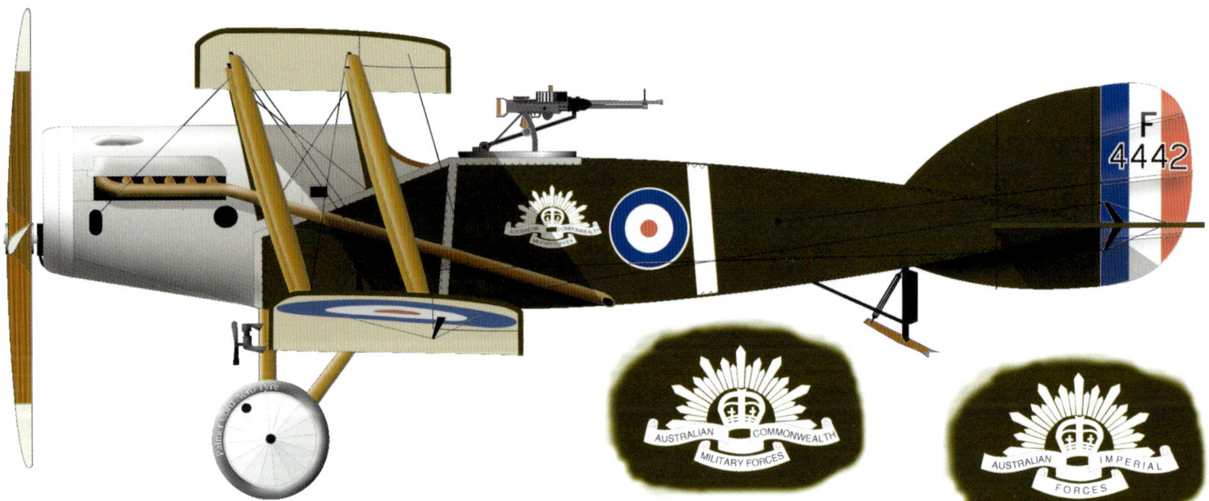

Bristol F2b F4442, Captain A Hepburn, A Flight, No.88 Sqdn. RAF. F4442 bore a representation of the Australian Imperial Forces badge below the observer"s cockpit. and carried the inscription "AUSTRALIAN COMMONWEALT.H MILITARY FORCES".

Sopwith Dolphin J9, No.91 Sqdn. RAF. No.91 Sqdn. was scheduled to arrive in France in November 1918 and used a large triangle as their marking.

RAF SE5a B104, No.92 Sqdn. RAF. Three diagonal white bars were carried by the SE5as of No.92 Sqdn. Possible flight marking of a black circle on the white wheel cover, this particular aircraft also has a blue headrest.

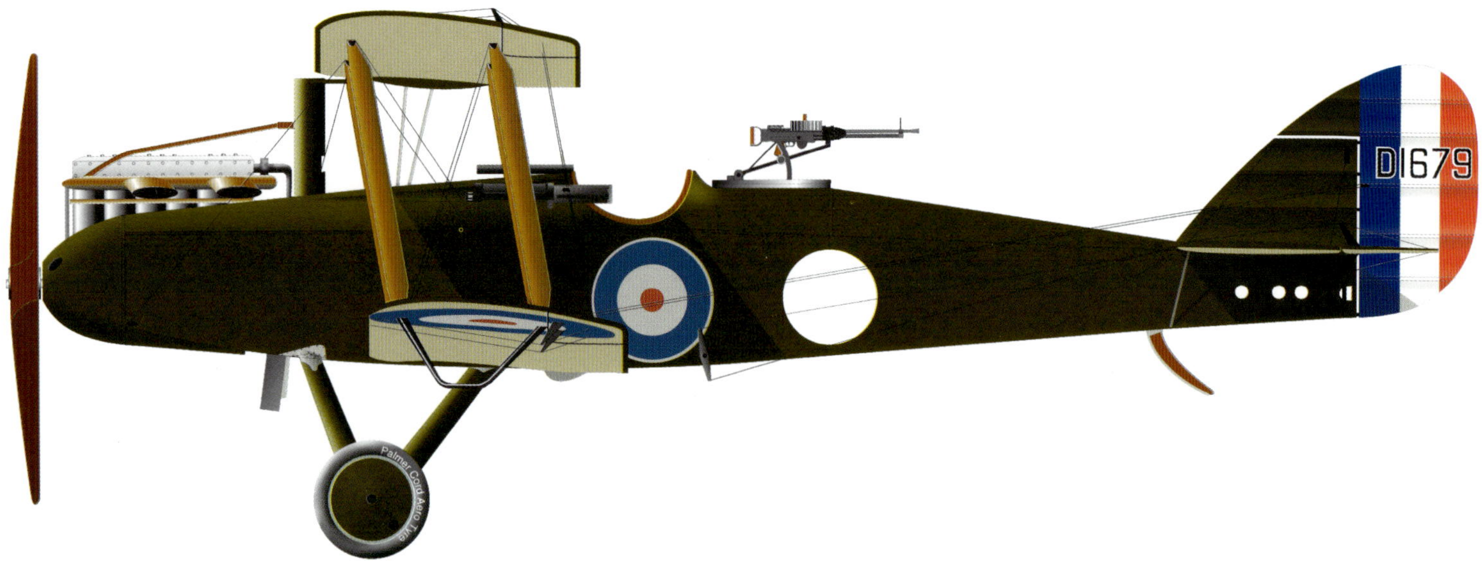

DeHavilland DH9 D1679, No.99 Sqdn. RAF. Even though unit markings were supposed to be removed in the post March 1918 period, No.99 Sqdn. continued to use a white disc.

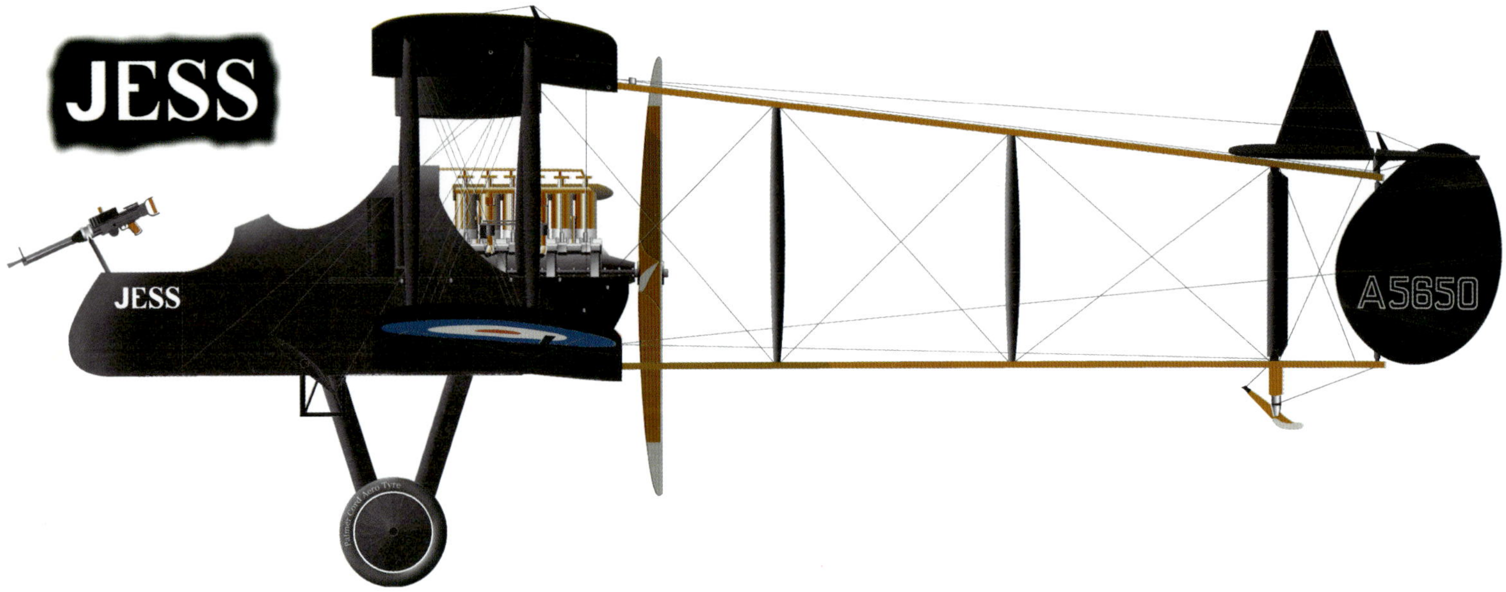

RAF FE2b A5650, No.100 Sqdn. RAF, August 1918. Overall black – including undersurfaces – typifies this night-bombing machine of No.100 Sqdn. RAF. There are no squadron markings, although the personal marking of "JESS" is carried.

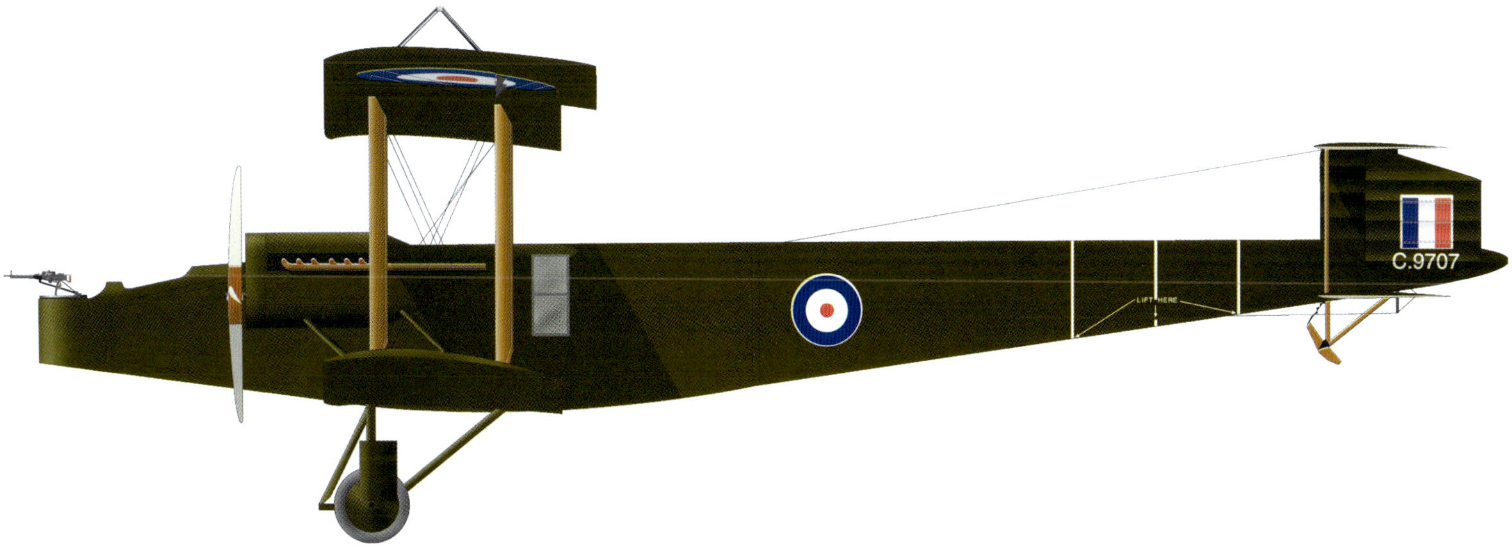

Handley Page 0/400 C9707, No.100 Sqdn. RAF. Overall PC10 - including undersurfaces. the vertical stripes on the aft fuselage are "Lift here" locations. The fin flash has a thin white outline to it.

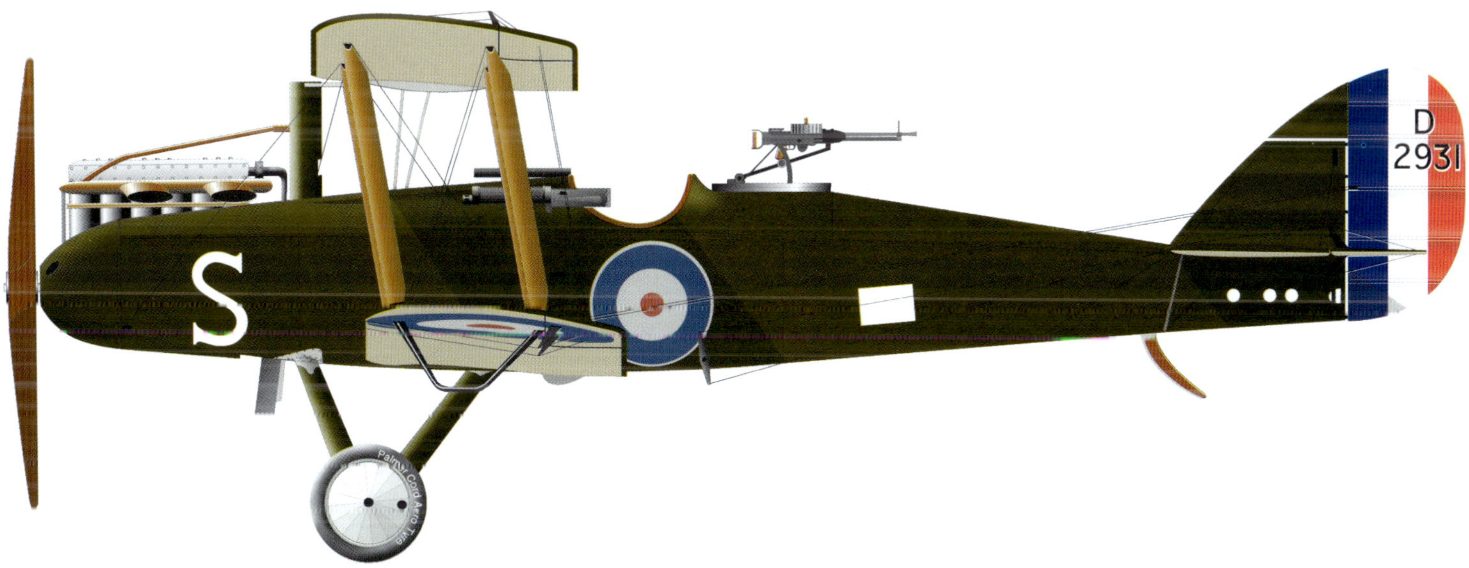

DeHavilland DH9 D2931, No.104 Sqdn. RAF. Although all two-seater units removed their markings in March 1918, No.104 added a small white rectangle to their aircraft. This overall PC10 DH9 was photographed in German hands in the summer of 1918.

RAF SE5a serial unknown, No.111 Sqdn. RFC. Overall PC10 (or possibly PC12), with a horizontal white stripe along the upper longeron.

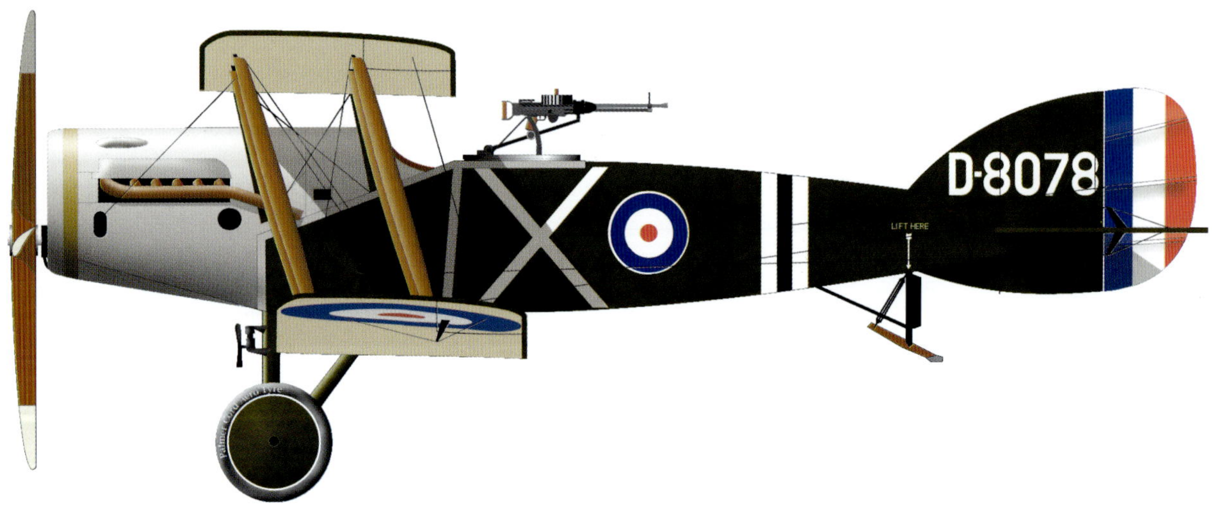

Bristol F2b D8078, No.139 Sqdn. RAF. The original marking of No.139 Sqdn. was two white bands separated by black. This was later expanded to five white and four black bands, and ultimately seven and six respectively.

Sopwith Camel B6313, Major William George Barker, OC, No.139 Sqdn. RAF. Upon assuming command of No.139 Sqdn., Barker was able to bring along his trusty Camel, B6313 and had it painted in a distinct style. Using the 139 b/w bands as a starting point, he added four white and three black bands as well as black nose, fin and flank panels. A red spinner and red heart pierced by a white arrow completed the picture.

Sopwith Camel B6313, Major William George Barker, OC, No.139 Sqdn. RAF, September 1918. The final appearance of B6313 found it with the cowl stripped of all paint, the stripes expanded to seven and six (the last of which didn"t quite fit and was a bit narrower), while the heart on the fin was now in the opposite direction. No spinner was carried at this time. There were also extra cooling holes in the front of the cowl.

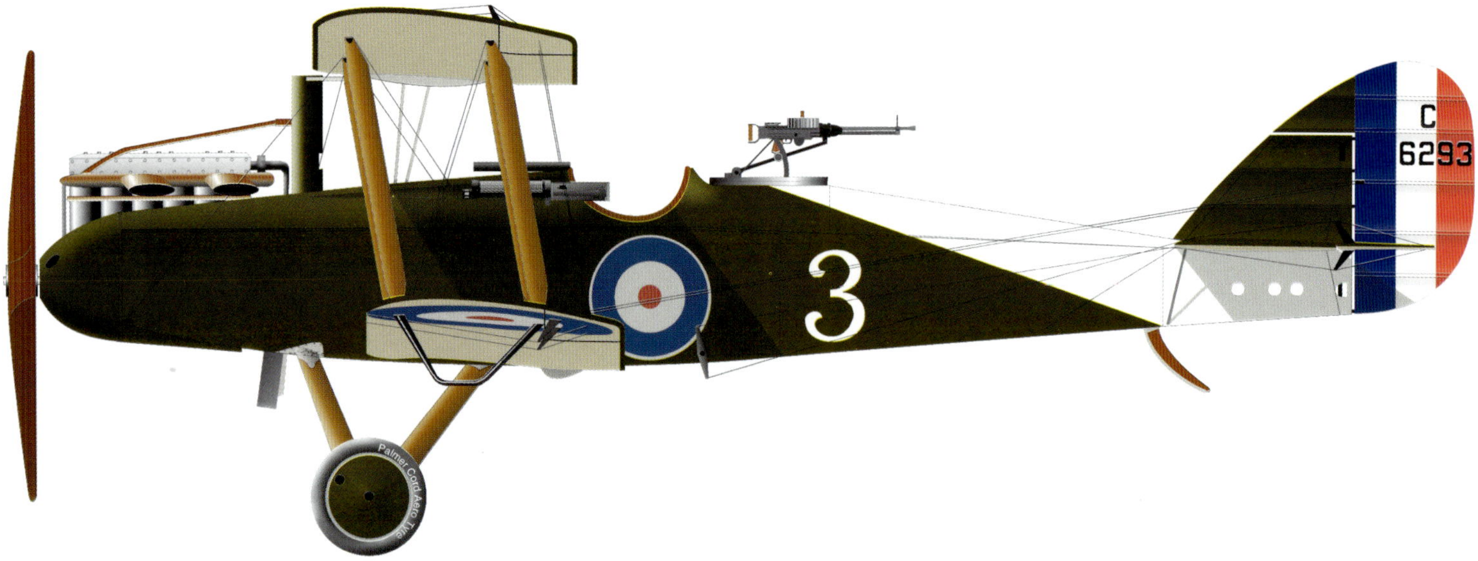

DeHavilland DH9 C6293, No.144 Sqdn. RAF. This Middle-East based DH9 has an interesting scheme of a white rear fuselage, however it is thought this was a personal rather than a unit marking.

Sopwith Triplane N5429, No.1(N) Sqdn. RNAS. PC10 overall with white cowl, fin and wheel covers. Flown by various pilots at No.1(N) Sqdn. RNAS between December 1916 and April 1917, later went to other RNAS units until lost 13 September 1917 with FSL JR Wilford of No.1(N) being taken POW.

Sopwith Triplane N5475, No.1(N) Sqdn. RNAS. PC10 overall. Squadron marking of two small white bars on aft fuselage

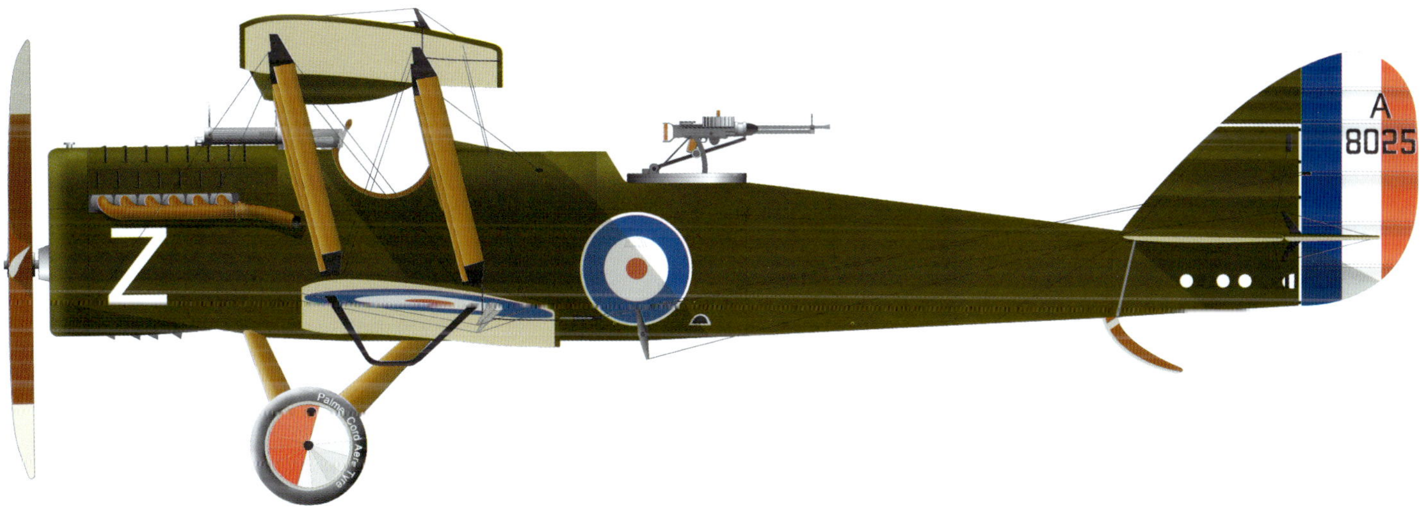

DeHavilland DH4 A8025, No.202 Sqdn. RAF. Overall PC10 with red/white wheel covers and individual marking "Z".

Sopwith Camel B3781, FSL AB Ellwood, No.3(N) Sqdn. RNAS, August 1917. At this stage No.3(N) Sqdn. used individual markings. The red/white heart on the fuselage was repeated on either side of the upperwing centre-section. Cowl is depicted as red, although it may be another dark colour.

Sopwith Camel B6378, Captain R Sykes, No.203 Sqdn. RAF, June 1918. The former RNAS squadrons continued to use colourful markings after amalgamation into the RFC, and No.203 was no exception. They carried various coloured bands on the rear fuselage with individual letter or Roman numerals within. This particular aircraft also appears to have blue cowl, wheel covers, and fin.

Nieuport "17b" 3956,FSL GG Simpson, No.8(N) Sqdn. RNAS. I had previously depicted this aircraft with French two-tone brown and green uppersurfaces, however closer examination of the photo tends to show that the brighter patch below the cockpit is in fact reflected light from the lower wing. Research by Les Rogers and Sqdn/Ldr. Joe Warne states that the camouflaged Nieuports bought from the French before November 1916 were in olive drab topsides with gray or aluminum cowls. Undersides were straw or creamy/buff. Various sources state that 3956 was named "BINKY" while at No 3(N), however I believe it was named as such while at Naval Eight a photograph of four aircraft of "A" flight, Naval Eight shows "BINKY" and another unclearly named Nieuport Ni.17B. Two other aircraft named "BINKY" served with Naval Eight.

Sopwith Pup N5185, No.8(N) Sqdn. RNAS. N5185 was named "BINKY II" and went to 8(N) on 20 December 1916 after prior service with 3(N), to which it returned on 3 February 1917. If "BINKY I & II" were indeed named while at 3(N) then N5185 "BINKY II" would have been named before 3956 "BINKY", as N5185 was supposedly named around 30 November prior to service with 8(N), and 3956 after transfer to 3(N) on 5 January. Hence my belief that they were in fact named while at Naval Eight.

Sopwith Triplane N5449, No.8(N) Sqdn. RNAS. The third of the "BINKY" trio was N5449. Arriving at 8(N) on 28 February and originally named "JOAN", "BINKY III" was photographed on its back after being overturned on landing by FSL J A M Allen on 15 March 1917.

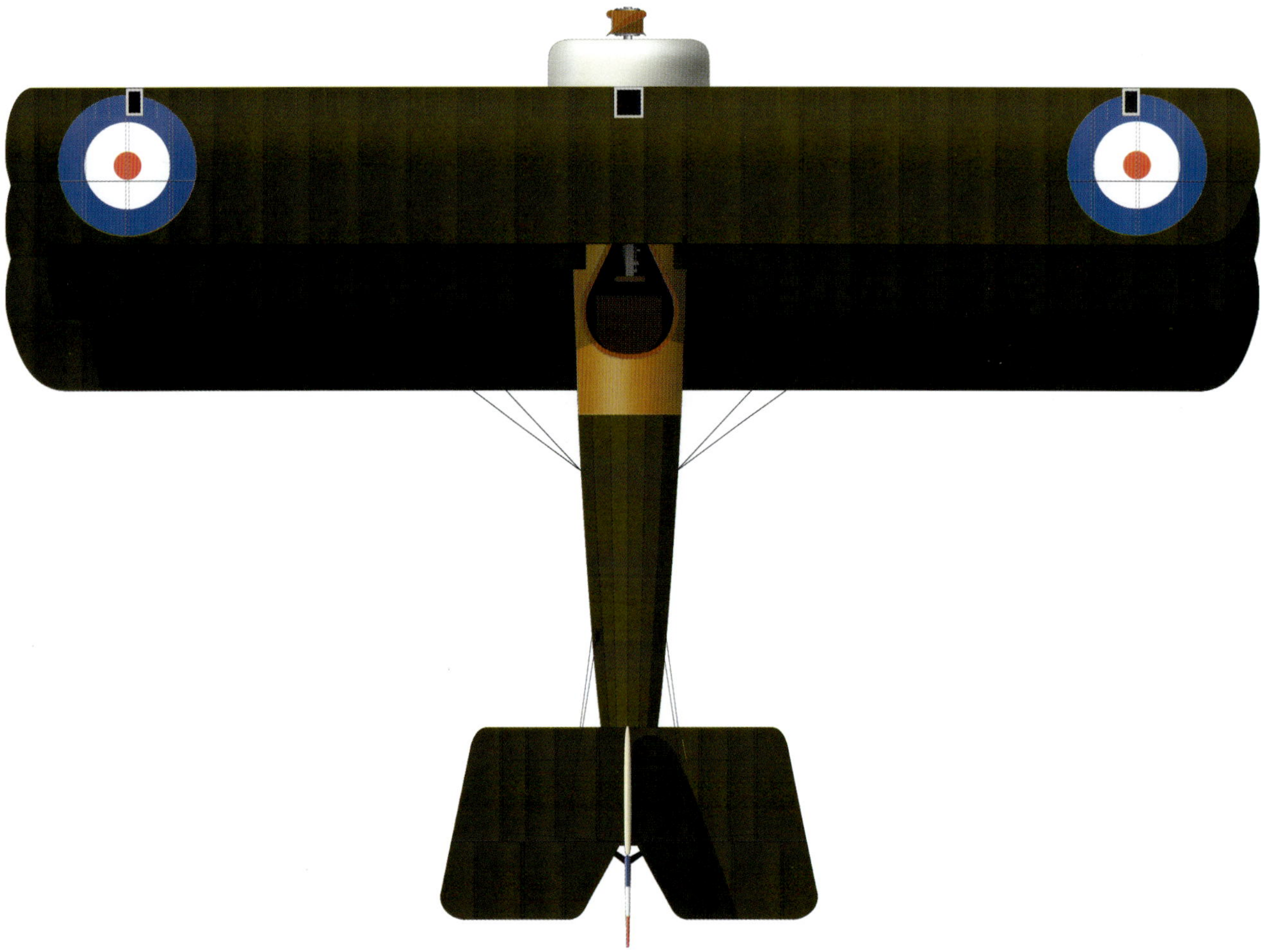

Sopwith Triplane N5493, No.8(N)Sqdn. RNAS. Formerly "BLYMP", the aircraft of R A Little, N5493 is seen here after he no longer flew it, in markings that weren"t his. Tho rod/white band on the fuselage is repeated on the rear decking to form a cross when viewed from above. Red heart on white fin.

Sopwith Camel B3921, FLt./Cdr R B Munday, A Flight, No.8(N) Sqdn. RNAS, Late 1917. No.8(N) Sqdn. used a white disc as their unit marking from December 1917 – March 1918. Individual markings were placed on the fin.

Sopwith Camel D1845, NO.208 Sqdn. RAF. After March 1918, the marking was changed to two sloping stripes behind the cockade. Of interest is a small scroll below the cockpit; unfortunately, details of this are lacking.

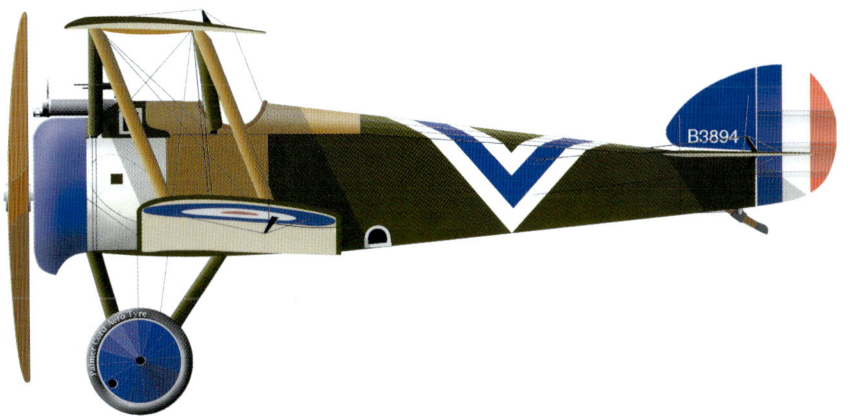

Sopwith Camel B3884, No.9(N) Sqdn. RNAS. Standard PC10 finish with natural metal flank panels and varnished ply. Blue cowl, fin and wheel covers. The tailplane is blue with white edging. White outlined blue diamond pattern repeats either side of centre-section. Other 9(N) Camels carried similar markings featuring other geometric shapes.

Sopwith Camel B7270, Captain Arthur Royal Brown, No.209 Sqdn. RAF, April 1918. The three vertical bars were used by the former No.9(N) as their marking from March 1918. In addition to the upper wing chevron, the photo seems to show a red stabilizer and white elevator. Photos of 209 Camels show the fuselage cockade and serial both visible and/or overpainted in various combinations. I have recently been informed that the reason for this was that during the time that their aircraft were photographed, they were all being repainted!

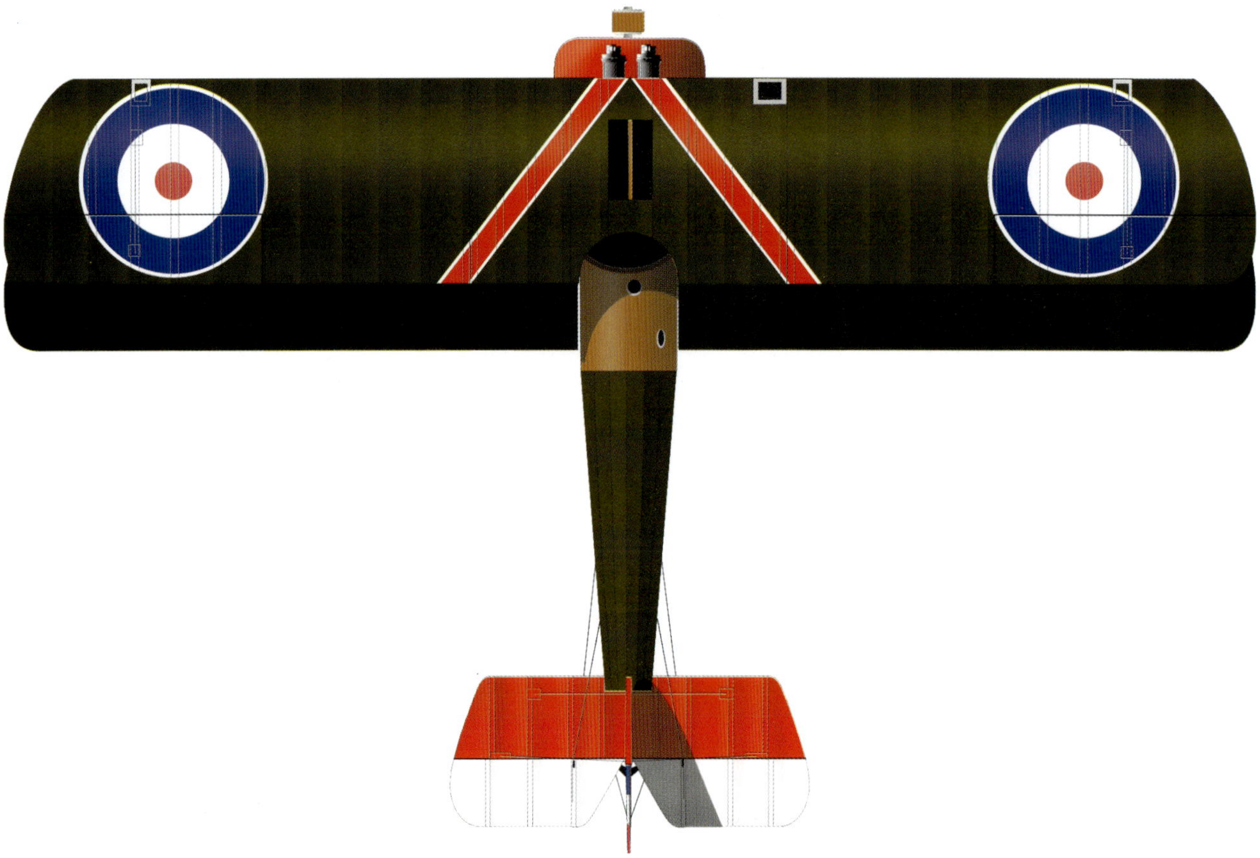

Sopwith Triplane N6307, FSL John E Sharman, No.10(N)Sqdn. RNAS. The Sopwith Triplanes of "B" Flight all bore a black cowl, metal panels and wheel covers. In addition each "Black Flight" Triplane was christened with a suitable sobriquet:

N5492 & N533
Collishaw
Black Maria

N5487
Alexander
Black Prince

N5483
Reid
Black Roger

N6307
Sharman
Black Death

N5376
Nash
Black Sheep

Supposedly the Triplanes of "A" and "C" flights were marked with red and blue cowls and wheel covers.

Sopwith Camel B5658, No.10(N) Sqdn. RNAS. This aircraft shows the typical 10(N) markings of two white stripes and the individual flight letter. Unlike other units, 10(N) kept the flight letter the same on each aircraft of the flight. Personal marking of "CLEADA" can be seen above the flight letter "B". The cowl colour is conjectural based on tonal values in the photo.

Sopwith Triplane N5358, FSL Robert Saunders, No.10(N) Sqdn. RNAS, June 1917. Saunders used the letter "Q" as Sharman had taken "S". Saunders was shot down and killed by Ltn. Groos of Jasta 11 on 24 June 1917.

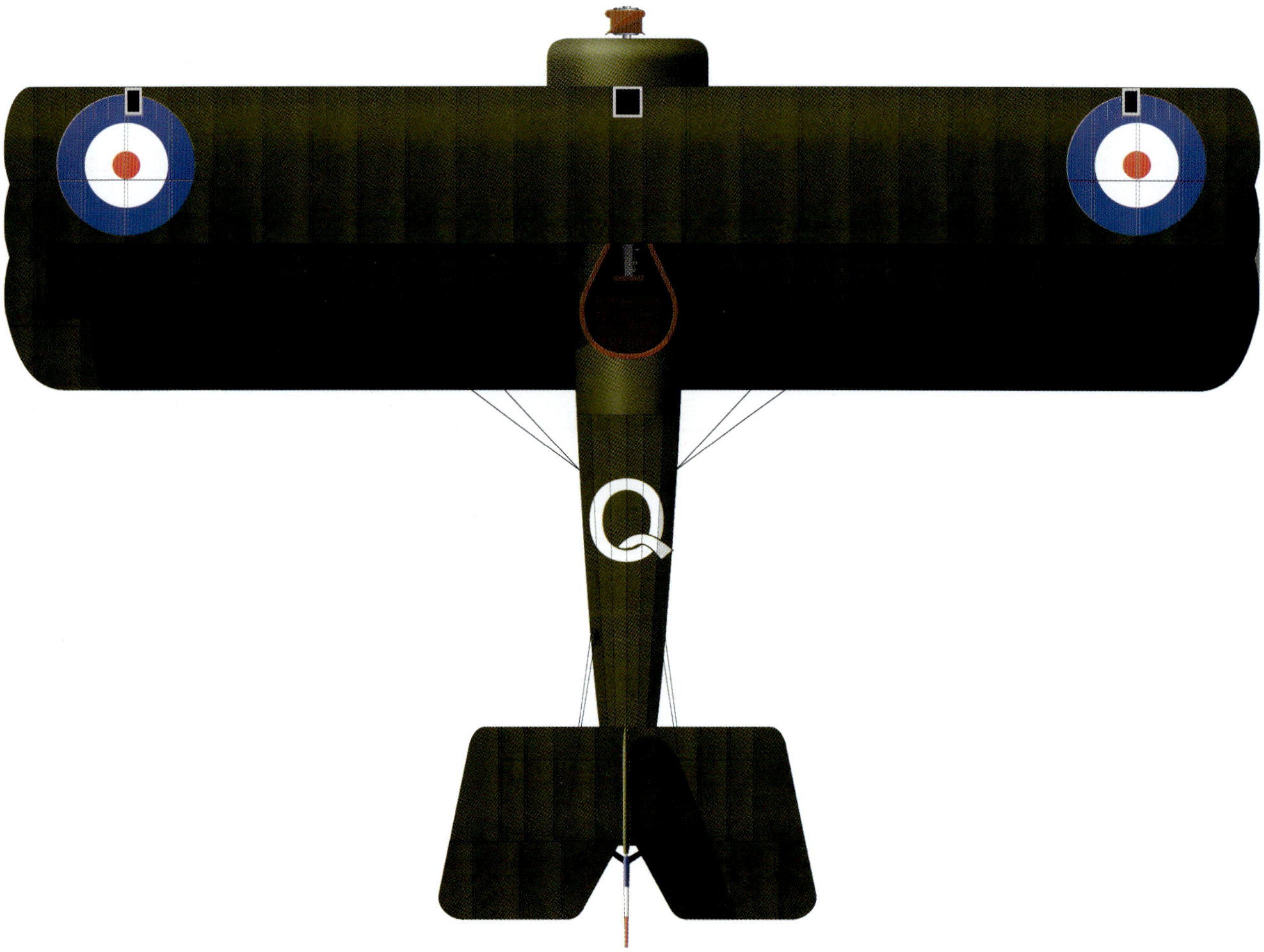

NAVAL TEN'S Striped Camels

The following nine profiles are based on correspondence with Stewart Taylor in which he had descriptions of the markings carried by various of the striped Camels. In addition, photos of an "A" flight lineup show the markings, and Stewart"s letter allowed the serials to be allocated. As per earlier practice, each aircraft of the same flight carried that Flight"s letter forward of the roundel; individual markings were carried on the wheel covers.

Sopwith Camel B6289, FSL HL Nelson, A Flight, No.10(N) Sqdn. RNAS. Nelson was credited with two aircraft while flying B6289. Black/white checkerboard wheel covers.

Sopwith Camel B6320, FSL FV Hall, A Flight, No.10(N)Sqdn. RNAS. Hall scored two victories while flying B6320. On 11 December 1917 he had his wheels and axle shot off while trench strafing. B6320 later went to No.9(N) Sqdn. in February 1918. Black/white wheel covers are divided into ten equal sections of "pie". The front undercarriage strut is also striped in black and white.

Sopwith Camel B5663, A flight, No.10(N) Sqdn. RNAS. Flown by various 10(N) pilots including FV Hall and WA Curtis – the later claiming a red Albatros on 5 December 1917 along with B6320 (FSL Hall). On 23 January 1918, FSL RA Blyth collided with an Albatros and both aircraft fell locked together with Blyth being killed. B5663 was claimed by Ltn. Wandelt of Jasta 36; whether he was the other pilot involved is unknown. Black/white striped wheel covers.

Sopwith Camel B6299, Captain NM MacGregor; B Flight, No.10(N) Sqdn. RNAS. The Sopwith Camel flown by FLt./Lt. Norman Miers MacGregor of No.10(N) Sqdn. RNAS has been the subject of numerous model kits and paintings with its red and white stripes on the cowl. However close examination of the 10(N) lineup shows that previous attempts at portraying B6299 have been incorrect, and fail to incorporate the stripe on the decking behind the cockpit. White wheel covers have the familiar red overlapping ovals.

Sopwith Camel B3950, FSL JG Manuel, B Flight, No.10(N) Sqdn. RNAS. Also flown by Flt. Cdr WM Alexander. Both Manuel and Alexander claimed a victory while flying B3950. Wheel covers have a red ring.

Sopwith Camel B6211, FSL HB Maund, B Flight, No.10(N) Sqdn. RNAS. Maund claimed an Albatros D.V OOC on 19 September 1917. Plain white wheel covers.

Sopwith Camel B5659, FSL AG Beattie, C Flight, No.10(N) Sqdn. RNAS Wheel covers are halved blue/white.

Sopwith Camel B5664, C Flight, No.10(N) Sqdn. RNAS. Solid blue wheel covers.

Sopwith Camel B6358, FSL LP Coombes, C Flight, No.10(N) Sqdn. RNAS. Blue wheel covers with a white ring.

Sopwith Camel F5914, No.210 Sqdn. RAF. The marking of No.10(N) was changed to a white disc in the big changeover of March 1918.

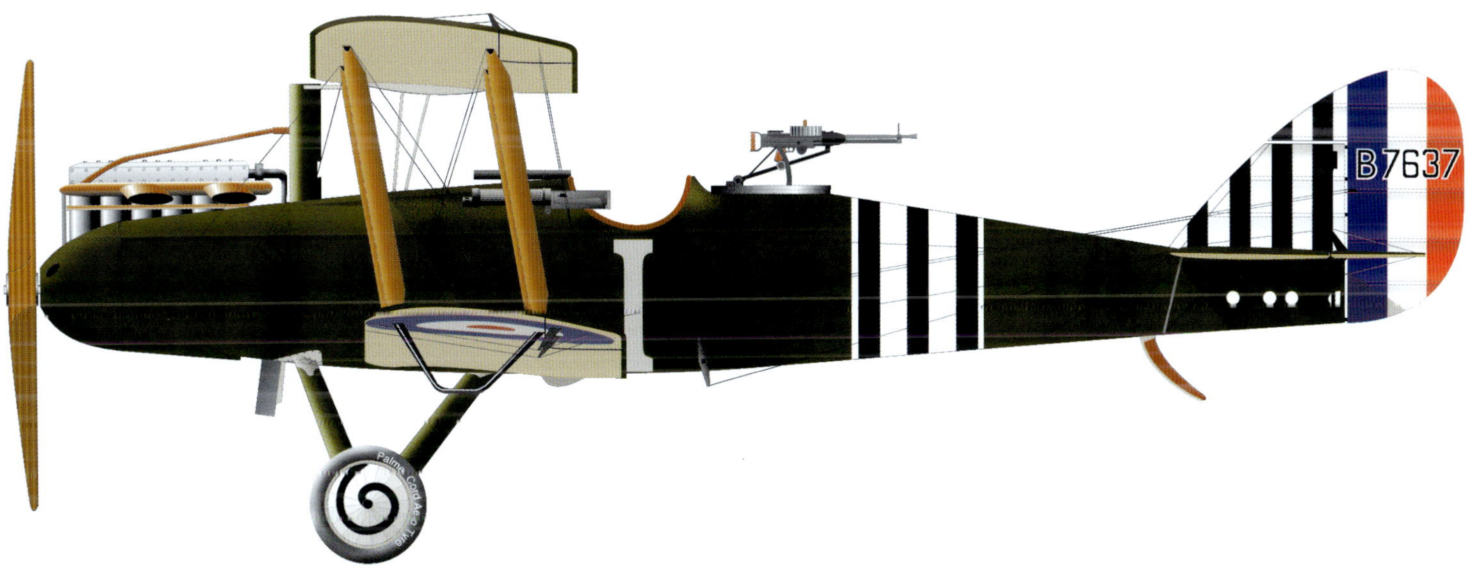

DeHavilland DH9 B7637 (?), No.211 Sqdn. RAF. Overall PC10 with black and white stripes on the fin and fuselage. Wheel covers have a black swirl on white.

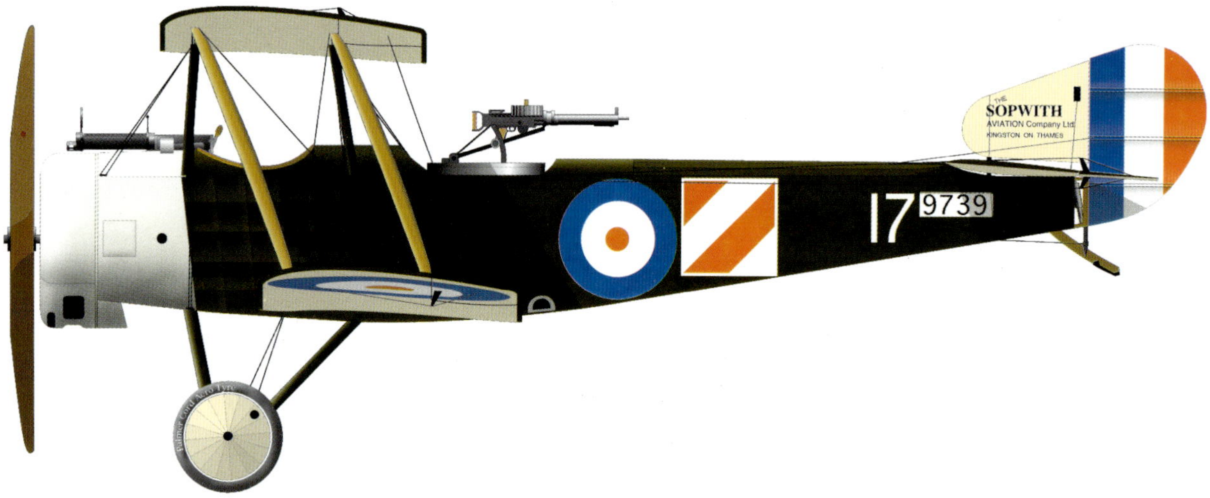

Sopwith 1 1/2 Strutter 9739, FSL RF Redpath/, No.3 Wing RNAS, Luxeuil-les-bains Aerodrome, October 1916. The Sopwith 1 1/2 Strutters of No.3 WIng RNAS bore a red or blue geometric design within a white square which repeats on both sides of the tailplane. Aircraft "17" was a presentation aircraft named "Britons in Egypt No.2", 9739 went to No.3 Wing, Manston on 28 August 1916, and arrived at Luxeuil on 22 September. 9739 was flown by many teams including F/S/L R. F. Redpath/AM Dell, F/S/L McNeil/AM Dell, Wg. Cdr. Davies and AM Pinchen. F/L C. B. Dalison/Sub.Lt. Fraser downed an EA on 24 November. On 25 February 1917, F/S/L L. E. Smith and AM R. S. Portsmouth were shot down by Off.Stv. Gottlieb Vothknecht of Jasta 24 for his first victory. Portsmouth was killed, while Smith was taken POW and later died of his wounds.

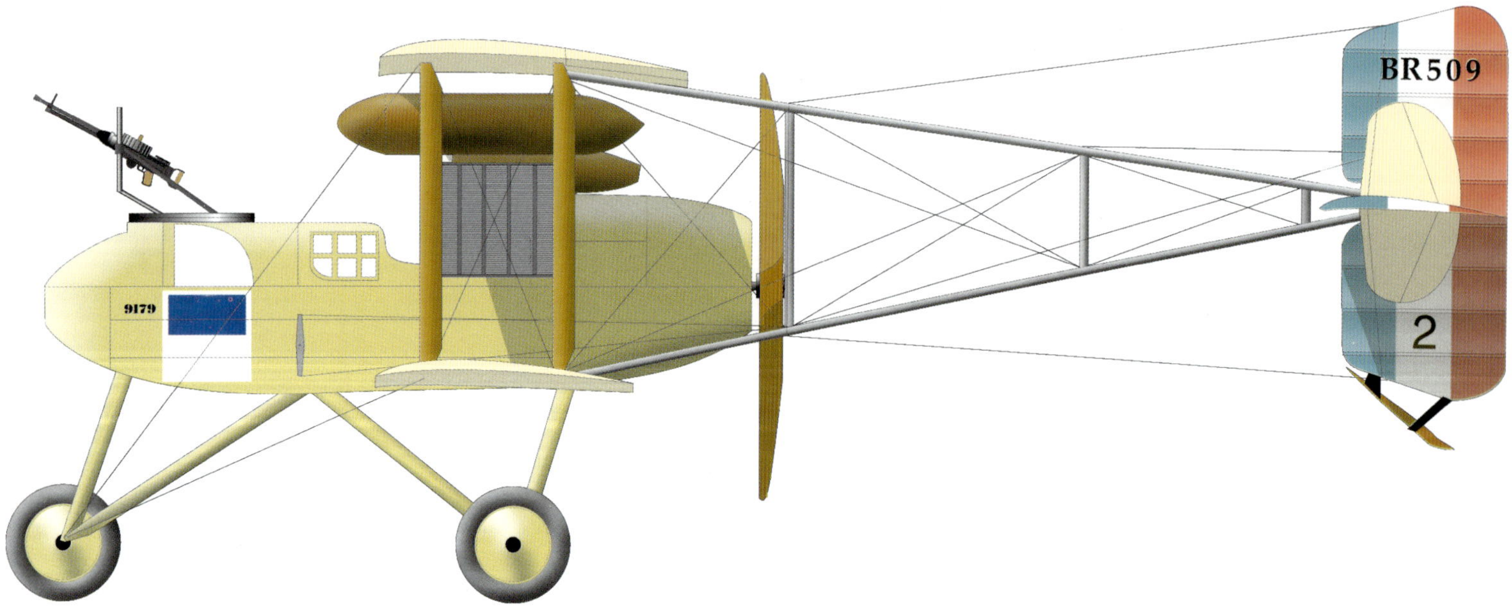

Breguet Br.V 9179, No.3 Wing RNAS Luxeuil-les-bains aerodrome, October 1916. Formerly the French BR.509, 9179 arrived at Luxeuil on 21 September and was deleted on 10 November. Reportedly aircraft "5", although the available photos don"t show its position, there is a small number "2" on the rudder. Close studies of the photos of 9179 and 9181 show the tailplane to be striped spanwise in the national colours with blue foremost. It is unknown whether the individual marking was repeated as on the Sopwith aircraft.

RAF SE5a D6995, Lt. F Alberry, No.2 Sqdn. AFC, September 1918. The unit marking carried by the various Australian squadrons was originally a boomerang on the rear fuselage, this was changed to a vertical bar in front of the cockpit at both Nos.2 and 4 squadron. Alberry had lost a leg in the Infantry, but transferred to the AFC rather than take his discharge. Of interest are the odd proportions to the fuselage cockade.

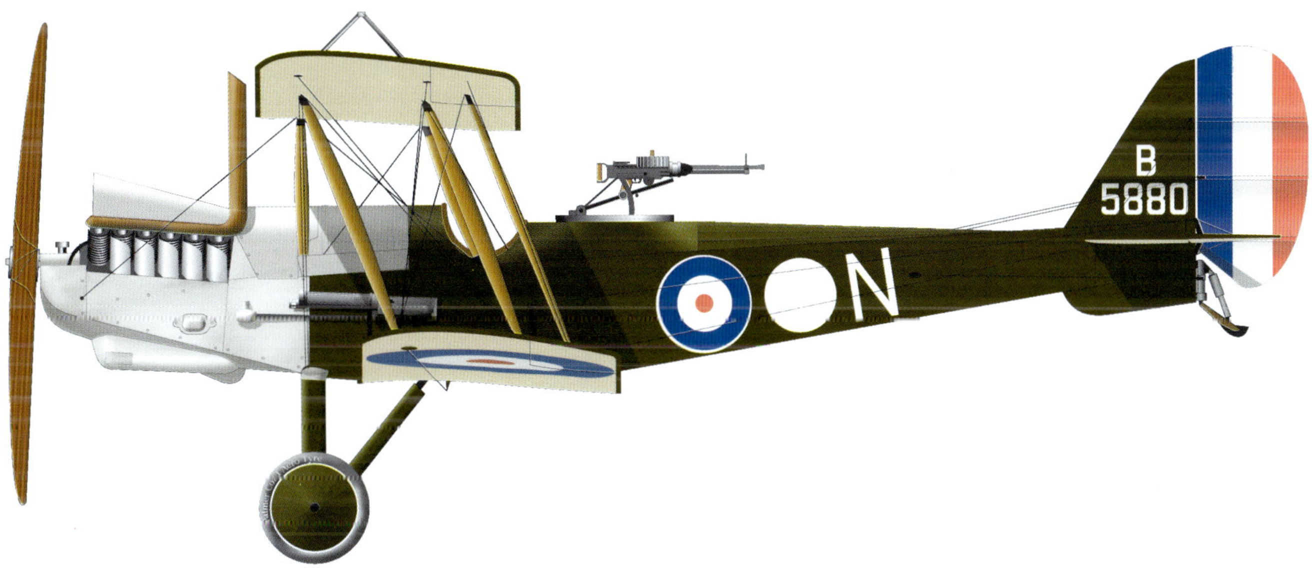

RAF RE8 B5880, No.3 Sqdn. AFC. A white disc is the marking for No.3 Sqdn. AFC.

Sopwith Camel B5592, 2/Lt. A Couston, No.4 Sqdn. AFC, February 1918. As mentioned above, the original marking of the AFC squadrons was the boomerang, seen here on B5592. Couston was shot down and taken prisoner on 21 February 1918 by Ltn. Matthei of Jasta 46.

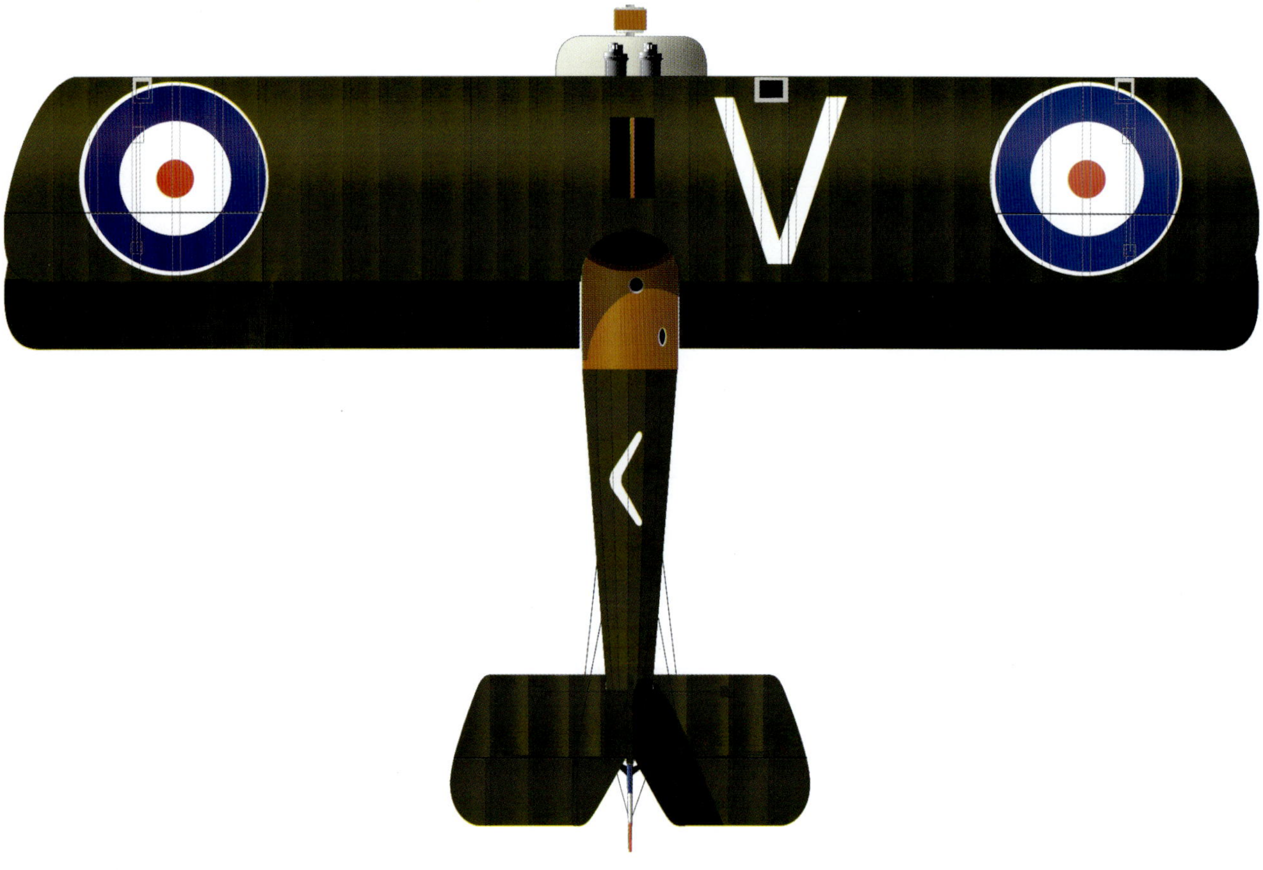

Sopwith 7F.1 Snipe E8069, No.4 Sqdn. AFC. After March 1918, the 4AFC marking became a vertical bar in front of the roundel. In common with other Snipes, E8069 has its cowl and ply panels in gray.

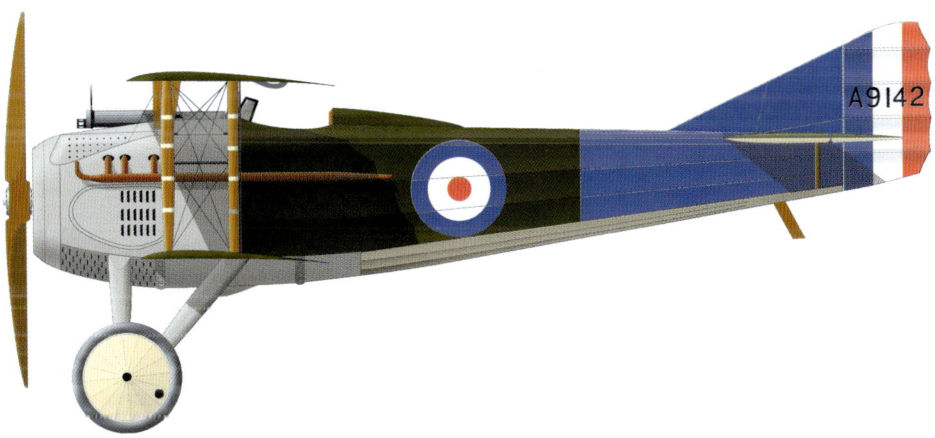

SPAD VII A4192, No.1 School of Aerial Fighting. PC10 overall with a grey cowl and blue tail.

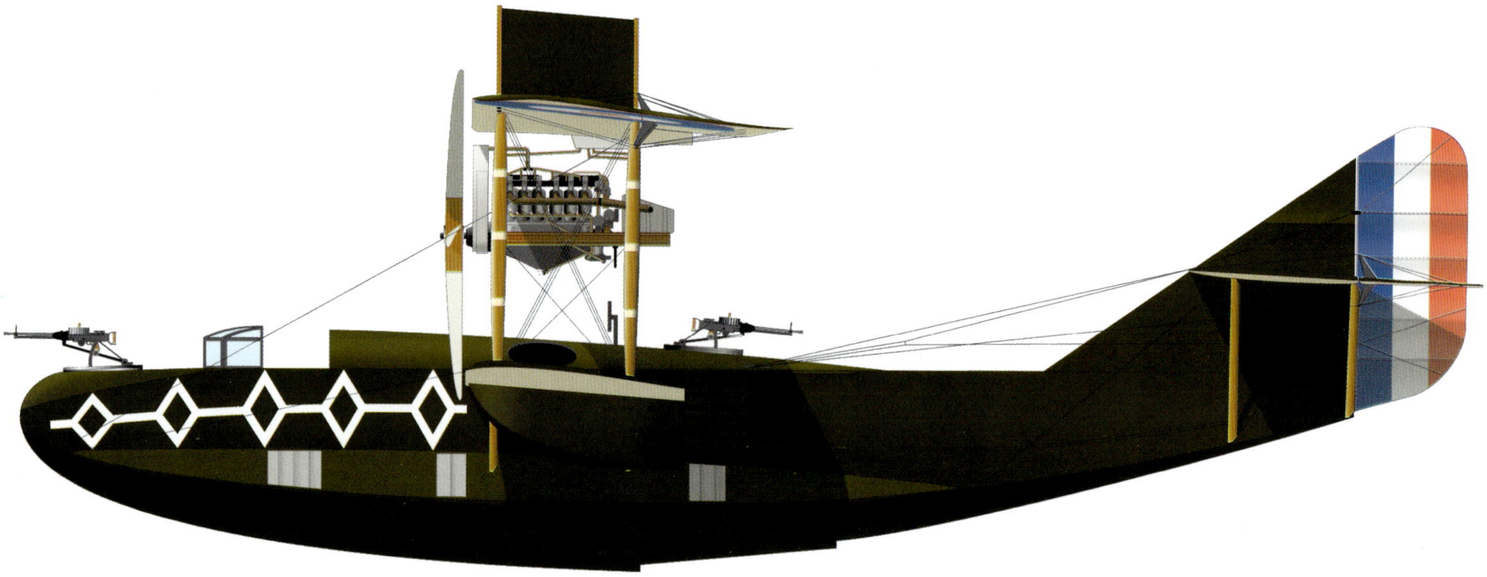

Curtiss H-16 N4072, Dundee NAS. Overall PC10 with white diamond pattern on nose.

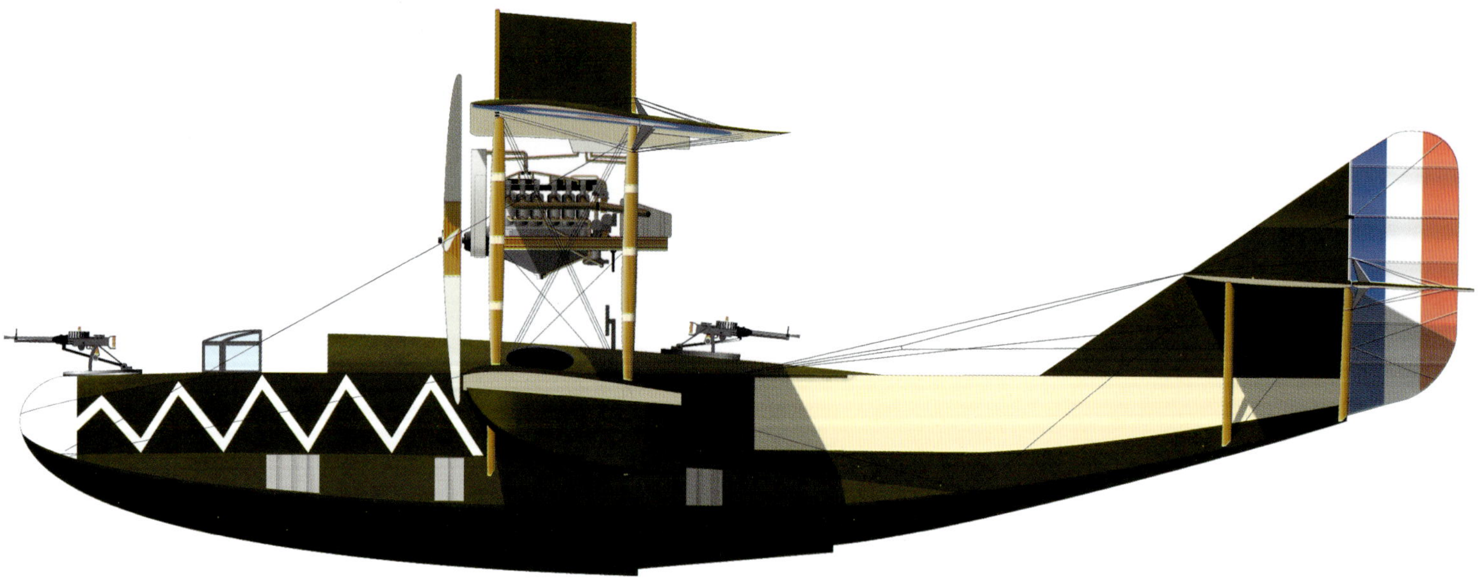

Curtiss H-16 serial unknown, Dundee NAS. I have had correspondence with Stuart Leslie over this boat and we both feel it is an H-16, not an F2A as reported elsewhere. The rear hull appears to have CDL fabric in place still.

Sopwith Schneider 3717, Felixstowe NAS. The only markings are the Union Jack and serial on the rudder. The serial is on a white rectangle

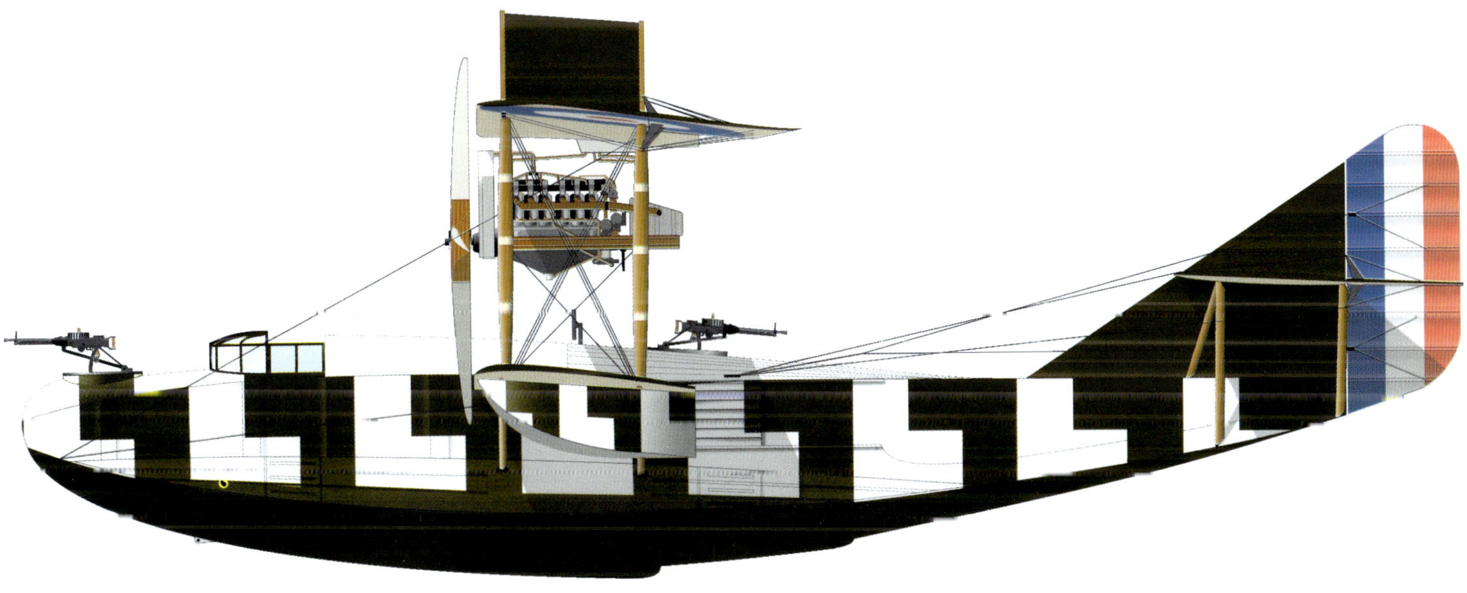

Felixstowe F2A serial unknown, Felixstowe NAS. This closed-cockpit boat featured a repeating pattern of white and PC10 interlocking shapes. The hull top is white, the bottom is shown as PC10, but this is conjectural.

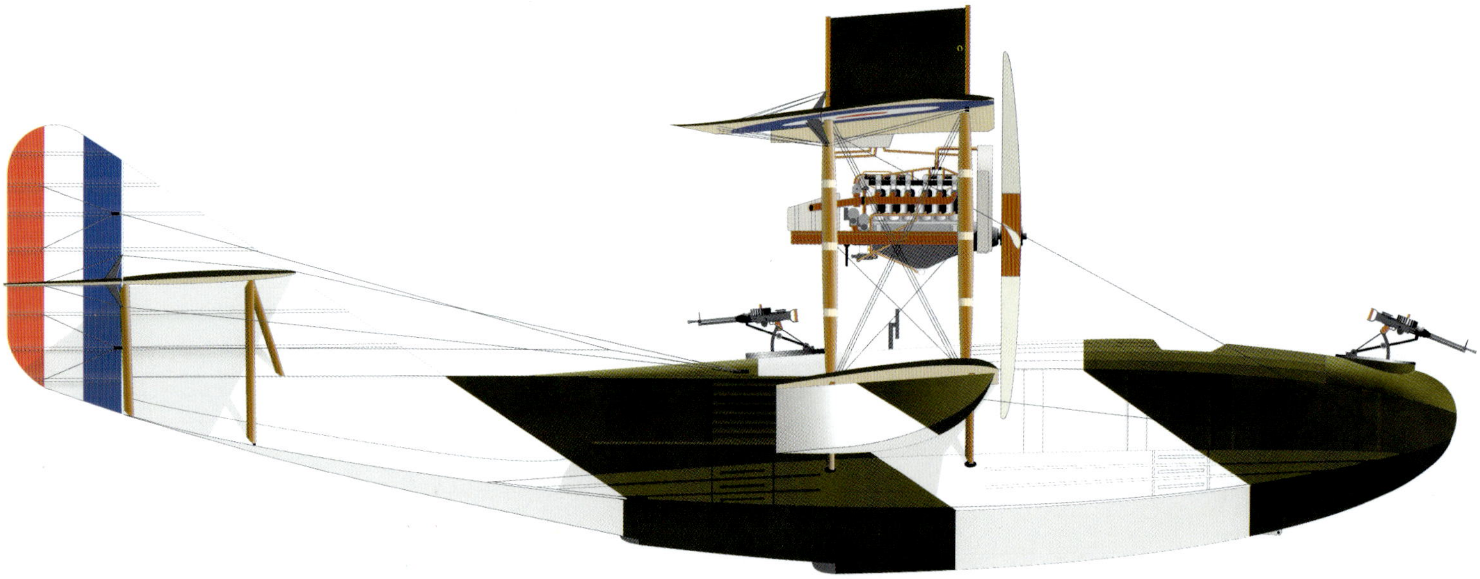

Felixstowe F2A N4087 (?), Felixstowe NAS. An open-cockpit boat, this F2A (possibly N4087) was dazzle-painted with white diagonal stripes on the hull and floats.

Felixstowe F2A N4297, Felixstowe NAS, November 1918. Blue and white stripes on bow, and chevrons on the rear hull. Top of hull is PC10. Hull bottom is conjecturally shown as PC10 as well, but may have been in blue and white.

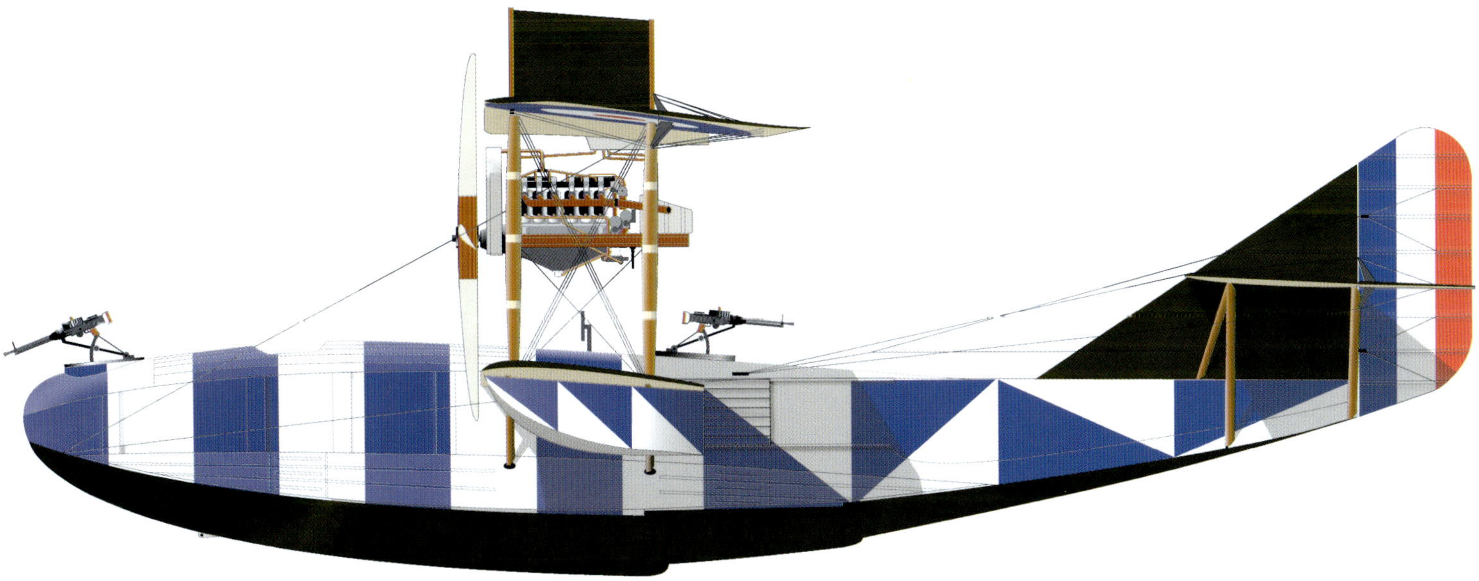

Felixstowe F2A serial unknown, Felixstowe NAS. This unknown boat features a blue and white striped nose and triangular pattern.

Felixstowe F2A serial unknown, Felixstowe NAS. Red and white marked Felixstowe. This boat bore a zig-zag pattern on the bow and vertical stripes on the rear hull and vertical tail surfaces.

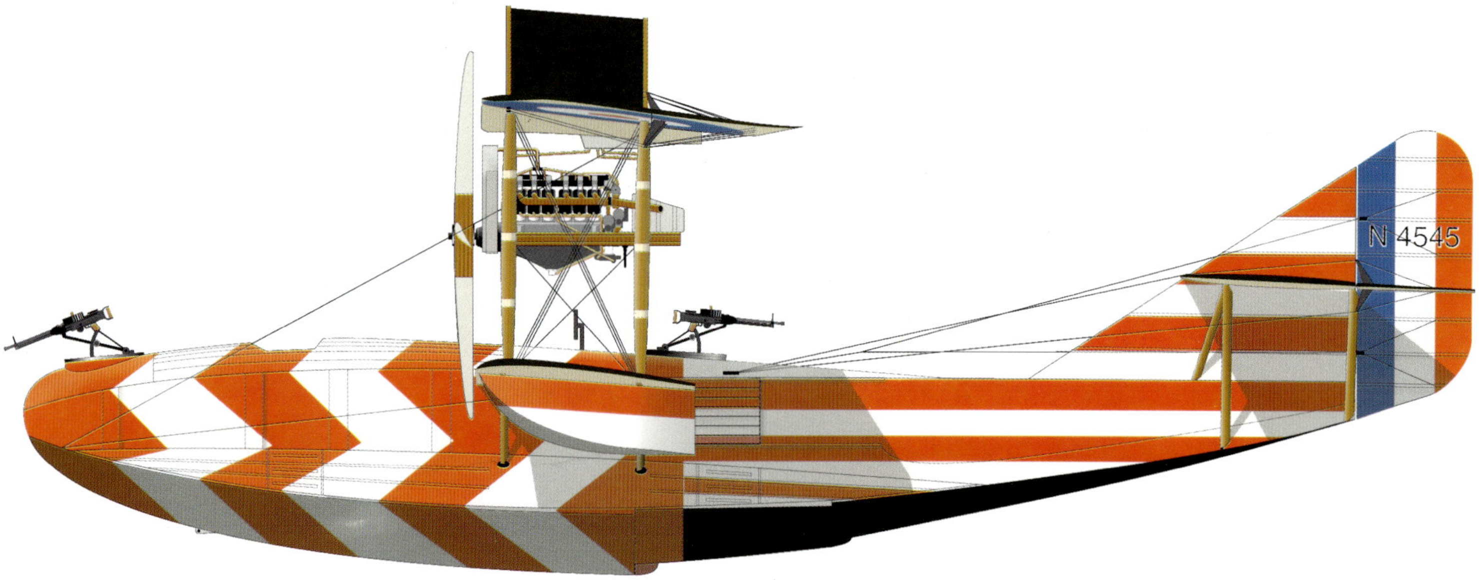

Felixstowe F2A N4545, Felixstowe NAS. Yet another red/white marked boat. N4545 has a zig-zagged nose and horizontally striped rear hull and fin.

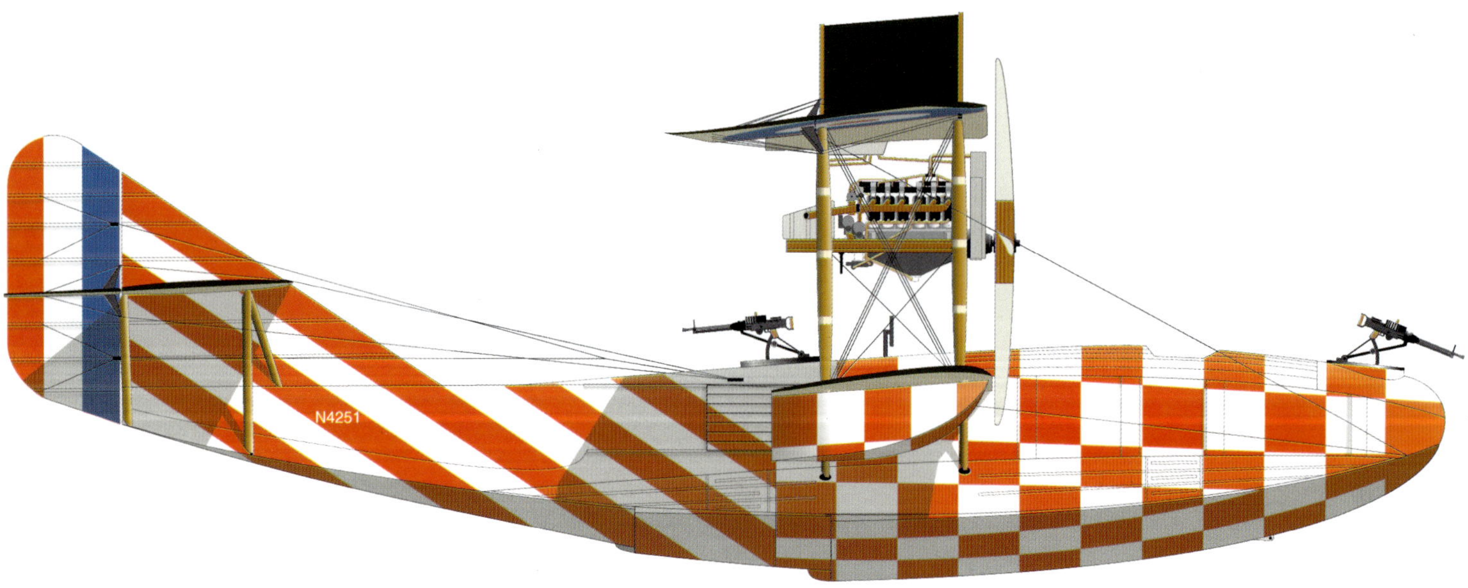

Felixstowe F3 N4251, Felixstowe NAS. A red and white checked nose was worn by this and the next boat. N4521 also had diagonal stripes on the rear surfaces.

Felixstowe F3 N4258, Felixstowe NAS. As with N4521, N4528 bore a red/white checked nose; however, this was the extent of its deviation from the PC10 norm. The rest of the boat was in PC10.

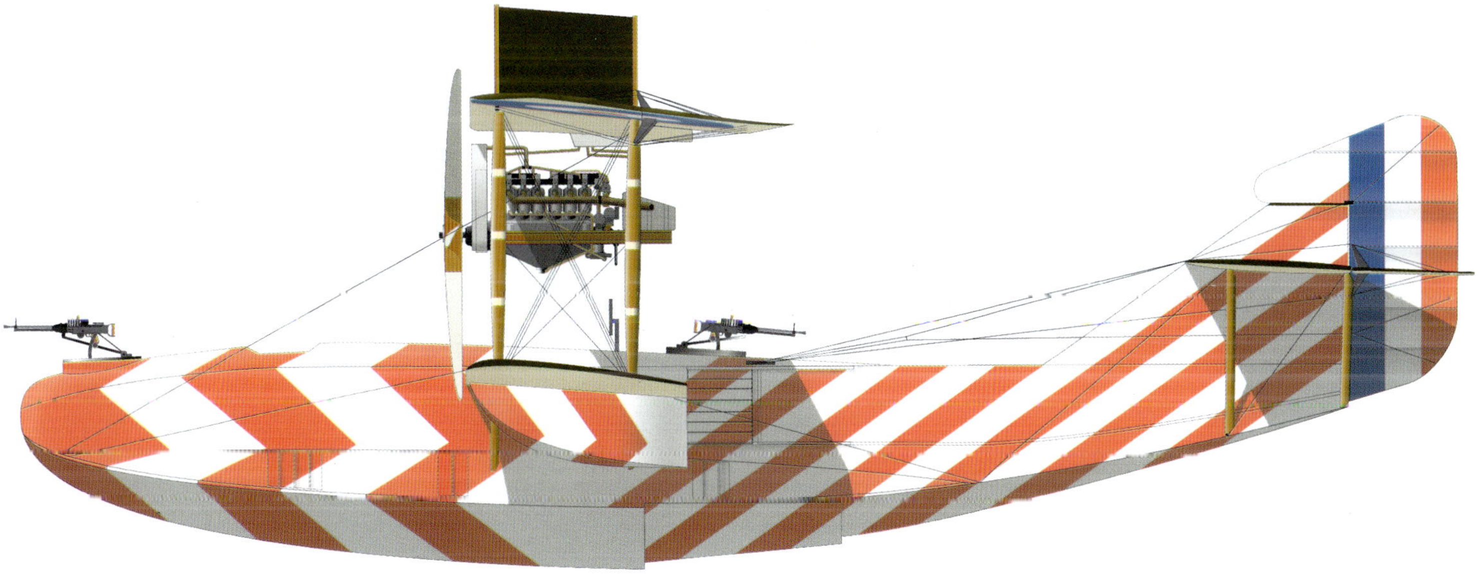

Curtiss H-16 N4060, Felixstowe NAS. One more of the colourful Felixstowe-based boats is N4060. It is shown here after having the control surfaces modified to include balances.

Sopwith Baby N1019 or 8157, Seaplane Defence Flight, Dunkerque NAS. Both this and the next profile carry two Lewis guns as armament, one over the centre-section, the other alongside the cockpit firing through the propeller arc. The fuselage cockades of both have a large centre and corresponding thinner outer ring.

Sopwith Baby N1017, Seaplane Defence Flight, Dunkerque NAS. As above.